# The Rich Get Richer and the Poor Get Prison

D0873192

# The Wiley Series in Deviance and Criminology

# The Rich Get Richer and the Poor Get Prison

## Ideology, Class, and Criminal Justice

### Second Edition

**Jeffrey H. Reiman**

*School of Justice and*
*Department of Philosophy and Religion*
*The American University*
*Washington, D.C.*

**John Wiley & Sons**

New York • Chichester • Brisbane • Toronto • Singapore

Cover Art by Kenny Beck

Copyright © 1979, 1984, by Jeffrey H. Reiman

All rights reserved. Published simultaneously in Canada.

Reproduction or translation of any part of
this work beyond that permitted by Sections
107 and 108 of the 1976 United States Copyright
Act without the permission of the copyright
owner is unlawful. Requests for permission
or further information should be addressed to
the Permissions Department, John Wiley & Sons.

*Library of Congress Cataloging in Publication Data:*

Reiman, Jeffrey H.
    The rich get richer and the poor get prison.
    (The Wiley series in deviance and criminology)
    Includes bibliographical references and index.
    1. Criminal justice, Administration of—United States.
2. Social classes—United States.  3. Ideology.
I. Title.  II. Series.
HV9471.R44  1984        364'.973    83–12551
ISBN 0–471–89029–4

Printed in the United States of America

10  9  8  7  6  5  4  3  2  1

For Sue

# Preface to the Second Edition

In revising *The Rich Get Richer and the Poor Get Prison*, I have had two primary goals. First, I have tried to bring the research findings and statistics up to date. Thus, I have drawn on studies published as recently as 1982. With regard to statistics, however, where I compare the relative danger to the public of criminal versus noncriminal harms (such as occupational and environmental hazards), I have generally used figures for 1980, since this was the latest year for which I could find adequate statistics on both criminal and noncriminal harms. Occasionally, where I have been unable to find precisely comparable figures, I have had to assume that earlier statistics still reflect continuing trends or to make projections from the past into the present. In all cases, I have made the most conservative assumptions in order to keep my argument on the most solid ground possible. In the years since the first edition was written, many things have changed. Most notably, the government is now much more restrained in its estimates of job-related deaths, and thus I have been more restrained as well. Nevertheless, the main thesis of the first edition continues to be supported by the facts. It is still true that acts that are not treated as crimes pose at least as great a danger to the public as acts that are, and often a considerably greater danger. Thus, the disproportionality between our heavy-handed response to crime and our kid-glove response to noncriminal dangers continues to need explanation. And, in my view, it is still true that this explanation is connected to the fact that the acts that are treated as crimes are largely acts of the poor, while the noncriminal dangers result from acts of the well-off. In short, it is still true that *the rich get richer and the poor get prison*.

Second, the first edition was sometimes accused of being a "conspiracy theory," implying that the criminal justice system's focus on the acts of the poor was the intentional design of the rich and powerful. Although I tried to avoid such a view in the first edition, I can see now that many passages did invite this interpretation. To combat this, I have rewritten these passages to make unambiguously clear both why I think conspiracy theories are unsatisfactory and why my explanation is not one. I call my explanation the "historical inertia" explanation because it aims to account for why criminal justice policy currently in motion tends to stay in motion. I supplement it with a Marxian explanation which, since it focuses on the structure of capitalist societies, is called a "structuralist" explanation. I have added it because I believe it sets the thesis of the book in a wider theoretical context. I am hopeful that instructors may find the section in which the structuralist explanation is presented a handy means to introduce their students to Marxian theory and its relation to criminology. Nevertheless, the historical inertia explanation can support the thesis of the book without the structuralist explanation.

Since I have revised rather than rewritten *The Rich Get Richer*, I am still thankful to those who helped me with the first edition (see *Acknowledgments*). But now I owe new debts of gratitude. I thank Professor Eleanor Miller at the University of Wisconsin, Milwaukee, who shared with me many helpful recommendations based on her experience with the first edition, and Professors Richard Bennett and Robert Johnson, my colleagues at The American University School of Justice, who read the revised manuscript and generously commented in detail on it. Many of their suggestions are incorporated in the book. My thanks also go to Marcia Trick, who served as my research assistant for some months during 1982. She gathered most of the data that I have used in updating the book; her fine job made mine much easier. I am grateful to the College of Public and International Affairs of The American University for providing the funds to hire Ms. Trick. Thanks also go to Ivan Cohen, who came in in the late innings and helped track down the last bits of information needed to put the finishing touches on the manuscript. And, as before, I am deeply appreciative of the support, encouragement, and continuing education that I receive from the staff and faculty of The American University School of Justice. It is also high time I thanked Carol Luitjens of John Wiley & Sons for her dependably good advice and good cheer.

While I was preparing this new edition, Richard A. Myren was preparing to step down as Dean of the School of Justice at The American University and turn full-time to the life of scholarship and teaching that he has spent so many years supporting and protecting for others. Though we have probably disagreed more than agreed, he is a man from whom I have learned much. For his belief in me and his unstinting support of my work, he has my gratitude. For the courage, academic integrity, and honest hard work with which he carried out his tasks as dean, he has my respect. In his pursuit of the joys of the scholarly life, much delayed and earned many times over, he has my best wishes for success.

Finally, for all the same reasons as before plus whatever is added by standing the test of time, this edition, like the first, is dedicated to Sue Headlee Hollis.

**Jeffrey H. Reiman**

# Preface to the First Edition

It is obvious that the American criminal justice system is failing in the war against crime, and equally obvious that American criminal justice policies often contribute to the very problem that they seek to solve. This book is an attempt to understand this failure: its dimensions, its mechanisms, its causes, and its moral implications.

It is today a commonplace of social analysis, as in the past it was a tenet of common sense, that if social practices endure, they must—even the most blatantly irrational of social practices—be serving some interests. With this as a starting point, I determine if there are any interests that might be served by the continuing failure of the American criminal justice system. I try to see if there is an angle from which this failure is a success, and find indeed that there is.

To understand this conclusion, it is necessary to see that the failure of the criminal justice system to protect us is not haphazard. It has a pattern. The criminal justice system devotes the lion's share of its crime-fighting resources to fighting against crimes like murder and mugging, crimes that are characteristically committed by the poor in our society. And, although our prisons are filled with poor criminals, little dent is made in the overall volume of their crimes. Indeed, there is reason to believe that prisons serve more as training grounds for future criminality than for good citizenship. But this failure of the system to stem the crimes of the poor must be viewed in the context of another and more easily overlooked failure: the failure to fight vigorously, moreover often the failure even to treat as criminal, the dangerous acts of the wealthy and powerful. We have a system shaped by economic bias from the start. The dangerous acts and crimes unique to the wealthy are either ignored or treated lightly, while for the so-called common crimes, the poor are far more likely than the well-off to be arrested, if arrested charged, if charged convicted, and if convicted sentenced to prison. Hence, the failure of the criminal justice system has a pattern: *the rich get richer and the poor get prison.*

But failure is in the eye of the beholder. This failure *succeeds* in conveying to the general public a message of enormous ideological value to those at the top in our society: the message that the greatest danger to the average citizen comes from below him or her on the economic ladder, not from above. For those at the top, this failure is a success.

No one who writes a book can be mindless of the power of words. In our own times, we have rightly been made conscious of the power of technically neutral nouns like "man" and pronouns like "he" to convey a picture of a world in which the actors are all male. Not only is this a distortion of the world in which we live, it is a link in the chain that bars women from full and active participation in social, economic, and political life. In this book I have therefore striven to avoid the use of words that are technically neutral but are effectively masculine. In a few instances, however, I use the masculine form even though the reference is to men and women. My reasoning is this. There are other evils in the world to be remedied besides sexism. The injustices visited on our fellow human beings in the name of criminal justice are among the gravest of these evils. This book is offered in the hope of contributing to the reduction of these evils. Only rarely, where there was no way to eliminate traditional masculine nouns or pronouns without weakening the force of what I consider to be an important statement, do I let the traditional forms stand. Readers may find my judgments here faulty but I hope they will accept my reasons.

**Jeffrey H. Reiman**

# Acknowledgments

This book is the product of seven years of teaching in the School of Justice (formerly, the Center for the Administration of Justice), a multidisciplinary criminal justice education program at The American University in Washington, D.C. I have had the benefit of the school's lively and diverse faculty and student body. And, although they will surely not agree with all that I have to say, I have drawn heavily on what I have learned from my colleagues over the years and stand in their debt. In addition, more than is ordinarily recognized, a teacher receives guidance from students as they test, confirm, reject, and expand what they learn in class in the light of their own experience. Here, too, I am deeply in debt. My thanks go to the hundreds of students who have shared some part of their world with me as they passed through The American University, and in particular to three students whose encouragement, loyalty, and wisdom are very much a part of the development of the ideas in this book: Elizabeth Crimi, Bernard Demczuk, and Lloyd Raines.

I express my gratitude to The American University for providing me with a summer research grant that enabled me to devote full time to the book in the summer of 1976, when most of the actual writing was done. I am also grateful to Bernard Demczuk who was my research assistant during the academic year 1975 to '76, and who gathered much of the research data. I owe thanks as well to Cathy Sacks for ably and carefully typing the final manuscript.

Drafts of the manuscript for this book were read in whole or in part by (or at) Bernard Demczuk, Sue Hollis, Richard Myren, Lloyd Raines, Phillip Scribner, I. F. Stone, and John Wildeman. I am grateful for their many comments and I incorporate many of their recommendations in the final version. I have made my mistakes in spite of them.

Finally, for teaching me about artichokes, the meaning of history, and countless other mysteries, this book is dedicated to Sue Headlee Hollis.

J. H. R.

# Contents

# Introduction: Criminal Justice Through the Looking Glass, or Winning by Losing

> *The inescapable conclusion is that society secretly wants crime, needs crime, and gains definite satisfactions from the present mishandling of it.*
>
> **Karl Menninger,** *The Crime of Punishment*

A criminal justice system is a mirror in which a whole society can see the darker outlines of its face. Our ideas of justice and evil take on visible form in it, and thus we see ourselves in deep relief. Step through this looking glass to view the American criminal justice system—and ultimately the whole society it reflects—from a radically different angle of vision.

In particular, entertain the idea that the goal of our criminal justice system is not to reduce crime or to achieve justice but to project to the American public a visible image of the threat of crime. To do this, it must maintain the existence of a sizable or growing population of criminals. And to do this, it must fail in the struggle to reduce crime.

You will rightly demand to know how and why a society such as ours would tolerate a criminal justice system "designed to fail" in the fight against crime. Indeed, a considerable portion of this book is devoted to answering this question. Right now, however, a short explanation of how this upside-down idea of criminal justice was born will best introduce it and myself.

Some years ago, I taught a seminar for graduate students, entitled The Philosophy of Punishment and Rehabilitation. Many of the students were already working in the field of corrections as probation officers or prison guards or halfway-house counselors. First we examined the various philosophical justifications for legal punishment, and then we directed our attention to the functioning of the actual correctional system. For much of the semester we talked about the myriad inconsistencies and cruelties and overall irrationality of the system. We discussed the arbitrariness with which offenders are sentenced to prison and the arbitrariness with which they are treated in prison. We discussed the lack of privacy and the deprivation of sources of personal identity and dignity, the ever-present physical violence, as well as the lack of meaningful counseling or job training within prison walls. We discussed the harassment of parolees, the inescapability of the "ex-con" stigma, the refusal of society to let a person finish paying his or her "debt to society," and the near-total absence of meaningful noncriminal opportunities for the ex-prisoner. We confronted time and again the bald irrationality of a society that builds prisons to prevent crime knowing full well that they do not and that does not even seriously try to rid its prisons and post-release practices of those features that guarantee a high rate of *recidivism*: the return to crime by prison alumni. How could we fail so miserably? We are neither an evil nor a stupid nor an impoverished people. How could we continue to bend our energies and spend our hard-earned tax dollars on cures we know are not working?

Toward the end of the semester I put before the students an idea that appears from time to time in the literature of sociology: Imagine that instead of designing a correctional system to reduce and prevent crime, we had to design one that would maintain and encourage the existence of a stable and visible "class" of criminals. What would it look like? The response was electrifying. In briefer and somewhat more orderly form, here is a sample of the proposals that emerged in our discussion:

*First.* It would be helpful to have a number of irrational laws on the books, such as laws against heroin or prostitution or gambling—laws that prohibit acts that have no clear victim and that really do not prevent the acts they make illegal. This would make many people "criminals" for what they regard as normal behavior and would increase their need to engage in *secondary* crime (the drug addict's need to steal to pay for drugs, the prostitute's need for a pimp, since police protection is unavailable, etc.).

*Second.* It would be good to give police, prosecutors, and judges broad discretion to decide who got arrested, who got charged, and who got sentenced to prison. This would mean that almost anyone who got as far as prison would know of others who committed the same crime but who either were not arrested or were not charged or were not sentenced to prison. This would assure us that a good portion of the prison population would experience their confinement as arbitrary and unjust and thus respond with rage, which would make them more "antisocial," rather than with remorse, which would make them feel more bound by social norms.

*Third.* The prison experience should be not only painful but also demeaning. The pain of loss of liberty might deter future crime. But demeaning and emasculating prisoners by placing them in an enforced childhood characterized by no privacy and no control over their time and actions, as well as by the constant threat of rape or assault, is sure to overcome any deterrent effect by weakening whatever capacities a prisoner had for self control.

*Fourth.* It goes almost without saying that prisoners should neither be trained in a marketable skill nor provided with a job after release. And, of course, their prison records should stand as a perpetual stigma to discourage employers from hiring them. Otherwise, they might be tempted *not* to return to crime after release.

*Fifth.* The ex-offenders' sense that they can never pay their debt to society, that they will always be different from "decent citizens," should be reinforced by the following means. They should be deprived for the rest of their lives of rights, such as the right to vote. They should be harassed by police as "likely suspects" and be subject to the whims of parole officers who can at any time threaten to send them back to prison for things no ordinary citizens could be arrested for, such as going out of town or drinking or fraternizing with the "wrong people."

*And so on.*

In short, *asked to design a system that would maintain and encourage the existence of a stable and visible "class of criminals," we "constructed" the American criminal justice system!*

What is to be made of this? First, it is, of course, only part of the truth. Some prison officials do try to treat their inmates with dignity and to respect their privacy and self-determination to the greatest extent possible within an institution dedicated to involuntary confinement. Minimum security prisons and halfway houses are certainly moves in this direction. Some prisons do provide meaningful job training, and some parole officers are not only fair but go out of their way to help their "clients" find jobs and make it "legally." And, of course, plenty of people are arrested for doing things that no society ought to tolerate, such as rape, murder, assault, or armed robbery, and many are in prison who might be preying on their fellow citizens if they were not. *All of this is true.* Complex social practices are just that: *complex.* They are neither all good nor all bad. But for all that, the "successes" of the system, the "good" prisons, the halfway houses that really help offenders make it, are still the exceptions. They are not even prevalent enough to be called the beginning of the trend of the future. *On the whole, most of the system's practices make more sense if we look at them as ingredients in an attempt to maintain rather than to reduce crime!*

This statement calls for an explanation. The one I will offer is that the practices of the criminal justice system keep before the public the *real* threat of crime and the *distorted* image that crime is primarily the work of the poor. The value of this *to those in positions of power* is that it deflects the discontent and potential hostility of middle America away from the classes above them and toward the classes below them. If this explanation is hard to swallow, it should be noted in its favor that it not only explains our dismal failure to reduce crime, but it also explains why the criminal justice system functions in a way that is biased against the poor at every stage from arrest to conviction. Indeed, even at the earlier stage, when crimes are defined in law, the system primarily concentrates on the predatory acts of the poor and tends to exclude or deemphasize the equally or more dangerous predatory acts of those who are well off. In sum, I will argue that *the criminal justice system fails to reduce crime while making it look like crime is the work of the poor.* And it does this in a way that conveys the image that the real danger to decent, law-abiding Americans comes from below them, rather than from above them, on the economic ladder. This image sanctifies the status quo with its disparities of wealth, privilege, and opportunity and thus serves the interests of the rich and powerful in America—the very ones who could change criminal justice policy if they were really unhappy with it.

Therefore, it seems appropriate to ask you to look at criminal justice "through the looking glass." On one hand, this suggests a reversal of common expectations. Reverse your expectations about criminal justice and entertain the notion that the system's real goal is the very reverse of its announced goal. On the other hand, the figure of the looking glass suggests the prevalence of image over reality. Indeed, my argument is that the system functions the way it does *because it creates a particular image of crime: the image that it is a threat from the poor.* Of course, for this image to be believable there must be a reality to back it up. The system must actually fight crime—or at least some crime—but only enough to keep it from getting out of hand and to keep the struggle against crime vividly and dramatically in the public's view—never enough to reduce or eliminate crime. I call this way of looking at criminal justice policy the *Pyrrhic defeat* theory.

It will prevent confusion later if the reader remembers the following two features of the Pyrrhic defeat theory of criminal justice: *First,* though I maintain that our failing criminal justice system exists in part because its failure provides benefits to those with power and wealth, I do not maintain that those with power and wealth intentionally make the system fail in order to gain those benefits. *Second,* central to my analysis of the criminal justice system is the claim that the acts that the system defines as criminal are not the only or even the most dangerous acts in our society—rather they are primarily the dangerous acts committed by poor people in our society. Thus, note that when I speak of the criminal justice system I mean more than the familiar institutions of police, courts, and prisons. I mean the entire system that runs from the decisions of lawmakers about what acts are criminal all the way to the decisions of judges and parole boards about who will be in prison to pay for these acts.

I claim no particular originality for the Pyrrhic defeat theory. It is a child of the marriage of several streams of western social theory. And although this will be discussed at greater length in what follows, it will serve clarity to indicate from the start the parents and the grandparents of this child. The idea that crime serves important functions for a society comes from Emile Durkheim. The notion that public policy can best be understood as serving the interests of the rich and powerful in a society stems from Karl Marx. From Kai Erikson is derived the notion that the institutions that are designed to fight crime serve instead to contribute to its existence. And from Richard Quinney comes the concept of the "reality" of crime as *created* in the process that runs from the definition of some acts as "criminal" in the law to the treatment of some persons as "criminals" by the agents of the law. The Pyrrhic defeat theory combines these ideas into the view that the failure of criminal justice policy becomes intelligible when we see that it creates the "reality" of crime as the work of the poor and thus projects an image that serves the interests of the rich and powerful in American society.

The Pyrrhic defeat theory veers away from traditional Marxist accounts of legal institutions insofar as such accounts generally emphasize the *repressive* function of the criminal justice system, while my view emphasizes its *ideological* function. On the whole, Marxists see the criminal justice system as serving the powerful by *successfully* repressing the poor. My view is that the system serves the powerful by its *failure* to reduce crime, not by its success. Needless to add, insofar as the system fails in some respects and succeeds in others, these approaches are not necessarily incompatible. Nevertheless, in looking at the ideological rather than the repressive function of criminal justice, I will focus primarily on the image its *failure* conveys rather than on what it actually *succeeds* in repressing. To these remarks should be added the recognition that since the 1960s, a new generation of Marxist theorists, primarily French, has begun to look specifically at the ideological functions performed by the institutions of the state. Most noteworthy in this respect is the work of Louis Althusser and Nicos Poulantzas.[1]

Having located the Pyrrhic defeat theory in its family tree, a word about the relationship between crime and economics is in order. It is my view that the social order (shaped decisively by the economic system) causes or promotes most of the crime that troubles us. This is true of all classes in the society, since a competitive economy that refuses to guarantee its members a decent living places pressures on all members to enhance their economic position by whatever means available. Nevertheless, these economic pressures work with particular harshness on the poor, since their condition of extreme need and their relative lack of access to opportunities for lawful economic advancement vastly intensify for them the pressures toward crime that exist at all levels of our society.

These views lead to others that, if not taken in their proper context, may strike you as paradoxical. Evidence will be presented showing that there is a considerable amount of crime in our society at all socioeconomic levels. At the same time, it will be argued that poverty is a *source* of crime—I say "source" rather than "cause" because the link between poverty and crime is not like a physical relationship between cause and effect. Many, perhaps most, poor people do not commit crimes. Nevertheless, there is evidence suggesting that the particular pressures of poverty lead poor people to commit a higher proportion of the crimes that people fear (such as homicide, burglary, and assault) than their number in the population. There is no contradiction between this and the recognition that those who are well off commit many more crimes than is generally acknowledged, both the crimes widely feared and those not widely feared (such as "white-collar" crimes). There is no contradiction here, because, as will be shown, the poor are arrested far more frequently than those who are well off when they have committed the same crimes; and the well-to-do are almost never arrested for white collar crimes. Thus, if arrest records were brought in line with the real incidence of crime, it is likely that those who are well off would appear in the records far more than they do at present, even though the poor would still probably appear in numbers greater than their proportion of the population in arrests for the crimes people fear. In addition to this, it will be argued that those who are well off commit acts that are not defined as crimes and yet that are as or more harmful than the crimes people fear. Thus, if we had an accurate picture of who is really dangerous to society, there is reason to believe that those who are well off would receive still greater representation. On this basis, the following propositions will be put forth, which may appear paradoxical if these various levels of analysis are not kept distinct.

1. Society fails to protect people from the crimes they fear by (among other things, documented in Chapter 1) refusing to alleviate the poverty that breeds them.
2. The criminal justice system fails to protect people from the most serious dangers by failing to define the dangerous acts of those who are well off as crimes (documented in Chapter 2), and by failing to enforce the law vigorously against the well-to-do when they commit crimes (documented in Chapter 3).
3. By virtue of these and other failures, the criminal justice system succeeds in creating the image that crime is almost exclusively the work of the poor, an image that serves the interests of the powerful (argued in Chapter 4).

The view that the social order is responsible for crime does not mean that individuals are wholly blameless for their criminal acts or that we ought not have a criminal justice system able to protect us against them. To borrow an analogy from Ernest van den Haag, it would be foolhardy to refuse to fight a fire because its causes were suspect. The fact that society produces criminals is no reason to avoid facing the realization that these criminals are dangerous and must be dealt with. Also, although blaming society for crime may require that we tone down our blame of individual criminals, it does not require that we deny entirely that they are responsible for their crimes. This is particularly important to remember in view of the fact that so many of the victims of the crimes of the poor are poor themselves. To point to the unique social pressures that cause the poor to prey on one another is to point to a mitigating, not an excusing, factor. Even the victims of exploitation and oppression have moral obligations not to harm those who do not exploit them or who share their oppression.

# 1

# Crime Control in America: Nothing Succeeds Like Failure

*My love she speaks softly*
*She knows there's no success like failure*
*And that failure's no success at all*

**Bob Dylan,** Love Minus Zero/No Limit

## DESIGNED TO FAIL

Something in the American grain keeps us from admitting defeat both to ourselves and to others. Perhaps it is the heady air of the long-closed frontier trapped in our lungs; whatever it is, it keeps us from confessing to anything more serious than the temporary elusiveness of victory. Americans never confess to having lost a war, although we do admit there are a few we did not win. And domestically, no public policy ever fails, although some do not succeed. Hence President Reagan's remarks about crime control in America can only be read as a confession of failure, *American style*:

> *The frightening reality—for all of the speeches of those of us in government, for all of the surveys, studies, and blue ribbon panels, for all of the 14-point programs and the declarations of war on crime, crime has advanced and advanced steadily in its upward climb, and our citizens have grown more and more frustrated, frightened, and angry.*[1]

9

Of course, we do not need a presidential announcement to know that our assaults on the crime problem are a failure anymore than we need a presidential announcement to know that Monday follows Sunday. Everyone knows that for all our efforts, intelligence, and money, serious crime remains an enormous social problem. Although rates for some crimes do occasionally decrease from one year to the next, the overall trend in recent decades has been *up*. In that same speech, Mr. Reagan said:

> In the past decade, violent crime reported to the police has increased by 59 percent. Fifty-three percent of our citizens say they're afraid to walk the streets alone at night. Eighty-five percent say they're more concerned today than they were five years ago about crime.
>
> Crime is an American epidemic. It takes the lives of nearly 25,000 Americans, it touches nearly one-third of American households, and it results in at least . . . $8.8 billion per year in financial losses.
>
> Just during the time that you and I are together today, at least 1 person will be murdered, 9 women will be raped, 67 other Americans will be robbed, 97 will be seriously assaulted, and 389 homes will be burglarized.

Indeed, President Reagan's remarks themselves no more than hint at the enduring and abysmal nature of our failure. In 1960, the average citizen had less than a 1-in-50 chance of being a victim of one of the crimes on the FBI Index (murder, forcible rape, robbery, aggravated assault, burglary, larceny, or auto theft). In 1970, that chance grew to 1-in-25. In 1980, the FBI reported nearly 5900 Index crimes per 100,000 citizens, a further increase in the likelihood of victimization to a 1-in-17 chance. And this only counts the crimes that are reported. Based on "victimization studies" (asking randomly selected citizens if they or anyone in their household had been a victim of a crime reported to the police or not), experts extimate that unreported crime is at least double the number of reported crimes, and in some cases as much as six times as great. For example, the FBI reported 875,910 crimes of violence in 1973, while victimization studies indicated over 5 million crimes of violence in that year. In 1980, the FBI reported 1,308,900 violent crimes, while victimization studies indicated nearly 6 million. And these figures span a seven-year period characterized by a toughened war on crime and approximately $150 billion spent on criminal justice across the nation.[2]

How are we to comprehend this monstrous failure? It appears that our government is failing to fulfill the most fundamental task of governance: keeping our streets and homes safe, ensuring us of what the Founding Fathers called "domestic tranquility," providing us with the minimal requirement of civilized society. It appears that our new centurions with all their modern equipment and know-how are no more able than the old Roman centurions to hold the line against the forces of barbarism and chaos. How are we to understand this failure?

One way, of course, is to look at the *excuses* that are offered for the failure. And this we will do—but mainly to show that they do not hold up! In general, these excuses fall into two categories. Some apologists point to some feature of modern life, such as urbanization or population growth (particularly the rapid increase in the number of individuals in the crime-prone ages of 15 to 24), and they say that this feature is responsible for the growth in crime. This means that crime cannot be reduced unless we are prepared to return to horse-and-buggy days or to abolish adolescence. *Translation:* We are failing to reduce crime because it is impossible to reduce crime.

The second batch of excuses tries to argue that we simply do not know how to reduce crime. *Translation:* Even though we are doing our best, we are failing to reduce crime because our knowledge of the causes of crime is still too primitive to make our boot good enough.

These excuses simply do not pass muster. Although increasing urbanization and a growing youth population account for some of the increase in crime, they by no means account for all the increase, and certainly not for the impossibility of reducing crime. Crime rates vary widely (and wildly) when we compare cities of similar population size and density. Some very large and densely populated cities have lower crime rates than small and sparse ones. Some cities are high in one type of crime and low in another, and so on. What this means is that growing crime is not a simple, unavoidable consequence of increasing urbanization. If crime rates vary between large cities, urbanization cannot explain away our inability to reduce crime *at least* to *the lowest* rates prevalent in large cities. Similarly, the crime rate has increased far more rapidly than the youth population has both in absolute numbers and as a fraction of the total population. This means that growing crime is not a simple, unavoidable consequence of a growing youth population. If crime rates are increasing faster than the young themselves are, then increasing youth itself is not the cause of increasing crime. We have to know why 15- to 24-year-old young people are committing more crimes now than they did in the past, and it is no answer to point to their youth. A

growing youth population cannot explain away our inability to reduce crime *at least* down to the rate at which the young are increasing (or, more recently, decreasing) in our population.

On the other hand, the excuse that we do not know how to reduce
crime also does not hold up. The bald truth is that we *do* know some
of the sources of crime and *we obstinately refuse to remedy them*! We
know that poverty increases the pressures to commit crimes in pursuit of property and that crimes to obtain property account for about
90 percent of the crime rate—and yet we do little to improve the conditions of our impoverished inner-city neighborhoods beyond click-
ing our tongues over the strange coincidence that these are also the
neighborhoods with the highest crime rates. We know that our
prisons undermine human dignity and that the "ex-con" stigma
closes the door to many lawful occupations—and yet we do little to
improve these conditions beyond shaking our heads over the fact
that so much crime is committed by *recidivists*: people who have already enjoyed the hospitality of our jails and penitentiaries. We
know that heroin addiction "forces" people into crime *because* of the
high prices of illegal heroin—and yet we refuse to make cheap heroin
legally available. We know that guns figure in most murders and
make possible many thefts—and yet we refuse to adopt effective gun
control. In other words, we may not know how to eliminate crime,
but we certainly know how to reduce crime and the suffering it produces. The simple truth is that, as with crime so with crime reduction, *ignorance is no excuse.*

Since the excuses do not explain our failure to reduce crime, we
are back at square one. The question "How will we comprehend this
monstrous failure?" still stares us in the face. Examining the excuses
has been of little avail. Indeed, it has produced a result opposite from
the one hoped for. It has suggested that our failure is an avoidable
one. What has to be explained is not why *we cannot* reduce crime *but
why we will not*! Oddly enough, this parodoxical result points us in
the direction of an answer to our question.

Failure is, after all, in the eye of the beholder. The last runner
across the finish line has failed in the race only if he or she wanted to
win. If the runner wanted to lose, the "failure" is, in fact, a success.
Here, I think, lies the key to understanding our criminal justice
system.

If we look at the system as "wanting" to reduce crime, it is an abysmal failure—and we cannot understand it. If we look at it as *not*
wanting to reduce crime, it a howling success—and all we need to
understand is why the goal of the criminal justice system is to fail to

reduce crime. If we can understand this, then the system's "failure," as well as its obstinate refusal to implement the policies that could remedy that "failure," becomes perfectly understandable.

*In other words, I propose that we can make more sense out of criminal justice policy by assuming that its goal is to maintain crime than by assuming that its goal is to reduce crime!*

I call this outrageous way of looking at criminal justice policy the *Pyrrhic defeat* theory. A "Pyrrhic victory" is one in which a military victory is purchased at such a cost in troops and treasure that it amounts to a defeat. The Pyrrhic defeat theory argues that the failure of the criminal justice system yields such benefits to those in positions of power that it amounts to success. In what follows, I will try to explain the failure of the criminal justice system to reduce crime by showing the benefits that accrue to the powerful in America from this failure. I will argue that from the standpoint of those with the power to make criminal justice policy in America: *Nothing succeeds like failure.* And I challenge you to keep an open mind and determine for yourself whether or not the Pyrrhic defeat thesis does not make more sense out of criminal justice policy and practice than the old-fashioned idea that the goal of the system is to reduce crime.

The Pyrrhic defeat thesis has several components. Above all, it must provide an explanation of *how* the failure to reduce crime could benefit anyone—anyone other than criminals, that is. This is the task of Chapter 4, which is entitled "To the Vanquished Belong the Spoils: Who Is Winning the Losing War Against Crime?" I argue there that the failure to reduce crime broadcasts a powerful *ideological* message to the American people, a message that benefits and protects the powerful and privileged in our society by legitimating the present social order with its disparities of wealth and privilege and by diverting public discontent and opposition away from the rich and powerful and onto the poor and powerless.

To provide this benefit, however, not just any failure will do. It is necessary that the failure of the criminal justice system take a particular shape. *It must take a dive in the fight against crime while making it look like serious crime and thus the real danger to society is the work of the poor.* Indeed, the system accomplishes this both by what it does and by what it refuses to do. In Chapter 2, "A Crime by Any Other Name," I argue that the criminal justice system refuses to label and treat as crime a large number of acts that produce as much or more damage to life and limb as the so-called crimes of the poor. In Chapter 3, ". . .And the Poor Get Prison," I show how, even among the acts that are treated as crimes, the criminal justice system is biased from start to finish in a way that guarantees that *for the same crimes* members of the lower classes are much more likely than members of the middle and upper classes to be arrested, convicted, and imprisoned—thus providing living "proof" that crime is a threat from the poor. (A statement of the main propositions that form the core of the Pyrrhic defeat theory is found in Chapter 2, in the section entitled *Criminal Justice as Creative Art.*)

*One caution is in order:* The argument in Chapters 1 through 4 is not a "conspiracy theory." It is the task of social analysis to find patterns in social behavior and then explain them. Naturally, when we find patterns, particularly patterns that serve someone's interests, we are inclined to think of these patterns as *intended* by those whose interests are served, as somehow brought into being *because* they serve these interests. This way of thinking is generally called a "conspiracy theory." Later I will have more to say about the shortcomings of this way of thinking, and will explain in detail how the Pyrrhic defeat theory differs from it. For the present, however, note that though I have (and will) speak of the criminal justice system as "not wanting" to reduce crime, and of the failure to reduce crime as resulting in benefits to the rich and powerful in our society, *I am not maintaining that the rich and powerful intentionally make the system fail in order to gather up the resulting benefits.* A closer approximation is this: The criminal justice system we have is characterized by beliefs about what is criminal and about what to do about crime that predate industrial society. Rather than being anyone's conscious plan, it reflects attitudes so deeply embedded in tradition as to appear natural. To understand why it persists even though it fails to protect us, all that is necessary is to recognize that, on the one hand, those who are most victimized by crime are not those in positions to make and implement policy. Crime falls more frequently and more harshly on the poor than on those who are better off (see Chapter 4). On the other hand, there are enough benefits to the wealthy from the identification of crime with the poor and the system's failure to reduce crime (see Chapter 4, the section called *The Poverty of Criminals and the Crime of Poverty*) that those with the power to make profound changes in the system feel no compulsion nor see any incentive in making them. In short, the criminal justice system came into existence in an earlier epoch and persists in the present because, even though it is failing, indeed because of the way it fails, it generates no effective demand for change. When I speak of the criminal justice system as "designed to fail," I mean no more than this. I call this explanation of the existence and persistence of our failing criminal justice system, the *historical inertia* explanation. In Chapter 4, I shall spell this explanation out in greater detail, and supplement it with a *structural* explanation.

In Chapter 5, I present in dialogue form an argument that the conditions described in Chapters 1, 2, and 3 (whether or not one accepts my explanation for them in Chapter 4) have the effect of undermining the essential moral difference between criminal justice and crime itself. In this chapter, called "Criminal *Justice* or *Criminal* Justice: A Matter of Moral Conviction," I make some recommendations for reform of the system. However, these are not offered as ways to "improve" the system but as the minimal conditions necessary to establish the moral superiority of that system to crime itself.

In the remainder of the present chapter, I explore in some detail the excuses for the failure to reduce crime and show that they will not suffice. In addition, I offer evidence to back up my assertion that there are policies that could reduce crime that we refuse to implement. I then briefly outline the relationship between the Pyrrhic defeat theory and the criminological theory of Kai Erikson and Emile Durkheim, to which it is akin.

## THREE EXCUSES THAT WILL NOT WASH, OR HOW WE COULD REDUCE CRIME IF WE WANTED TO

On July 23, 1965, President Lyndon Johnson signed an Executive Order establishing the President's Commission on Law Enforcement and Administration of Justice to investigate the causes and nature of crime, to collect existing knowledge about our criminal justice system, and to make recommendations about how that system might better meet "the challenge of crime in a free society." The commission presented its report to the President early in 1967, thick with data and recommendations. Since we are a nation higher on commissions than on commitments, it should come as no surprise that for all the light cast on the crime problem by the President's Commission, little heat has been generated and virtually no profound changes in criminal justice policy have taken place in the nearly 20 years since the report was issued.

During this period, however, more and more money has been poured into crime control with the bleak results I have already outlined. When the commission wrote, it estimated that over $4 billion was being spent annually at the national, state, and local levels to pay for police, courts, and correction facilities in the fight against crime.[3] Since that time the total number of reported Index Crimes grew from 4,710,800 in 1965 to a staggering 13,295,400 in 1980.[4] The annual cost to the public of this brand of domestic tranquility reached $25,871,357,000 for fiscal year 1979, with over a million and a quarter persons employed by the criminal justice system, 701,092 of them providing "police protection."[5] Needless to say, dollar-for-dollar, crime control is hardly an impressive investment.

Nevertheless, multiplying almost as fast as crime and anticrime dollars are excuses for our failure to stem the rapid growth of crime (not to say the failure to actually reduce it) in the face of increased expenditure, personnel, research, and data. Three excuses (or, more charitably, "explanations") have sufficient currency to make them worthy of consideration as well as to set in relief the Pyrrhic defeat thesis, which I propose in their place.

### First Excuse

One excuse is that crime is an inescapable companion of any complex, populous, industrialized society. As we become more complex, more populous, more industrialized, and particularly more *urbanized*, we will have more crime as inevitably as we will have more ulcers and more traffic. These are the costs of modern life, the benefits of which abound and clearly outweigh the costs. Growing crime then takes its place alongside death and taxes. We can fight it, but we cannot win, and we should not tear our hair out about it.

It takes little reflection to see that this is less an explanation than a recipe for resignation. Furthermore, it does not account for the fact that other complex, populous, and highly industrialized nations such as Japan have crime rates that are not only lower than ours but that do not accelerate as quickly as ours. In 1971, the total number of criminal offenses known to the police in Japan was 1,244,168, a little more than 1000 offenses for every 100,000 inhabitants. In other words, about *one-fifth* the number of serious offenses known to the police in America that year occurred in a country with *half* the population of the United States crowded onto a land less than *one-twentieth* the size of the United States. More striking, however, is that while American crime was soaring in the 1970s, Japan reports that offenses known to the police decreased to 1,191,549 in 1973.

Reporting the results of her study of the relationship between crime and modernization around the world, Louise Shelley writes, "Although both societies have undergone urbanization and industri-

alization, Japan and Switzerland have been exempt from many of the
crime problems that currently plague the other developed countries.
. . . Most other developed countries have considerably higher rates of
crime commission than these two societies, but few developed countries have as high rates of crime commission as the United States."[6]
This generalization is borne out strikingly by comparing homicide
rates in the United States with those in other modern nations. In
1977, Japan had a homicide rate of 1.2 (homicides per 100,000 inhabitants), Switzerland had a rate of .9, France 1.0, West Germany 1.2,
England .9, Spain .7. For the same year, the homicide rate in the
United States was 9.2![7]

Moreover, the "costs of modern life" or urbanization excuse does
not account for the striking differences in the crime rates *within* our
own modern complex, populous, and urbanized nation. Within the
United States in 1980, the homicide rate ranged from .7 per 100,000
inhabitants in South Dakota to 16.9 in Texas and 20 per 100,000 in
Nevada.[8] Discussing the homicide rate in a 1968 issue, *Time* magazine reported that "in some Northern ghettos it hits 90, just as it did
some years ago in the [Martin Luther] King murder city of Memphis.
Texas, home of the shoot-out and divorce-by-pistol, leads the U.S.
with about 1000 homicides a year, more than 14 other states combined. Houston is the U.S. murder capital: 244 last year, more than in
England, which has 45 million more people."[9] By 1980, however,
Texas with 2392 homicides was in second place behind California
with 3411, and New York was close behind Texas with 2228—Houston's glory as the murder capital had clearly faded. Houston reported
633 homicides in 1980, roundly outdone by Los Angeles with 1010
and Chicago with 863, and left far behind by New York City, which
captured the 1980 murder title with an astounding 1812 (35 killings a
week).[10]

And such variations are not limited to murder. A comparison of
crime rates (incidence of FBI Index Crimes per 100,000 inhabitants)
for standard metropolitan statistical areas (areas "made up of a core
city with a population of 50,000 or more inhabitants and the surrounding county or counties which share certain metropolitan characteristics") reveals a striking *lack* of correlation between crime rate
and population size (which we can take as a reasonable, though
rough, index of urbanization and the other marks of modernity, such
as complexity and industrialization, that are offered as explanations
for the intractability of crime). Citizens of the New York City metropolitan area (population 9,080,777) have only a slightly greater
chance of being victimized by an Index Crime (8952.8 per 100,000

population) than citizens living in and around Tucson, Arizona, where the population is 531,896 and the crime rate is 8840.8 per 100,000, and a slightly smaller chance than citizens in the area of Tallahassee, Florida, where the population is 157,076 and the crime rate is 9,072.7 per 100,000. Consider the relationship between crime rates in the New York City metropolitan area and the Chicago metropolitan area. Metropolitan New York City's population is almost 30 percent greater than metropolitan Chicago's 7,057,853. However, a New Yorker is *three times more likely* than a Chicagoan to be a victim of a violent crime and *40 percent more likely* to be a victim of a property crime, since the violent crime rate around Chicago is 585 per 100,000 (compared to N.Y.'s 1710.6) and the property crime rate around Chicago is 5136.8 (compared to N.Y.'s 7242.3). On the other hand, a New Yorker is considerably safer than a resident of the Miami, Florida area (population 1,572,842; violent crime rate 1919.5; property crime rate 9662.3). Indeed, Miami has the highest overall crime rate, 11,581.8 per 100,000 population, of any metropolitan area in the United States—almost twice the national crime rate of 6757.6.[11]

There is, of course, no denying that crime becomes more of a problem once we reach cities with populations of over 50,000 or 100,000 persons. However, this is about all that can be said. If crime were an unavoidable and intractable consequence of urbanization, we should expect crime rates to be higher wherever population or population density (number of persons per square mile) is higher. But the facts do not bear this out. Instead, they indicate a striking *lack of correlation* between a city's crime rate and its population or population density (see Table 1).[12]

In other words, classifying crime with death and taxes and saying that it is an inevitable companion of modernity or urbanization just will not explain our failure to reduce it. Even if death and taxes are inevitable (although unfortunately not in that order), some die prematurely and some die suspiciously and some pay too much in taxes and some pay none at all. And none of these variations is inevitable or unimportant. So too with crime. Even if crime is inevitable in modern societies, its rates and types vary extensively—and this is neither inevitable nor unimportant. Indeed, the variations in crime rates between modern cities and nations is proof that the *extent* of crime is not a simple consequence of urbanization. Other factors must explain the differences. And it is these differences that suggest that although some crime may be an ineradicable consequence of urbanization, this in no way excuses our failure to reduce crime at least to the lowest rates reported in modern cities and nations.

## TABLE 1

*Metropolitan Areas by Population and Crime Rate*

| Ten Standard Metropolitan Statistical Areas by Population | Overall Crime Rate Rank (Number of FBI Index Crimes per 100,000 persons) | Violent Crime Rate Rank (Number of FBI Index Violent Crimes per 100,000 persons) | Property Crime Rate Rank (Number of FBI Index Property Crimes per 100,000 persons) |
|---|---|---|---|
| New York, N.Y.– N.J. (9,080,777) | 3rd (8952.8) | 2nd (1710.6) | 3rd (7242.3) |
| Los Angeles– Long Beach, Cal. (7,444,521) | 4th (8418.7) | 3rd (1339.6) | 4th (7079.1) |
| Chicago, Ill. (7,057,853) | 7th (5721.8) | 9th (585.0) | 7th (5136.8) |
| Philadelphia, Pa.–N.J. (4,700,996) | 10th (5357.8) | 8th (637.9) | 10th (4719.8) |
| Detroit, Mich. (4,339,768) | 6th (7582.3) | 5th (859.6) | 6th (6722.8) |
| Cleveland, Ohio (1,895,391) | 8th (5634.4) | 6th (794.1) | 9th (4840.3) |
| Miami–Fla. (1,572,842) | 1st (11,581.8) | 1st (1919.5) | 1st (9662.3) |
| Phoenix, Ariz. (1,511,552) | 2nd (9308.4) | 7th (743.7) | 2nd (8564.6) |
| Milwaukee, Wis. (1,392,872) | 9th (5364.2) | 10th (306.1) | 8th (5058.2) |
| Kansas City, Mo.–Kans. (1,322,156) | 5th (7720.3) | 4th (869.4) | 5th (6850.9) |

*Source:* Federal Bureau of Investigation, *Uniform Crime Reports*—1980.

## Second Excuse

A second excuse takes the form of attributing the growth in crime to young people—particularly young men between the ages of 15 and 24. This explanation goes as follows: Young people in our society, especially males, find themselves emerging from the security of childhood into the frightening chaos of adult responsibility. Little is or can be done by the adult society to ease the transition by providing meaningful outlets for the newly bursting youthful energy aroused in still immature and irresponsible youngsters. Hence, these youngsters both mimic the power of manhood and attack the society that frightens and ignores them by resorting to violent crime. Add to this the rapid increase of people in this age group since the baby boom of the 1940s, and we have another explanation that amounts to a recipe for resignation: We can no more expect to reduce crime than we can hope to eradicate adolescence. We can fight crime, but it will be with us until we figure out a way for people to get from childhood to adulthood without passing through their teens.

There can be no doubt that youngsters show up disproportionately in arrest figures. In 1965, persons between the ages of 11 and 24 constituted 23.4 percent of the nation's population. They represented, however, 50 percent of those arrested for willful homicide, rape, robbery, and aggravated assault; and a staggering 75.2 percent of those arrested for larceny, burglary, and motor vehicle thefts.[13] Using more recent statistics, *Time* reports that "forty-four percent of the nation's murderers are 25 or younger, and 10 percent are under 18. Of those arrested for street crimes, excluding murder, fully 75 percent are under 25 and 45 percent are under 18."[14]

However, there are many problems with this explanation. First and most obvious is that the crime rate has grown much faster than either the absolute number of young people or their percentage of the population. Neither the number nor the percentage of youngsters has doubled between 1965 and 1971, although serious crime has. Nor has the number or percentage of teenagers jumped 17 percent between 1973 and 1974, although serious crime has.

From 1960 to 1974, the number of Americans aged 15 to 24 climbed from 24.5 million to 39.5 million, an increase of about 60 percent. As a fraction of the total population, they increased about 50 percent, from 13.6 percent to 18.7 percent of the total populace. Neither figure comes close to explaining the fact that reported crimes *tripled* in that same period, going from 3,360,000 in 1960 to over

10,000,000 in 1974. Neither figure comes close to explaining the fact that the number of youngsters aged 15 to 24 who were arrested also *tripled* in that same period.[15] Similarly, from 1974 to 1980, the number of Americans aged 15 to 24 climbed from 39.5 million to 42.5 million, an increase of about 8 percent (their fraction of the total population remained unchanged at 18.7 percent). During this same period of 1974 to 1980, reported crimes increased by over 30 percent, from 10,000,000 to 13,295,399—a change far greater than the change in the number of 15 to 24 year olds.[16] In other words, there is every reason to suspect that both the overall volume of crime and the number of crimes committed by 15 to 24 year olds has increased at a much faster rate than the number of youngsters in this age bracket has increased.

Note that I am not denying that a large number of crimes are committed by young people. Thus there is undoubtedly truth in the claim that some of the decreases in crime rates that have recently been noted can be attributed to the end of the "baby boom" and the resultant decrease in the number of persons in the 15 to 24-year-old group.[17] My point is only that when this group was growing, the crime rates were growing faster than it was. If crime has increased faster than the youth population, then that increase cannot be explained by the increase in youths. If crime *among* these youngsters has increased, then this certainly is not explained by their youth. Something other than their youth or their numbers must explain why they are committing more crimes than people their age did in other periods. In neither case does the increase in young people provide an excuse for failing to reduce the growth of crime at least to the rate at which the number of young people is (or was) growing. Moreover, this remains a failure even when declining youth population leads to declining crime rates, since neither decline can be credited to criminal justice polices. So another excuse for our failure fails to excuse.

### Third Excuse

The third excuse is the hardest to swallow. This excuse, in its crudest form, is that we simply are not yet smart enough to solve the problem. We have tried and continue to try in good faith, but we can only go as far as our own lights, and they have not yet lit the path to the solution of the crime problem. In differing forms and in differing degrees of despair, this excuse is proffered by experts—both academic and professional—in the various divisions of the criminal justice system. An article by Joel D. Weisman, entitled "Chicago Reflects Police Frustration in Fight Against Crime," in the *Washington Post* gives a good sampling of this view among experts on the police:

> There is controversy over whether police departments can significantly affect crime. Boston Police Commissioner Robert J. diGrazia claims police can only displace crime—not reduce or eliminate it. "It's like squeezing a balloon," said [David] Fogel [executive director of the Illinois Law Enforcement Commission]. "You push the air away from where you're squeezing but it expands the rest of the balloon."
>
> James Q. Wilson, a professor of political science at Harvard University and author of the book Thinking About Crime, said police can contribute to reducing crime but it is unclear by how much. The data is too unreliable, he contended.
>
> "All those answers the sociologists had for us in the 1960s aren't so definite now," said [Franklin] Zimring [head of the University of Chicago's Center for Studies in Criminal Justice]. "For that matter, all of the law enforcement answers weren't so right either."[18]

An article by Leroy Aarons, also in the *Washingon Post*, entitled, "U.S. Penal System 'Truths' Questioned," reflects similar bewilderment among correctional officials. Reporting the conclusions of a "recent issue of *Corrections* magazine," which "devoted 27 pages to an article on the current ferment in the field," Aarons writes:

> The article concluded, based on interviews with wardens, administrators and students of corrections around the country that:
>
> • There is little or no evidence that correctional "treatment" programs work.
> • The gradual restructuring of the correctional system over the last 50 years around the notion of individualized and enforced treatment for all offenders was a mistake.
> • A radically new approach is needed that will provide both better protection for the public and a more realistic view of what can and cannot be done to cut recidivism, the return to criminal behavior.
>
> "What the new approach should include is a matter of dispute," the article said.

Aarons concludes his own article with an observation drawn from current doubts among corrections experts but applicable to the whole criminal justice system:

> It seems clear that, in the long run, solutions to the age-old problem of what to do with those individuals deemed law-breakers still elude society.[19]

This excuse says, in short, that growing crime is not inherently intractable, as is claimed by the partisans of excuses one and two—but it might as well be. It might as well be because we simply do not know what to do about it. And so we fail, and we cannot be blamed for our failure.

To believe this excuse, you must believe the following: That the United States, with virtually limitless resources, capable of spending hundreds of billions of dollars to fight a hardly believable "threat" in Vietnam, cannot summon the resources and will to do battle with a threat that haunts almost everyone in our society and makes them fearful to walk the streets and hardly more secure at home; that the United States, with technology and information beyond the dreams of any previous generation, indeed any previous civilization, capable of placing a human being on the moon and a heart in a human being, cannot figure out at least *some* of the causes of some crime and eliminate those causes; and that the United States, with over a million law enforcement and criminal justice personnel with training and literally billions of work-hours of experience in the "fight against crime," has not developed the expertise even to dent the rising crime rate much less actually to reduce it. This is just too much to swallow.

*But there is more.* There are, in fact, things that we do know about the sources of crime. Note that I have said "sources" rather than "causes," because the kind of knowledge we have is far from the precise knowledge that a physicist has about how some event *causes* another. We know that poverty, slums, and unemployment are *sources* of street crime. We do not know if (or how) they *cause* crime, because we know as well that many, if not most, poor, unemployed slumdwellers do not engage in street crime. And yet to say that this means we do not know that such conditions increase the likelihood of an individual resorting to violent crime is like saying that we do not know that a bullet in the head is deadly because some people survive or because we do not fully understand the physiological process that links the wound with the termination of life.

Those 15 to 24 year olds who figure so prominently in arrest statistics are not drawn equally from all economic strata. Although there is much reported and even more unreported crime among middle-class youngsters, the street crime that is attributed to this age group and that makes our city streets a perpetual war zone is largely the work of poor ghetto youth. This is the group at the lowest end of the economic spectrum. This is a group among whom unemployment approaches 50 percent with underemployment (the rate of persons either jobless or with part-time, low-wage jobs) still higher. This is a group with no realistic chance (for any but a rare individual) to enter college or amass sufficient capital (legally) to start a business or to get into the union-protected, high-wage, skilled job markets. This much we do know, just as we know that of the over 1 million persons processed through the criminal justice system on any given day, fully 80 percent come from the lowest 15 percent of the economic spectrum.[20] We know that poverty is a *source* of crime, even if we do not know how it *causes* crime—and yet we do virtually nothing to improve the life chances of the vast majority of the inner-city poor. They are as poor as ever and are facing cuts in welfare and other services. Indeed, the gap between rich and poor widened during the decade of the seventies. In 1970, the poorest 5 percent of the nation received 5.4 percent of the nation's aggregate income, while the richest 5 percent received 40.9 percent. In 1979, the poorest 5 percent received 5.3 percent, while the share of the richest 5 percent increased to 41.6 percent.[21]

Moreover, the Reagan administration's strategy of fighting inflation by cutting services to the poor while reducing the taxes of the wealthy is only accelerating this process. In September 1982, a group of 34 prominent economists sharply criticized Reagan's economic policies as "extremely regressive in its impact on our society, redistributing wealth and power from the middle class and the poor to the rich, and shifting more of the tax burden away from business and onto low- and middle-income consumers."[22] In that same month, a study released by the Urban Institute concluded that "the Reagan administration's policies are not only aiding upper-income families at the expense of the working poor, but also are widening the gulf between affluent and poorer regions of the country."[23] The study maintained that Reagan's tax cuts required sacrifices of low-income families, while yielding small gains for middle-income families and large gains for the upper-income families; and that the combined effect of the administration's tax and social service spending cuts was "to penalize working families near the poverty line who receive some federal benefits . . . creating 'major work disincentives.' " Further, as unemployment grows during the current recession, unemployment at the bottom of society grows faster than the national average. One indication of this is that in 1970, when 4.9 percent of all American workers were unemployed, the percentage for whites was 4.5 and that for nonwhites 8.2, or 1.8 times that for whites. In 1981, when 7.6 percent of all American workers were unemployed, the percentage for whites was 6.7 and that for nonwhites 14.2, or 2.1 times that for whites.[24] And in September of that same year, unemployment among black teenagers reached a record 50.7 percent.[25]

There are other things we know as well. We know that prison produces more criminals than it cures. We know that more than 70 percent of the inmates in the nation's prisons or jails are not there for the first time. We know that prison inmates are denied autonomy and privacy and subjected to indignities, mortifications, and acts of violence as regular features of their confinement. The result, as delineated by Robert Johnson and Hans Toch in *The Pains of Imprisonment*, "is that the prison's survivors become tougher, more pugnacious, and less able to feel for themselves and others, while its nonsurvivors become weaker, more susceptible, and less able to control their lives."[26] Prisoners are thus bereft of both training and capacity to handle daily problems in competent and socially constructive ways, inside or outside of prison. And once on the outside, rarely trained in a marketable skill and burdened with the stigma of a prison record, they find few opportunities for noncriminal employment open to them. Should we then really pretend that we do not *know* why they turn to crime? Can we honestly act as if we do not know that our prison system (combined with our failure to ensure a meaningful post-release noncriminal alternative for the ex-con) is a *source* of crime? Recidivism does not happen because ex-cons miss their alma mater. In fact, if prisons are built to deter people from crime, one would expect that ex-prisoners would be most deterred because the deprivations of prison are more real to them than to the rest of us. Recidivism is thus a doubly poignant testimony to the job that prison does in preparing its graduates for crime—and yet we do little to change the nature of prisons or to provide real services to ex-convicts.

We know that it is about as difficult to obtain a handgun in the United States as a candy bar. We know that there are more than 100 million guns in private use in this country. In 1968 Franklin Zimring tried to estimate the numbers of guns in civilian hands by using both the results of public opinion polls and the available figures on domestic production, as well as foreign import of firearms for civilian use. He concluded that:

> Survey results thus indicate ownership of approximately 80 million firearms, while production and import totals indicate approximately 100 million. We can do no better than average these two figures and conservatively estimate the number of firearms now in civilian hands in this country . . . 35 million rifles, 31 million shotguns, and 24 million handguns—in 60 million households.[27]

Speaking before the Law Enforcement Executives Narcotics Conference, former Attorney Gerneral Edward Levi, estimated that the number of handguns in the United States is over 40 million "and that the number increases each year by 2.5 million."[28] The President's Crime Commission reported that in 1965, "5,600 murders, 34,700 aggravated assaults and the vast majority of the 68,400 armed robberies were committed by means of firearms. All but 10 of 278 law enforcement officers murdered during the period 1960–65 were killed with firearms." The commission concluded over a decade ago that

> *more than one-half of all willful homicides and armed robberies, and almost one-fifth of all aggravated assaults, involve use of firearms.* As long as there is no effective gun-control legislation, violent crimes and the injuries they inflict will be harder to reduce than they might otherwise be.[29]

The situation has worsened since the commission's warning. The FBI's annual report on crime in the United States for 1980 indicates that 10.2 of every 100,000 Americans were murdered in 1980, 5.2 percent more than in 1979, and 62.4 percent of the homicides were committed through the use of firearms, 50 percent with handguns.[30] In the face of these facts—indeed, in the face of his own nearly fatal shooting by a would-be assassin—President Reagan has refused to support any legislative attempts to control the sale of handguns.[31]

Can we believe that a president sincerely wants to cut down on violent crime and the injuries it produces when he opposes even as much as *registering* guns or *licensing* gun owners, much less actually restricting the sale and movement of guns as a matter of national policy? Are we to believe that the availability of guns does not contribute to our soaring crime rate? Zimring's study indicates that areas with a high number of privately owned guns have more crimes involving guns than do areas with lower numbers of privately owned firearms. His data also indicate that cities that experience an increase in legal gun sales also experience an increase in gun-related suicides, accidents, and crimes.[32]

But this is hardly more than what common sense would lead us to expect. Can we really believe that if guns were less readily available, violent criminals would simply switch to other weapons to commit the same amount of crimes and do the same amount of damage? Is there a weapon other than the handgun that works as quickly, that allows it user so safe a distance, or that makes the criminal's physical strength (or speed or courage for that matter) as irrelevant? Could a bank robber hold a row of tellers at bay with a switchblade? Would an escaping felon protect himself from a pursuing police officer with a hand grenade? In fact, Zimring's studies also indicate that if gun users switched to the next deadliest weapon—the knife—and attempted the same number of crimes, we could still expect *80 percent fewer fatalities*, since the fatality rate of the knife is roughly one-fifth that of the gun. In other words, even if guns were eliminated and crimes not reduced, we could expect to save as many as four out of every five persons who are now the victims of firearm homicide!

Finally, the United States has a massive heroin-addiction problem. The number of users is hard to estimate because we only know of the ones who get caught and because there are a large but unknown number of individuals who (contrary to popular mythology) shoot up occasionally without becoming addicts—a practice known as "chipping." In his book *The Heroin Solution*, Arnold Trebach indicates that this number may be as high as 3.5 million.[33] Nevertheless some reasonable methods of arriving at a ballpark estimate of the number of addicts—that is, regular users who have developed a physical need for heroin and who therefore experience painful withdrawal symptoms if they do not shoot up regularly—have been concocted, and the most conservative figure that emerges is 250,000, with estimates ranging as high as 600,000.[34]

As shocking as this statistic may be, it must be at least as shocking to discover that there is little evidence proving that heroin is a *dangerous drug*. There is no evidence conclusively establishing a link between heroin and disease or tissue degeneration such as that which has been established for tobacco and alcohol. On the basis of the scientific evidence available, there is every reason to suspect that we do our bodies more damage, more *irreversible* damage, by smoking cigarettes and drinking liquor. Most of the physical damage that is associated with heroin use is probably attributable to the trauma of withdrawal—and this, of course, is a product not so much of heroin but of its unavailability.

It might be said that the evil of heroin is that it is *addicting*, since this is a bad thing even if the addicting substance is not itself harmful.[35] It is hard to deny that the image of a person enslaved to a chemical is rather ugly and is repugnant to our sense that the dignity of human beings lies in their capacity to control their destinies. More questionable however, is whether this is, in the case of adults, anybody's business but their own. But even so, suppose we agree that addiction is an evil worthy of prevention. Doesn't that make us hypocrites? What about all our other addictions? What about nicotine addiction, which is, like heroin, a physical need the body develops for a chemical that, unlike heroin, we know contributes to cancer and heart disease? What about the 9 or 10 million alcoholics in the nation who are working their way through their livers and into their graves? And what about the people who cannot get started without a caffeine fix in the morning, and those who, once started, cannot slow down without their alcohol fix in the evening? Are they not addicts? Suffice it to say, then, at the very least, our attitudes about heroin are inconsistent and irrational, although there is reason to believe they are outrageous and hypocritical. But even if this were not so, even if we could be much more certain that heroin addiction was a disease worth preventing, the fact would remain that the "cure" we have chosen is worse than the disease. We *know* that treating the possession of heroin as a criminal offense produces more crime than it prevents.

In its report entitled *Social Cost of Drug Abuse*, the Special Action Office for Drug Abuse Prevention uses recent figures on the average cost per day of a heroin habit to estimate the amount of theft that heroin addicts must engage in to support their habits. They compute a variety of totals using a combination of different assumptions and then average them to produce their final estimate. They assume that the average addict must supply his or her habit 255 days a year, allowing some time for being in jail or in the hospital; that they must resort to crime to obtain funds for between 33 and 60 percent of their drug needs; and that they must steal three times the dollar value they need, since they must convert their booty into cash through a fence. They assume, then, that there are between 250,000 and 600,000 addicts, who must steal to supply between 33 and 60 percent of habits costing between $43 and $51.50 per day. Using eight combinations of these assumptions, they calculate eight totals reflecting the combination of the lowest to the combination of the highest assumptions. Their totals range from a low of $2.7 billion to a high of $14.2 billion. They drop the lowest two and the highest two as unrealistic in both directions and then compute the average of the middle four:

> The average cost of these alternatives is $6.3 billion, which we shall use as an approximation of cost due to theft related to heroin use.[36]

These figures should be seen in relation to the total dollar value of stolen property across the nation. In the *Uniform Crime Reports* for 1980, the FBI sets the value of stolen property at $8.6 billion. Moreover, the figure of $6.3 billion is a conservative one on many counts. First of all, it is an estimate of what it cost addicts to support their habits in 1974, without adjustment for the effects of inflation between 1974 and 1980, the year for which the FBI's figures on stolen property are given. Second, it does not take into account the expenses that addicts have other than their drugs. In 1977, Dr. Robert DuPont said, "Our latest data at NIDA [National Institute on Drug Abuse] suggest that, during the time the addict is involved in crime . . . [his] annual income exceeds $24,000—58 percent of which (or $14,000) is required to cover the cost of drugs. Of course, the actual value of goods stolen is generally estimated to be 3 to 4 times the amount obtained through fences. So we estimate that a single heroin addict may cost society up to $100,000 a year in property loss."[37] Trebach adds, about these comments, that if "DuPont's $100,000 loss figure were to be multiplied by 200,000, our minimum estimated number of addicts not in treatment, annual property loss would amount to $20 billion, an improbable figure."[38] Even if we accept that this is an improbable figure, and even if we also assume that the FBI's estimate of the value of stolen property would increase dramatically if we knew the value of unreported theft, we cannot escape the conclusion that theft by heroin addicts—who have no other means of supporting their habits—accounts for an astounding amount of property crime. And note that nearly 60,000 inmates of state corrections facilities in 1979 reported regular use of heroin prior to incarceration, and 23,000 inmates of local jails in 1978 reported daily use of heroin prior to incarceration.[39]

It is essential to recognize that it is not the "disease" of heroin addiction that leads to property crime. There is, writes Trebach, "nothing in the pharmacology, or physical and psychological impact, of the drug that would propel a user to crime."[40] Nor is there anything about heroin itself that makes it extremely costly. The heroin that an addict pays $50 or more a day for could be legally produced at a cost of a few cents for a day's supply. Thus, it is not the "disease" of heroin addiction but its "cure" that leads to property crime. *It is our steadfast refusal to provide heroin through legal sources that, for approximately a quarter of a million individuals on the streets, translates a physical need for a drug into a physical need to steal over $6,000,000,000 worth of property a year.*

Prior to 1914, when anyone could go into a drugstore and purchase heroin and other opiates the way we buy aspirin today, hundreds of thousands of upstanding law-abiding citizens were hooked.[41] Opiate addiction is not in itself a *cause* of crime—if anything, it is a pacifier.[42] However, once sale or possession of heroin is a serious criminal offense, a number of consequences follow. First, since those who supply it face grave penalties, they charge wildly high prices to make the risk worthwhile. And since those who need it face grave pains of withdrawal and have no alternative source, they pay the wildly high prices. What an addict pays $50 a day for could be produced and sold legally for pennies (as is the case in Great Britain, where heroin is dispensed to addicts by government-controlled clinics). Second, since the supply (and the quality) of the drug fluctuates depending on how vigorously the agents of the law try to prevent it, the addict's life is continuously unstable. Addicts live in constant uncertainty about the next fix and must devote much of their wit and energy to getting it and to getting enough money to pay for it. They do not, then, fit easily into the routines of a 9-to-5 job even if they could get one that would pay enough to support their habits. Finally, all the difficulties of securing the drug add up to an incentive to be not merely a user of heroin but a dealer as well, since this both earns money and makes one's own supply more certain. Addicts thus have an incentive to find and encourage new addicts, which they would not have if heroin were legally and cheaply available. If we add to this the fact that heroin addiction has increased in spite of all our law enforcement efforts, can we doubt that the cure is worse than the disease? Can we doubt that the cure is a *source* of crime?

Against this conclusion, it is sometimes countered that studies show that a large proportion of criminal heroin addicts were criminal before they were addicts. But such studies would only refute the claim that the illegality of heroin is a source of crime if the claim was that heroin addiction turns otherwise law-abiding citizens into thieves. Rather the claim is that the illegality of heroin (and thus its limited availability and almost unlimited price) places addicts in situations in which they *must* engage in theft continually and at a high level in order to keep a step ahead of the pains of withdrawal. Thus, even for addicts who already were criminals, heroin addiction must increase the amount they need to steal and must work to make them virtually immune to any attempts to wean them from a life of crime. Consequently, even if all criminal heroin addicts were criminals before they were addicts, the illegality of heroin would still be a source of crime because of the increased pressure it places on the addict to steal much and often.

In the face of all this, it is hard to believe that we do not know how to reduce crime at all. It is hard not to share the frustration expressed by Norval Morris, dean of the University of Chicago Law School: "It is trite but it remains true that the main causes of crime are social and economic. The question arises whether people really care. The solutions are so obvious. *It's almost as if America wished for a high crime rate.*"[43]

In summary, then, American criminal justice has failed to reduce crime. The failure cannot be excused by claiming that our growing crime problem is intractable or impossible to solve. The failure cannot be excused by claiming that we do not know what to do to reduce crime. Both of these excuses fly in the face of the obvious fact that the crime rate varies under different social conditions and that there are some things we really do know about reducing crime. The second excuse also asks us to believe that the makers of criminal justice policy are more ignorant than we can possibly imagine. Therefore, if a solution is possible and we know it and we can institute it and we do not, what are we left to believe? It must be that we do not want to "solve" the crime problem, or at least some people who are strategically placed do not want to. And if this is so, then the *system's failure is only in the eye of the victim: For those in control, it is a roaring success!*

## HOW CRIME PAYS: ERIKSON AND DURKHEIM

Kai T. Erikson has suggested in his book *Wayward Puritans* that societies derive benefit from the existence of crime and thus there is reason to believe that social institutions work to maintain rather than to eliminate crime. Since the Pyrrhic defeat theory draws heavily upon this insight, it will serve to clarify my own view if we compare it with Erikson's.

Professor Erikson's theory is based on the view of crime that finds expression in one of the classic books on sociological theory, *The Division of Labor in Society*, by Emile Durkheim. Writing toward the end of the nineteenth century, Durkheim "had suggested that crime (and by extension other forms of deviation) may actually perform a needed service to society by drawing people together in a common posture of anger and indignation. The deviant individual violates rules of conduct which the rest of the community holds in high respect; and when these people come together to express their outrage over the offense and to bear witness against the offender, they develop a tighter bond of solidarity than existed earlier."[44]

The solidarity that holds a community together, in this view, is a function of the intensity with which the members of the community share a living sense of the group's cultural identity, of the boundary between acceptable and unacceptable behavior that gives the group its distinctive nature. It is necessary, then, for the existence of a community *as a community* that its members learn and constantly relearn the location of its "boundaries." And, writes Erikson, these boundaries are learned in dramatic confrontations with *policing agents whose special business it is to guard the cultural integrity of the community. Whether these confrontations take the form of criminal trials, excommunication hearings, courts-martial, or even case conferences, they act as boundary-maintaining devices in the sense that they demonstrate to whatever audience is concerned where the line is drawn between behavior that belongs in the special universe of the group and behavior that does not.*[45]

In brief, this means not only that a community makes good use of unacceptable behavior *but that it positively needs unacceptable behavior.* Not only does unacceptable behavior cast in relief the terrain of behavior acceptable to the community but also it reinforces the intensity with which the members of the community identify that terrain as their shared territory. On this view, *deviant behavior is an ingredient in the glue that holds a community together.* "This," Erikson continues,

> *raises a delicate theoretical issue. If we grant that human groups often derive benefit from deviant behavior, can we then assume that they are organized in such a way as to promote this resource? Can we assume, in other words, that forces operate in the social structure to recruit offenders and to commit them to long periods of service in the deviant ranks?. . .*
>
> *Looking at the matter from a long-range historical perspective, it is fair to conclude that prisons have done a conspicuously poor job of reforming the convicts placed in their custody; but the very consistency of this failure may have a peculiar logic of its own. Perhaps we find it difficult to change the worst of our penal practices because we expect the prison to harden the inmate's commitment to deviant forms of behavior and draw him more deeply into the deviant ranks.*[46]

In other words, based on Durkheim's recognition that societies benefit from the existence of deviants, Erikson entertains the view that societies have institutions whose unannounced function is to recruit and maintain a reliable supply of deviants. Modified for our purposes, Erikson's view would become the hypothesis that the American criminal justice system fails to reduce crime because a visible criminal population is essential to maintaining the "boundaries" that mark the cultural identity of American society and to maintaining the solidarity between those who share that identity. In other words, in its failure, the criminal justice system succeeds in providing some of the cement necessary to hold American society together as a society.

It is not my intention to do battle with the Durkheim-Erikson thesis. Rather, my aim is to acknowledge my debt to that thesis and state the difference between it and the view that I will defend. The debt is to the insight that societies may promote behavior that they seem to desire to stamp out, that failure to eliminate deviance may be a success of some sort.

The difference, on the other hand, is this. Both Durkheim and Erikson jump from the *general* proposition that the failure to eliminate deviance promotes social solidarity to the *specific* conclusion that the form in which this failure occurs in a particular society can be explained by the contribution that that failure makes to promoting consensus on shared beliefs and thus feelings of social solidarity. This is a "jump" because it leaves out the important question of how it is that a social group forms its particular consensus around one set of shared beliefs rather than another. That is, Durkheim and Erikson implicitly assume that a consensus already exists (at least virtually) and that deviance is promoted in order to manifest and reinforce it. This leads to the view that social institutions reflect beliefs that are already in people's heads and already largely and spontaneously shared by all of them. In my view, even if it is granted that societies work to strengthen feelings of social solidarity, the set of beliefs about the world around which those feelings will crystallize are by no means already in people's heads and spontaneously shared. A consensus is made, not born, although, again, I do not mean that it is made intentionally. It is created by social institutions, not just reflected by social institutions. Thus, the failure to stamp out deviance does not simply reinforce a consensus that already exists; it is part of the process by which a very particular consensus is created. In developing the Pyrrhic defeat theory, I try to show how the failure of criminal justice works to create and reinforce a very particular set of beliefs about the world, about what is dangerous and what is not, who is a threat and who is not. And this does not merely shore up general feelings of social solidarity; it allows those feelings to be attached to a social order characterized by striking disparities of wealth, power, and privilege; and considerable injustice.

# 2

# A Crime by Any Other Name

> If one individual inflicts a bodily injury
> upon another which leads to the death
> of the person attacked we call it man-
> slaughter; on the other hand, if the
> attacker knows beforehand that the
> blow will be fatal we call it murder.
> Murder has also been committed if
> society places hundreds of workers in
> such a position that they inevitably
> come to premature and unnatural ends.
> Their death is as violent as if they had
> been stabbed or shot. . . . Murder has been
> committed if society knows perfectly
> well that thousands of workers cannot
> avoid being sacrificed so long as these
> conditions are allowed to continue.
> Murder of this sort is just as culpable
> as the murder committed by an
> individual.
>
> **Frederick Engels**, The Condition of the
> Working Class in England

## WHAT'S IN A NAME?

If it takes you an hour to read this chapter, by the time you reach the last page, two of your fellow citizens will have been murdered. During that same time, at least 4 Americans will die as a result of unhealthy or unsafe conditions in the workplace! Although these work-related deaths could have been prevented, they are not called murders. Why not? Doesn't a crime by any other name still cause misery and suffering? What's in a name?

The fact is that the label "crime" is not used in America to name all or the worst of the actions that cause misery and suffering to Americans. It is primarily reserved for the dangerous actions of the poor.

In the March 14, 1976 edition of the *Washington Star*, a front-page article appeared with the headline: "Mine Is Closed 26 Deaths Late." The article read in part:

> *Why, the relatives [of the 26 dead miners] ask, did the mine ventilation fail and allow pockets of volatile methane gas to build up in a shaft 2,300 feet below the surface?*
>
> *Why wasn't the mine cleared as soon as supervisors spotted evidence of methane gas near where miners were driving huge machines into the 61-foot-high coal seam? . . .*
>
> *In Washington, Sen. Harrison Williams, D-N.J., said investigators of the Senate Labor and Welfare Committee which he chairs have found that there have been 1,250 safety violations at the 13-year-old mine since 1970. Fifty-seven of those violations were serious enough for federal inspectors to order the mine closed and 21 of those were in cases where federal inspectors felt there was imminent danger to the lives of the miners working there, he said. . . .*
>
> *Federal inspectors said the most recent violations found at the mine were three found in the ventilation system on Monday—the day before 15 miners were killed.*[1]

Next to the continuation of this story was another, headlined: "Mass Murder Claims Six in Pennsylvania."[2] It described the shooting death of a husband and wife, their three children, and a friend in a Philadelphia suburb. This was murder, maybe even mass murder. My only question is, why wasn't the death of the miners also murder.

Why do 26 dead miners amount to a "disaster" and 6 dead suburbanites a "mass murder"? "Murder" suggests a murderer, while "disaster" suggests the work of impersonal forces. But if over 1000 safety violations had been found in the mine—three the day before the first explosion—was no one responsible for failing to eliminate the hazards? Was no one responsible for *preventing* the hazards? And if someone could have prevented the hazards and did not, does that person not bear responsibility for the deaths of 26 men? Is he less evil because he did not want them to die although he chose to leave them in jeopardy? Is he not a murderer, perhaps even a *mass* murderer?

These questions are at this point rhetorical. My aim is not to discuss this case but rather to point to the blinders we wear when we look at such a "disaster." Perhaps there will be an investigation. Perhaps someone will be held responsible. Perhaps he will be fined. But will he be tried for *murder*? Will anyone think of him as a murderer? *And if not, why not*? Would the miners not be safer if such people were treated as murderers? Might they not still be alive? Will a president of the United States address the Yale Law School and recommend mandatory prison sentences for such people? Will he mean these people when he says,

> *These relatively few, persistent criminals who cause so much misery and fear are really the core of the problem. The rest of the American people have a right to protection from their violence[?]*[3]

Didn't those miners have a right to protection from the violence that took their lives? *And if not, why not*?

Once we are ready to ask this question seriously, we are in a position to see that the reality of crime—that is, the acts we label crime, the acts we think of as crime, the actors and actions we treat as criminal—is *created*: It is an image shaped by decisions as to *what* will be called crime and *who* will be treated as a criminal.

## THE CARNIVAL MIRROR

It is sometimes coyly observed that the quickest and cheapest way to eliminate crime would be to throw out all the criminal laws. There is a thin sliver of truth to this view. Without criminal laws, there would indeed be no "crimes." There would, however, still be dangerous acts. And this is why we cannot really solve our crime problem quite so simply. The criminal law *labels* some acts "crimes." In doing this, it identifies those acts as so dangerous that we must use the extreme methods of criminal justice to protect ourselves against them. But this does not mean that the criminal law *creates* crime—it simply "mirrors" real dangers that threaten us. And what is true of the criminal law is true of the whole justice system. If police did not arrest or prosecutors charge or juries convict, there would be no "criminals." But this does not mean that police or prosecutors or juries create criminals any more than legislators do. They *react* to real dangers in society. The criminal justice system—from lawmakers to law enforcers—is just a mirror of the real dangers that lurk in our midst. *Or so we are told.*

How accurate is this mirror? We need to answer this in order to know whether or how well the criminal justice system is protecting us against the real threats to our well-being. The more accurate a mirror, the more the image it shows is created by the reality it reflects. The more misshapen a mirror is, the more the distorted image it shows is created by the mirror, not by the reality reflected. It is in this sense that I will argue that the image of crime is created: The American criminal justice system is a mirror that shows a distorted image of the dangers that threaten us—an image created more by the shape of the mirror than by the reality reflected. What do we see when we look in the criminal justice mirror?

On the morning of September 16, 1975, the *Washington Post* carried an article in its local news section headlined "Arrest Data Reveals Profile of a Suspect." The article reported the results of a study of crime in Prince George's County, a suburb of Washington, D.C. It read in part that

> *The typical suspect in serious crime in Prince George's County is a black male, aged 14 to 19, who lives in the area inside the Capital Beltway where more than half of the county's 64,371 reported crimes were committed in 1974. . . .*
>
> *[The study] presents a picture of persons, basically youths, committing a crime once every eight minutes in Prince George's County.*[4]

This report is hardly a surprise. The portrait it paints of "the typical suspect in serious crime" is probably a pretty good rendering of the image lurking in the back of the minds of most people who fear crime. Furthermore, although the crime rate in Prince George's County is somewhat above the national average and its black population somewhat above that of the average suburban county, the portrait generally fits the national picture presented in the FBI's *Uniform Crime Reports* for the same year, 1974. In Prince George's County, "youths between the ages of 15 and 19 were accused of committing nearly half [45.5 percent] of all 1974 crimes."[5] For the nation in 1974, the FBI reported that persons in this age group accounted for 39.5 percent of arrests for the FBI Index Crimes (criminal homicide, forcible rape, robbery, aggravated assault, burglary, larceny, and motor vehicle theft.)[6] In 1980, this age group made up 39.0 percent of Index Crime arrests.[7] In Prince George's County, where blacks make up approximately 25 percent of the population, "blacks were accused of 58 percent of all serious crimes."[8] In the nation, where blacks made up 11.4 percent of the population in 1974, they accounted for 34.2 percent of arrests for Index Crimes.[9] In 1980, blacks made up 11.7 percent of the nation's population and 32.8 percent of Index Crime arrests.[10] This, then, is the Typical Criminal, the one whose portrait President Reagan has described as "that of a stark, staring face, a face that belongs to a frightening reality of our time—the face of a human predator, the face of the habitual criminal. Nothing in nature is more cruel and more dangerous."[11] This is the face that we see in the criminal justice mirror. Whose face is it? Let us look more closely.

He is, first of all, a *he*.[12] Second, he is a *youth*—most likely under the age of 20. Third, he is predominantly *urban*—although increasingly suburban.[13] Fourth, he is disproportionately *black*—blacks are arrested for Index Crimes at a rate three times that of their percentage in the national population. And finally, he is *poor*: "Of the 1.3 million criminal offenders handled each day by some agency of the United States correctional system, the vast majority (80 percent on some estimates) are members of the lowest 15-percent income level—that percent which is below the 'poverty level' as defined by the Social Security Administration."[14] The President's Commission reports that "from arrest records, probation reports, and prison statistics, a 'portrait' of the offender emerges that progressively highlights the disadvantaged character of his life. The offender at the end of the road in prison is likely to be a member of the lowest social and economic groups in the country."[15]

This is the Typical Criminal feared by most law-abiding Americans. His crime, according to former Attorney General John Mitchell (who is by no means a typical criminal), is forcing us "to change the fabric of our society," "forcing us, a free people, to alter our pattern of life," "to withdraw from our neighbors, to fear all strangers and to limit our activities to 'safe' areas."[16] These poor, young, urban (disproportionately) black males comprise the core of the enemy forces in the war against crime. They are the heart of a vicious, unorganized guerrilla army, threatening the lives, limbs, and possessions of the law-abiding members of society—necessitating recourse to the ultimate weapons of force and detention in our common defense. They are the "career criminals" President Reagan had in mind when he told the International Association of Chiefs of Police, assuring them of the tough stance that the Federal Government would take in the fight against crime, that "a small number of criminals are responsible for an enormous amount of the crime in American society."[17]

And how do we know who the criminals are who so seriously endanger us that we must stop them with force and lock them in prisons?

"From the arrest records, probation reports, and prison statistics," the authors of *The Challenge of Crime in a Free Society* tell us, the "'portrait' of the offender emerges."[18] *But these sources are not merely objective readings taken at different stages in the criminal justice process: Each of them represents human decisions.* "Prison statistics" and "probation reports" reflect *decisions* of juries on who gets convicted and decisions of judges on who gets probation or prison and for how long. "Arrest records" reflect decisions about which crimes to investigate and which suspects to take into custody. And all of these decisions rest on the most fundamental of all *decisions:* the decisions of legislators as to which acts shall be labeled "crimes" in the first place.

The reality of crime as the target of our criminal justice system and as perceived by the general populace is not a simple objective threat to which the system reacts: *It is a reality that takes shape as it is filtered through a series of human decisions running the full gamut of the criminal justice system*—from the lawmakers who determine what behavior shall be in the province of criminal justice to the law enforcers who decide which individuals will be brought within that province.

Note that by emphasizing the role of "human decisions," I do not mean to suggest that the reality of crime is voluntarily and intentionally "created" by individual "decision-makers." Their decisions are themselves shaped by the social system, much as a child's decision to become an engineer rather than a Samurai warrior is shaped by the social system. Thus, to have a full explanation of how the reality of crime is created, we have to understand how our society is structured in a way that leads people to make the decisions that they do. In other words, these decisions are part of the social phenomena to be explained—they are not the explanation.

For the present, however, I emphasize the role of the decisions themselves, for the following reasons: First, they are conspicuous points in the social process, easy to spot and verify empirically. Second, since they are decisions aimed at protecting us from the dangers in our midst, we can compare the decisions to the real dangers and determine whether or not they are responding to the real dangers. Third, since the reality of crime—the real actions labeled crimes, the real individuals identified as criminals, the real faces we watch in the news as they travel from arrest to court to prison—results from these decisions, we can determine whether that reality corresponds to the real dangers in our society. Where that reality does correspond to the real dangers, we can say that the reality of crime simply reflects the real dangers in society. Where the reality of crime does not correspond to the real dangers, we can say that it is a reality *created* by those decisions—although, ultimately this is a shorthand way of saying that it is a reality created by the social system that leads people to make the decisions that they do.

It is to capture this way of looking at the relation between the reality of crime and the real dangers "out there" in society that I refer to the criminal justice system as a "mirror." Who and what we see in this mirror is a function of the decisions about who and what are criminal, and so on. Our poor, young, urban, black male, who is so well-represented in arrest records and prison populations, appears not simply because of the undeniable threat he poses to the rest of society. As dangerous as he may be, he would not appear in the criminal justice mirror *if* it had not been decided that the acts he performs should be labeled "crimes," *if* it had not been decided that he should be arrested for those crimes, *if* he had access to a lawyer who could persuade a jury to acquit him and perhaps a judge to expunge his arrest record, and *if* it had not been decided that he is the type of individual and his the type of crime that warrants imprisonment. *The shape of the reality we see in the criminal justice mirror is created by all these decisions.* What we want to know is how accurately the reality we see in this mirror reflects the real dangers that threaten us in society.

It is not my view that this reality is created out of nothing. The mugger, the rapist, the murderer, the burglar, the robber all pose a definite threat to our well-being, and they ought to be dealt with in ways that effectively reduce that threat to the minimum level possible (without making the criminal justice system itself a threat to our lives and liberties). Of central importance, however, is that the threat posed by the Typical Criminal is not the greatest threat to which we are exposed. The acts of the Typical Criminal are not the only acts that endanger us, nor are they the acts that endanger us the most. We have a greater chance (as I show below) of being killed or disabled, for example, by an occupational injury or disease, by unnecessary surgery, by shoddy emergency medical services than by aggravated assault or even homicide! Yet even though these threats to our well-being are graver than that posed by our poor, young, urban, black males, they do not show up in the FBI's Index of serious crimes. And the individuals who are responsible for them do not turn up in arrest records or prison statistics. *They never become part of the reality reflected in the criminal justice mirror, although the danger they pose is at least as great and often greater than those who do!*

Similarly the general public loses more money *by far* (as I show below) from price-fixing and monopolistic practices, and from consumer deception and embezzlement, than from all the property crimes in the FBI's Index combined. Yet these far more costly acts are either not criminal, or if technically criminal, not prosecuted, or if prosecuted, not punished, or if punished, only mildly. In any event, although the individuals responsible for these acts take more money out of the ordinary citizen's pocket than our Typical Criminal, they rarely show up in arrest statistics and almost never in prison populations. *Their faces rarely appear in the criminal justice mirror, although the danger they pose is at least as great and often greater than those who do.*

The inescapable conclusion is that the criminal justice system does not simply *reflect* the reality of crime; it has a hand in *creating* the reality we see.

The criminal justice system is like a mirror in which society can see the face of the evil in its midst. But because the system deals with some evil and not with others, because it treats some evils as the gravest and treats some of the gravest evils as minor, the image it throws back is distorted like the image in a carnival mirror. Thus, the image cast back is false, not because it is invented out of thin air, but because the proportions of the real are distorted: Large becomes small and small large; grave becomes minor and minor grave. And like a carnival mirror, although nothing is reflected that does not exist in the world, the image is more a creation of the mirror than a picture of the world.

If criminal justice really gives us a carnival-mirror image of "crime," we are doubly deceived. First, we are led to believe that the criminal justice system is protecting us against the gravest threats to our well-being when, in fact, the system is only protecting us against some threats and not necessarily the gravest ones. We are deceived about how much protection we are receiving and thus left vulnerable. But, in addition, we are deceived about what threatens us and are, therefore, unable to take appropriate defensive action. The second deception is just the other side of the first one. If people believe that the carnival mirror is a true mirror—that is, if they believe that the criminal justice system simply *reacts* to the gravest threats to their well-being—they come to believe that whatever is the target of the criminal justice system must be the greatest threat to their well-being. In other words, if people believe that the most drastic of society's weapons are wielded by the criminal justice system *in reaction to* the gravest dangers to society, they will believe the reverse as well: that those actions that call forth the most drastic of society's weapons *must be* those that pose the gravest dangers to society.

There is a strange alchemy that takes place when people uncritically accept the legitimacy of their institutions: What *needs* justification becomes *proof* of justification. People come to believe that prisoners must be criminals *because* they are in prison and that the inmates of insane asylums must be crazy *because* they are in insane asylums.[19] The criminal justice system's use of extreme measures— such as force and imprisonment—is thought to be justified by the extreme gravity of the dangers it combats. But by this alchemy, these extreme measures become *proof* of the extreme gravity of those dangers, and the first deception, which merely misleads the public about how much protection the criminal justice system is actually providing, is transformed into the second, which deceives the public into believing that the acts and actors that are the target of the criminal justice system pose the gravest threats to its well-being. Thus the system may not only fail to protect us from dangers as great or greater than those listed in the FBI Crime Index, but it may do still greater damage by creating the false security of the belief that only the acts on the FBI Index really threaten us and require control.

In the following discussion, I describe how and why the criminal justice carnival mirror distorts the image it creates.

## CRIMINAL JUSTICE AS CREATIVE ART

In Chapter 1, I introduced the Pyrrhic defeat explanation for the "failure" of criminal justice in America: Criminal justice *fails* (or, what amounts to the same thing, crime is maintained) in order to project a particular *image* of crime.

It is the task of this chapter and the next to prove that the reality of crime is *created* and that it is created in a way that promotes a particular *image* of crime: *The image that serious crime—and therefore the greatest danger to society—is the work of the poor.* The notion that the reality of crime is created is derived from Richard Quinney's theory of *the social reality of crime.*[20] Since the meaning I attribute to this notion is somewhat different from the meaning Quinney gives it, it will help in presenting my view to compare it to Quinney's.

Quinney maintains that crime has a "social reality" rather than an objective reality. What he means can be explained with an example. Wherein lies the reality of money? Certainly not in the "objective" characteristics of green printed paper. It exists rather in the "social" meaning attributed to that paper and the pattern of "social" behavior that is a consequence of that meaning. If people did not act as if that green printed paper had value, it would be just green paper, not real money. The reality of a crime *as a crime* does not lie simply in the objective characteristics of an action. It lies in the "social" meaning attached to that action and the pattern of "social" behavior—particularly the behavior of criminal justice officials—that is a product of that meaning. I think Quinney is right in this. When I speak of the reality of crime, I am referring to much more than physical actions like stabbing or shooting. I mean the reality that a society gives those physical actions by labeling them and treating them as criminal.

Quinney further maintains that this reality of crime is *created*. By this he means that crime is a definition of behavior applied by lawmakers and other criminal justice decision makers. "Crime," Quinney writes, "is a *definition* of behavior that is conferred on some persons by others. Agents of the law (legislators, police, prosecutors, and judges), representing segments of a politically organized society, are responsible for formulating and administering criminal laws. Persons and behaviors, therefore, become criminal because of the *formulation* and *application* of criminal definitions. Thus, *crime is created*."[21]

Now this is *not* what I have in mind when I say that the reality of crime is created. Here is the difference. Quinney's position amounts to this: Crimes are established by the criminal law and the criminal law is a human creation; ergo, crime is created. This is true, but it does not take us very far. After all, who can deny that crime is created *in this sense*? Only someone who has been hypnotized into forgetting that law books are written by lawmakers could deny that "crime" is a label that human beings apply to certain actions. What *is* controversial, however, is whether or not the label is applied appropriately. "Crime" after all is not merely a sound—it is a word with a generally accepted meaning. It means roughly "an intentional action that is harmful to society." (Now, of course, "crime" has a technical definition, namely, "an act prohibited by a criminal law." But the point of prohibiting an act by the criminal law is to protect society from an injurious act. Thus, though any act prohibited by criminal law is rightly labeled a crime in the technical sense, not every act so prohibited is rightly prohibited, and thus not every act labeled crime is appropriately labeled. To determine whether the label crime is applied appropriately, we must use the more general definition.) The label is applied appropriately when it is used to identify all, or at least the worst of, the acts that are harmful to society. The label is applied inappropriately when it is attached to any harmless act or when it is not attached to seriously harmful acts. When I argue that the reality of crime is created, what I mean is that the label "crime" has not been applied appropriately.

One might ask why the inappropriate use of the label "crime" is a reason for saying that crime is created. My answer is this: By calling something *created*, we call attention to the fact that human actors are responsible for it. By calling crime created, I point to human actors rather than objective dangers as determining the shape that the reality of crime takes in our society. If the label "crime" is consistently applied to the most dangerous or harmful acts, then it is misleading to point to the fact that human decision makers are responsible for how the label is applied, since their decisions are dictated by compelling objective reasons. Rather than creating a reality, their decisions simply ratify a reality that already exists. On the other hand, if the label is not applied appropriately, it is sensible to assume that it is applied for reasons that lie with the decision makers and not in the realm of objective dangers. This means that when the label "crime" is applied inappropriately, it is essential to call attention to the fact that human actors are responsible for it. In other words, it is precisely when the label "crime" is applied inappropriately, that it is important to point out that the reality of crime is *created*.

By calling crime created, I want to emphasize the human responsibility for the shape of crime, not in the trivial sense that humans write the criminal law, *but rather to call attention to the fact that decisions as to what to label and treat as crime are not compelled by objective dangers, and thus that to understand the reality of crime, we must look to the social processes that shape those decisions.*

By calling crime created, I suggest that our picture of crime—the portrait that emerges from arrest statistics, prison populations, politician's speeches, news media, and fictionalized presentations, the portrait that in turn influences lawmakers and criminal justice policymakers—is not a photograph of the real dangers that threaten us. Its features are not simply traced from the real dangers in the social world. Instead, it is a piece of creative art. It is a picture in which some dangers are portrayed and others omitted. And since it cannot be explained as a straight reflection of real dangers, we must look elsewhere to understand the shape it takes.

This argument, which will occupy us in this chapter and the next leads to *five hypotheses* about the way in which criminal justice policy is made. To demonstrate that the reality of crime is created, that the criminal justice system is a carnival mirror that gives us a distorted image of the dangers that threaten us, I will try to prove that at each of the crucial decision-making points in criminal justice, the decisions made do not reflect the real and most serious dangers we face.

1.  **Of the Decisions of Legislators**    That the definitions of crime in the criminal law do not reflect the only or the most dangerous of antisocial behaviors.
2.  **Of the Decisions of Police and Prosecutors**    That the decisions on whom to arrest or charge do not reflect the only or the most dangerous behaviors legally defined as "criminal."
3.  **Of the Decisions of Juries and Judges**    That criminal convictions do not reflect the only or the most dangerous individuals among those arrested and charged.
4.  **Of the Decisions of Sentencing Judges**    That sentencing decisions do not reflect the goal of protecting society from the only or the most dangerous of those convicted by meting out punishments proportionate to the harmfulness of the crime committed.
5.  **And of All These Decisions Taken Together**    That what criminal justice policy decisions (in hypotheses 1 to 4) *do* reflect is the implicit identification of crime with the dangerous acts of the poor.

The Pyrrhic defeat theory is composed of these five hypotheses, *plus* the proposition that the criminal justice system is failing in avoidable ways to reduce crime (argued in Chapter 1), *plus* the *historical inertia* and *structural* explanations of how this failure is generated and left uncorrected because of the ideological benefits it produces (argued in Chapter 4). In presenting these explanations, I try to show how the decisions that create the reality of crime are caused by historical and structural forces, and left unchanged because the particular distribution of costs and benefits to which those decisions give rise serves to make the system self-reinforcing.

## A CRIME BY ANY OTHER NAME . . .

Think of a crime, any crime. Picture the first "crime" that comes into your mind. What do you see? The odds are you are not imagining a mining company executive sitting at his desk, calculating the costs of proper safety precautions, and deciding not to invest in them. Probably what you do see with your mind's eye is one person physically attacking another or robbing something from another on the threat of physical attack. Look more closely. What does the attacker look like? It's a safe bet he (and it is a *he*, of course) is not wearing a suit and tie. In fact, my hunch is that you—like me, like almost anyone in America—picture a young, tough, lower-class male when the thought of crime first pops into your head. You (we) picture someone like the Typical Criminal described above. And the crime itself is one in which the Typical Criminal sets out to attack or rob some specific person.

This last point is important. What it indicates is that we have a mental image not only of the Typical Criminal, but also of the Typical Crime. If the Typical Criminal is a young lower-class male, the Typical Crime is *one-on-one harm*—where harm means either physical injury or loss of something valuable or both. If you have any doubts that this is the Typical Crime, look at any random sample of police or private eye shows on television. How often do you see Jim Rockford or Matt Houston investigate consumer fraud or failure to remove occupational hazards? In fact, since portraying young lower-class males becomes rather humdrum after a steady diet, while one-on-one harm is apparently inexhaustibly interesting, the networks are much more likely to diverge from the Typical Criminal than from the Typical Crime. So even when a TV show such as "Columbo" specializes in crimes by the well-to-do in the California "castle circuit," the crimes they commit are basically the same as those that occupy the Hill Street cops on grubby urban sidestreets: crimes of one-on-one harm. A recent study of TV crime shows by The Media Institute in Washington, D.C., indicates that, while the fictional criminals portrayed on television are on the average both older and wealthier than the real criminals who figure in the FBI Uniform Crime Reports, "TV crimes are almost 12 times as likely to be violent as crimes committed in the real world."[22] In short, TV crime shows broadcast the double-edged message that the "one-on-one" crimes of the poor are the typical crimes of all and thus not uniquely caused by the pressures of poverty; *and* that the criminal justice system pursues rich and poor alike—thus when the criminal justice system happens mainly to pounce on the poor in real life, it is not out of any class bias.

It is important to identify this model of the Typical Crime because it functions like a set of blinders. It keeps us from calling a mine disaster a mass murder even if 26 men are killed, even if someone is responsible for the unsafe conditions in which they worked and died. In fact, I argue that this particular piece of mental furniture so blocks our view that it keeps us from using the criminal justice system to protect ourselves from the greatest threats to our persons and possessions.

What keeps a mine disaster from being a mass murder in our eyes is the fact that it is not one-on-one harm. What is important here is not the numbers but the *intent to harm someone.* An attack by a gang on one or more persons or an attack by one individual on several fits the model of one-on-one harm. That is, for each person harmed there is at least one individual who wanted to harm that person. Once he selects his victim, the rapist, the mugger, the murderer, all want this person they have selected to suffer. A mine executive, on the other hand, does not want his employees to be harmed. He would truly prefer that there be no accident, no injured or dead miners. What he does want is something legitimate. It is what he has been hired to get: maximum profits at minimum costs. If he cuts corners to save a buck, he is just doing his job. If 26 men die because he cut corners on safety, we may think him crude or callous but not a killer. He is, at most, responsible for an *indirect harm,* not a one-on-one harm. For this, he may even be criminally indictable for violating safety regulations—but not for murder. The 26 men are dead as an unwanted consequence of his (perhaps overzealous or undercautious) pursuit of a legitimate goal. And so, unlike the Typical Criminal, he has not committed the Typical Crime. Or so we generally believe. As a result, 26 men are dead who might be alive now if cutting corners of the kind that leads to loss of life, whether suffering is specifically intended or not, were treated as murder.

This is my point. Because we accept the belief—encouraged by our politician's statements about crime and by the media's portrayal of crime—that the model for crime is one person specifically intending to harm another, we accept a legal system that leaves us unprotected against much greater dangers to our lives and well-being than those threatened by the Typical Criminal. Before developing this point further, let us anticipate and deal with a likely objection. The defender of the present legal order is likely to respond to my argument at this point with irritation. Since this will surely turn to outrage in a few pages, let us talk to him now while the possibility of rational communication still exists.

The Defender of the Present Legal Order (I'll call him "the Defender" for short whenever it is necessary to deal with his objections in the future) is neither a foolish nor an evil person. He is not a racist, nor is he oblivious to the need for reform in the criminal justice system to make it more even-handed and for reform in the larger society to make equal opportunity a reality for all Americans. In general, his view is that—given our limited resources, particularly the resource of human altruism—the political and legal institutions we have are the best that can be. What is necessary is to make them work better and to weed out those who are intent on making them work shoddily. His response to my argument at this point is that the criminal justice system *should* occupy itself primarily with one-on-one harm. Harms of the sort exemplified in the "mine disaster" are really *not* murders and are better dealt with through stricter government enforcement of safety regulations. He would admit that this enforcement has been rather lax and recommend that it be improved. But basically he thinks this division of labor is right because it fits our ordinary moral sensibilities. In other words, according to our ordinary moral notions, someone who wants to do another harm and does is really more evil than someone who jeopardizes others while pursuing legitimate goals but wishes no one harm. And thus the former is rightfully in the province of the criminal justice system with its drastic weapons, while the latter is appropriately dealt with by milder forms of regulation.

Moreover, the Defender insists, the crimes identified as such by the criminal justice system are imposed on their victims totally against their will, while the victims of occupational hazards chose to accept their risky jobs and thus have in some degree consented to subject themselves to the dangers. Where dangers are consented to, the appropriate response is not blame but correction, and this is most efficiently done by regulation rather than with the guilt-seeking methods of criminal justice.

I think that the Defender's argument rests on three errors. First, he overestimates the reality of the "free consent" with which workers enter their jobs. Though no one is forced at gunpoint to accept any particular job, virtually everyone is forced by the requirements of necessity to take some job. Thus, at best, workers can choose among the dangers present at various worksites, and not choose to face no danger at all. Moreover, workers can only choose jobs where there are openings, which means they cannot simply pick their place of employment at will. Consequently, for all intents and purposes, most workers *must* face the dangers of the jobs that are available to them. (I will have more to say about the matter of free consent in the final section of Chapter 4).

Second, the Defender's argument errs by treating our ordinary notions of morality as a single consistent fabric rather than the crazy quilt of conflicting values and ideals it is. In other words, even if it fits some of our ordinary moral notions to believe that one-on-one harm is more evil than indirect harm, other aspects of our ordinary moral sensibilities lead to the opposite conclusion. For instance, it is a feature of both our moral sensibilities and our legal system, that we often hold people culpable for harms they have caused through negligence or recklessness, even though they wished to harm no one— thus the kid-glove treatment meted out to those responsible for occupational hazards and the like is no simple reflection of our ordinary moral sensibilities, as the Defender claims. Moreover, compare the mine executive who cuts corners to the typical murderer. Most murders, we know, are committed in the heat of some garden-variety passion like rage or jealousy. Two lovers or neighbors or relatives find themselves in a heated argument. One (usually it is a matter of chance *which* one) picks up a weapon and strikes the other a fatal blow. Such a person is clearly a murderer and rightly subject to punishment by the criminal justice system. But is this person more evil than the executive who chooses not to pay for safety equipment? I think a perfectly good case can be made that starts with our ordinary moral notions and ends up with the opposite conclusion.

The one who kills in a heated argument kills from passion. What he does he probably would not do in a cooler moment. He is likely to feel "he was not himself." The one he killed was someone he knew, a specific person who at the time seemed to him to be the embodiment of all that frustrates him, someone whose very existence makes life unbearable. I do not mean to suggest that this is true of all killers, although there is reason to believe it is true of many. Nor do I mean to suggest that such a state of mind justifies murder. What it does do, however, is suggest that the killer's action, arising out of passion, does not show general disdain for the lives of his fellows. Here is where he is different from the doer of *indirect harm*. Our absentee killer intended harm to no one in particular, but he *knew his acts were likely to harm someone*—and once someone is harmed, he (the victim) is someone in particular. Nor can our absentee killer claim that "he was not himself." His act is done, not out of passion, but out of cool reckoning. And precisely here his evil shows. In his willingness to jeopardize the lives of unspecified others who pose him no real or imaginary threat in order to make a few dollars, he shows his general disdain for all his fellow human beings. In this light, it is surely absurd to hold that he is less evil than one who kills from passion. My point will be made if you merely agree that both are equally wicked.

The Defender's argument errs a third time by overlooking the role of legal institutions in shaping our ordinary moral notions. Many who defend the criminal justice system do so precisely because of its function in educating the public about the difference between right and wrong. The great historian of English law, Sir James Fitzjames

Stephens, held that a "great part of the general detestation of crime which happily prevails amongst the decent part of the community in all civilized countries arises from the fact that the commission of offences is associated in all such communities with the solemn and deliberate infliction of punishment wherever crime is proved."[23] In other words, one cannot simply appeal to ordinary moral notions to defend the criminal law, since the criminal law has already had a hand in shaping ordinary moral notions. At least one observer has argued that making narcotics use a crime in the beginning of this century *caused* a change in the public's ordinary moral notions about drug addiction, which prior to that time had been viewed as a medical problem.[24] It is probably safe to say that in our own time, civil rights legislation has sharpened the public's moral condemnation of racial discrimination. Hence we might speculate that if the criminal justice system began to prosecute—and if the media began to portray—those who inflict *indirect harm* as serious criminals, our ordinary moral notions would change on this point as well.

I think this disposes of the Defender for the time being, although we will surely hear from him again. We are left with the conclusion that there is no moral basis for treating *indirect harm* as less evil than *one-on-one harm*. What matters, then, is whether the purpose of the criminal justice system will be served by including, in the category of serious crime, actions that are predictably likely to produce serious harm, yet which are done in pursuit of otherwise legitimate goals and without the desire to harm someone.

What is the purpose of the criminal justice system? No esoteric answer is required. Norval Morris and Gordon Hawkins write that "the prime function of the criminal law is to protect our persons and our property."[25] *The Challenge of Crime in a Free Society*, the report of the President's Commission on Law Enforcement and Administration of Justice, tells us that "any criminal justice system is an apparatus society uses to enforce the standards of conduct necessary to protect individuals and the community."[26] Whatever else we think a criminal justice system should accomplish, I doubt if anyone would deny that its central purpose is to protect us against the most serious threats to our well-being. I argue that this purpose is seriously undermined by taking one-on-one harm as the model of crime. Excluding harm caused without the intention to harm prevents the criminal justice system from protecting our persons and our property from dangers at least as great as those posed by one-on-one harm. This is so because, as I will show, there are a large number of actions that are not labeled *criminal* but that lead to loss of life, limb, and possessions on a scale comparable to those actions that are represented in the

FBI Crime Index. And a crime by any other name still causes misery
and suffering.

*     *     *

   In the remainder of this section I identify some acts that are *crimes
by any other name*—that is, acts, that cause harm and suffering comparable to that caused by acts called crimes. My purpose is to confirm the first hypothesis: that the definitions of crime in the criminal
law do not reflect the only or the most dangerous behaviors in our society. To do this, we will need some measure of the harm and suffering caused by crimes with which we can compare the harm and suffering caused by non-crimes. Our measure need not be too refined,
since my point can be made if I can show that there are some acts
that we do not treat as crime but that cause harm *roughly comparable*
to that caused by acts that we do treat as crimes. Thus it is not necessary to compare the harm caused by noncriminal acts to the harm
caused by *all* crimes. I need only show that the harm produced by
some noncriminal acts is comparable to the harm produced by *any*
serious crime. Since the harms caused by noncriminal acts fall into
the categories of death, bodily injury (including the disabling effects
of disease), and property loss, I will compare these harms to the injuries caused by the crimes of murder, aggravated assault, and theft.
   According to the *FBI Uniform Crime Reports*, in 1980 there were
23,040 murders and nonnegligent manslaughters. During that year,
there were 654,960 reported cases of aggravated assault. "Murder
and nonnegligent manslaughter" includes "all willful felonious
homicides as distinguished from deaths caused by negligence." "Aggravated assault" is defined as "assault with intent to kill or for the
purpose of inflicting severe bodily injury by shooting, cutting, stabbing, maiming, poisoning, scalding, or by the use of acids, explo-
sives, or other means."[27] Thus, as a measure of the physical harm
done by crime in 1980, I will assume that reported crimes led to
roughly 23,000 deaths and 650,000 instances of serious bodily harm
short of death. As a measure of property loss due to crime, we can
use $8,628,330,000—the total value of property stolen in 1980 accord-
ing to the UCR.[28] Whatever the shortcomings of these reported crime
statistics, they are the statistics upon which public policy has tradi-
tionally been based. Since it is my aim to analyze the difference between public policy regarding crime and that regarding other dangers, it is appropriate to use the reported figures. Thus I will consider
any actions that lead to loss of life, physical harm, and property loss
comparable to the figures in the UCR as actions that pose grave dangers to the community comparable to the threats posed by crimes.

They are surely precisely the kind of harmful actions from which a criminal justice system whose purpose is to protect our persons and property ought to protect us. *They are crimes by other names.*

Once we use these figures, it is hard to avoid the conclusion that the most dangerous American crime ring since the days of Al Capone is the U.S. government. The Vietnam War, based on a history of deception predating even the lies we were told about the so-called Gulf of Tonkin incident,[29] stands without peer in recent years in the annals of unnecessary carnage wrought by American hands. Few observers of Vietnamese history doubt that the present condition—more or less peaceful consolidation of South and North Vietnam under a more or less independent Communist regime—could have been achieved by negotiations with Ho Chi Minh many years, many lives, and many dollars ago. Furthermore, we need not doubt that those who consistently lied to the American public—as the Pentagon Papers amply document—knew that the American people would not willingly send their sons to defend a dictator like Nguyen Van Thieu against his own people. Thus, those who perpetrated this war have on their hands the blood of 57,939 young Americans, all of whose names are now listed on a somber memorial just footsteps away from the offices of those who sent them to their needless deaths. In addition to almost 60,000 dead Americans, they are responsible for several hundred thousand wounded Americans, many permanently injured, as well as several hundred thousand (some estimates give over a million) South Vietnamese who were killed by our troops and bombers as we fought to make their land safe for democracy!

I mention the Vietnam War, not because I believe that its perpetrators are likely to be brought to justice for the suffering they caused—or for the roughly $164 billion they took from the pockets of American taxpayers to finance their carnage—but because I wish to inject a note of humility that is often missing in discussions of our "crime problem." As indignant as we may be at muggers or rapists or murderers, we should never forget that they are small change compared to our own leaders when it comes to causing needless suffering, and much more likely to suffer before and as a result of their acts than our leaders ever will.

Coming closer to home, we can show that there are noncriminal actions that are more dangerous than the crimes on the FBI Index just by looking at occupational hazards in America.

### Work May be Dangerous to Your Health

Since the publication of *The President's Report on Occupational Safety and Health*[30] in 1972, numerous studies have documented both the astounding incidence of disease, injury, and death due to hazards in the workplace *and* the fact that much or most of this carnage is the consequence of the refusal of management to pay for safety measures and of government to enforce safety standards.[31]

In that 1972 report, the government estimated the number of job-related illnesses at 390,000 per year and the number of annual deaths from industrial disease at 100,000.[32] In *The Report of the President to the Congress on Occupational Safety and Health* for 1980, these estimates were rather sharply reduced to 148,900 job-related illnesses and 4950 work-related deaths.[33] Note that the latter figure is not limited to death from occupational disease but includes all work-related deaths including those resulting from accidents on the job.

Before considering the significance of these figures, it should be mentioned that all sources including the just-mentioned report as well the U.S. Department of Labor's *Interim Report to Congress on Occupational Diseases* indicate that occupational diseases are seriously underreported. *The Report of the President* states that "recording and reporting of illnesses continue to present measurement problems, since employers (and doctors) are often unable to recognize some illnesses as work-related. The annual survey includes data only on the visible illnesses of workers. To the extent that occupational illnesses are unrecognized and, therefore, not recorded or reported, the illness survey estimates may understate their occurrence."[34] The Labor Department's *Interim Report* states that

> Traditional sources of data [on the extent of occupational disease] include: employer records required by OSHA [the Occupational Health and Safety Administration], state workers' compensation records, and physician reports. Employer records understate the occupational disease problem because affected workers may no longer be employed by the firm where exposure occurred. In addition, some employers are reluctant to report occupational diseases when they are diagnosed because of their potential financial liability. Workers' compensation data understate the problem for similar reasons. . . . Physician-based records also understate the problem because few physicians are trained to recognize chronic occupational diseases and cancer.[35]

For these reasons, plus the fact that OSHA's figures on work-related deaths are only for workplaces with 11 or more employees, we must supplement the OSHA figures with other reported figures. One study conservatively estimates the number of annual cancer deaths attributable to occupational factors at 17,000.[36] Richard Schweiker, U.S. Secretary of Health and Human Services, states that "current estimates for overall workplace-associated cancer mortality vary within a range of five to fifteen percent."[37] With annual cancer deaths at 400,000, that translates into between 20,000 and 60,000 cancer deaths per year associated with the workplace. A report for the American Lung Association estimates 25,000 deaths a year from job-caused respiratory diseases.[38] None of these figures include deaths from heart disease, America's number one killer, a substantial portion of which are likely caused by stress and strain on the job.[39] Thus even if we discount the OSHA's 1972 estimate of 100,000 deaths a year due to occupational disease, we would surely be erring in the other direction to accept the figure of 4950. We can hardly be overestimating the actual toll if we set it at 25,000 deaths a year resulting from occupational disease.

As for the OSHA estimate of 148,900 job-related illnesses, here too there is reason to assume that the figure considerably underestimates the real situation. Once study suggests that it may represent no more than half of the actual number.[40] However, since this figure is probably less inaccurate than the figure for job-related deaths, it will suffice for our purposes. Let us assume, then, that there are annually in the United States approximately 150,000 job-related illnesses and 25,000 deaths from occupational diseases. How does this compare to the threat posed by crime? Before jumping to any conclusions, note that the risk of occupational disease and death falls only on members of the labor force, while the risk of crime falls on the whole population, from infants to the elderly. Since the labor force is less than half the total population (96,800,000 in 1980, out of a total population approaching 230,000,000), to get a true picture of the *relative* threat posed by occupational diseases compared to that posed by crime we should *halve* the crime statistics when comparing them to the figures for industrial disease and death. Using the 1980 statistics, this means that the *comparable* figures would be:

|                     | Occupational Disease | Crime (halved) |
| ------------------- | -------------------- | -------------- |
| Death               | 25,000               | 11,500         |
| Other physical harm | 150,000              | 325,000        |

If it is argued that this paints an inaccurate picture because so many crimes so unreported, my answer is this. First of all, homicides are by far the most completely reported of crimes. For obvious reasons, the general underreporting of crimes is not equal among crimes. It is much easier or tempting to avoid reporting a rape or a mugging than a corpse. Second, aggravated assaults are among the better-reported crimes, although not the best. Based on victimization studies, it is estimated that 54 percent of aggravated assaults were reported to the police in 1980, compared to 26.9 percent of thefts.[41] On the other hand we should expect more—not less—underreporting of industrial than criminal victims because diseases and deaths are likely to cost firms money in the form of workdays lost and insurance premiums raised, occupational diseases are frequently first seen by company physicians who have every reason to diagnose complaints as either non-job-related or malingering, and many occupationally caused diseases do not show symptoms or lead to death until after the employee has left the job.

*A survey conducted last year by the University of Washington reported that one in four Americans currently suffers an occupational disease. The report also disclosed that only one of the 10 workers with an occupational disease had been included in either OSHA [Occupational Safety and Health Administration] statistics or in the state's workmen's compensation records.*[42]

In sum, both occupational and criminal harms are underreported. Consequently, it is reasonable to assume that the effect of underreporting is probably balanced out, and the figures that we have give as accurate a picture of the *relative* threats of each as we need.

It should be noted further that the statistics given so far are *only* for occupational *diseases* and deaths from those diseases. They do not include death and disability from work-related injuries. Here too, the statistics are gruesome. The National Safety Council reported that in 1980, work-related accidents caused 13,000 deaths and 2.2 million disabling work injuries; 245 million man-days lost during that year because of work accidents, plus another 120 million man-days that will be lost in future years because of these accidents; and a total cost to the economy of $30 billion.[43] This brings the number of occupation-related deaths to 38,000 a year. If, on the basis of these additional figures, we recalculated our chart comparing occupational to criminal dangers, it would look like this:

|  | Occupational Hazard | Crime (halved) |
| --- | --- | --- |
| Death | 38,000 | 11,500 |
| Other physical harm | 2,350,000 | 325,000 |

Can there be any doubt that workers are more likely to stay alive and healthy in the face of the danger from the underworld than in the face of what their employers have in store for them on the job? If any doubt lingers, consider this. Lest we falter in the struggle against crime, the FBI includes in their annual *Uniform Crime Reports* a table of "crime clocks," which graphically illustrates the extent of the criminal menace. For 1980, the crime clock shows a murder occurring ever 23 minutes. If a similar clock were constructed for occupational deaths—using the conservative estimate of 38,000 cited above and remembering that this clock ticks only for that half of the population that is in the labor force—this clock would show an occupational death about every 14 minutes! In other words, in roughly the time it takes for one murder on the crime clock, two workers have died *just from trying to make a living.*

To say that some of these workers died from accidents due to their own carelessness is about as helpful as saying that some of those who died at the hands of murderers asked for it. It overlooks the fact that where workers are careless, it is not because they love to live dangerously. They have production quotas to meet, quotas that they themselves do not set. If quotas were set with an eye to keeping work at a safe pace rather than to keeping the production-to-wages ratio as high as possible, it might be more reasonable to expect workers to take the time to be careful. Beyond this, we should bear in mind that the vast majority of occupational deaths result from disease, not accident, and disease is generally a function of conditions outside a worker's control. Examples of such conditions are the level of coal dust in the air (about 10 percent of all active coal miners have black lung disease),[44] or textile dust (some 85,000 American cotton textile workers presently suffer breathing impairments due to acute byssinosis or brown lung, and another 35,000 former mill workers are totally disabled with chronic brown lung),[45] or asbestos fibers (a study of 632 asbestos-insulation workers between 1943 and 1971 indicates that 11 percent have died of asbestosis and 38 percent of cancer; two doctors who have studied asbestos workers conclude "we can anticipate three thousand excess respiratory, cardiopulmonary deaths and cancers of the lung—three thousand excess deaths *annually* for the next twenty or thirty years"),[46] or coal tars ("workers who had been employed five or more years in the coke ovens died of lung cancer at a rate three and a half times that for all steelworkers"; coke oven workers also develop cancer of the scrotum at a rate five times that of the general population).[47] Also some 800,000 people suffer from occupationally related skin disease each year (according to a 1968 estimate by the U.S. surgeon general)[48] and "the number of American workers experiencing noise conditions that may damage their hearing is estimated [in a 1969 Public Health Service publication of the Department of Health, Education and Welfare] to be in excess of 6 million, and may even reach 16 million."[49]

To blame the workers for occupational disease and deaths is simply to ignore the history of governmental attempts to compel industrial firms to meet safety standards that would keep dangers (such as chemicals or fibers or dust particles in the air) that are outside of the worker's control down to a safe level. This has been a continual struggle, with firms using everything from their own "independent" research institutes to more direct and often questionable forms of political pressure to influence government in the direction of loose standards and lax enforcement. So far, industry has been winning because OSHA has been given neither the personnel nor the mandate to fulfill its purpose. It is so understaffed that "in 1973, when 1500 Federal sky marshalls guarded the nation's airplanes from hijackers, only 500 OSHA inspectors toured the nation's workplaces." By 1980, OSHA employed 1581 compliance safety and health officers but this still enables inspection of only roughly 2 percent of the 2.5 million establishments covered by Federal OSHA. OSHA's budget is also an indication of the low priority given occupational health and safety: "The Federal government this year [1976] has budgeted $116 million for the Occupational Safety and Health Administration compared with $148 million to support commissaries on U.S. military bases." The Office of Management and Budget cut the fiscal 1976 budget request for $43 million for researching job-related health hazards to $32 million: "The bulk of the cuts involved research programs on occupationally caused cancers."[50] In addition to this, although OSHA has the power to levy fines for safety violations, its major thrust is on *voluntary compliance*, but since the chance of inspection is low and since fines are low when they are levied, there is little reason for firms to comply voluntarily, and so there is little voluntary compliance. Commenting on OSHA's enforcement difficulties, the Department of Labor's *Interim Report to Congress on Occupational Diseases* states:

> Data from the National Occupational Hazard Survey indicates that one in every four workers in the U.S. is potentially exposed to an OSHA-regulated health hazard—approximately 25 million workers. Only 500,000 workers are in worksites inspected by OSHA health inspectors each year.
>
> Another problem in the enforcement area is that the maximum penalty for violation of an OSHA standard ($1,000 for a serious violation) is often a minor cost factor for a firm faced with major expenditures for environmen-

*tal and engineering controls. Combined with a small probability of being in-*
*spected these relatively small fines are not likely to provide adequate eco-*
*nomic incentives for firms to reduce exposure to industrial health hazards.*[51]

Bitter Wages, the Nader Group's report, recounts a similar tale at
the level of state enforcement of safety standards. In 25 states sam-
pled in 1968 by the AFL-CIO, "one and a half times as many game
wardens as safety inspectors" were employed.[52] The Nader Group
sums up the situation at the state level in these terms:

> *The real weakness in the administration of state safety codes stems from the*
> *philosophical approach to enforcement taken by virtually all the states. The*
> *strange notion has become deeply rooted that corporate lawbreakers should*
> *not be penalized, but merely warned, in order to give them the opportunity*
> *for "voluntary compliance" with safety regulations. . . . The record indi-*
> *cates that this hope remains unfulfilled. Employers have little incentive to*
> *take any initiative to root out unsafe work conditions and practices. Instead,*
> *they can subject their employees to all kinds of hazards, to be corrected only*
> *if discovered by state inspectors—if and when the plant is visited.*[53]

Over and over again, the same story appears. Workers begin to
sicken and die at a plant. They call on their employer to lower the
level of hazardous material in the air, and their employer responds
first by denying that a hazard exists. As the corpses pile up, the firm's
scientists "discover" that some danger does exist but that it can be
removed by reducing the hazardous material to a "safe" level—
which is still above what independent and government researchers
think is really safe. At this point, government and industry spar
about "safe" levels and usually compromise at a level in between—
something less dangerous than industry wants but still dangerous.
This does not mean that the new levels are met, even if written into
the law. So government inspectors and compliance officers must
come in, and when (and if) they do, their efforts are too little and too
late:

- Federal officials cited the Beryllium Corporation for 26 safety violations and 5 "serious violations" for "excessive beryllium concentration in work place areas." Fine: $928. The corporation's
  net sales for 1970 were $61,400,000.[54]
- On request from the Oil, Chemical and Atomic Workers Union,
  OSHA officials inspected the Mobil Oil plant at Paulsboro, New
  Jersey. Result: citations for 354 violations of the Occupational
  Health and Safety Act of 1970. Fine: $7350 (about $20 a violation).[55]

- In 1972, a fire and explosion at the same Mobil plant killed a worker. Fine: $1215.[56]
- In 1968, there were 24,845 safety violations in Massachusetts, 28 prosecutions, 12 fines. Average fine: $88.[57]
- That same year, New York employers committed over 10,000 safety violations. The State Division of Inspection and Safety referred 442 cases for prosecution. Result: six fines.[58]
- In 1980, OSHA found 128,760 violations, for which penalties totaling $24,369,700 were proposed. Average penalty per violation: $189.26.[59]
- "In 1981, a Labor Department study found nearly 2 million Americans were severely or partially disabled from an occupational disease; the lost income is estimated at $11.4 billion. Yet, the study found, only 5 percent of the severely disabled received workers' compensation."[60]
- "OSHA recently offered to reduce the penalties against the operator of a grain elevator in Galveston, where an explosion killed 18 workers, and injured 22, from $126,000 to $8000—a mere $444 for each employee killed."[61]
- "Federal mine inspectors are issuing fewer violation notices, closing fewer mines for safety reasons and collecting less in fines at a time when fatalities from mine accidents appear to be on the rise. . . . A total of 153 miners were killed in 1981, the highest annual rate since 1975. . . . Assessments—civil penalties paid by mine operators—dropped from $19.5 million in calendar 1980 to $14.2 million in calendar 1981, or 27 percent."[62]

*And things seem to be getting worse rather than better.* The Reagan administration has given every indication that it believes that OSHA's regulatory activity has been too aggressive and should be toned down! Under the new administration, OSHA "has announced yet another policy change that should please most employers. OSHA will no longer automatically inspect a company accused of violating safety or health codes. Instead, OSHA will limit its inspections to companies that are accused of 'violations which pose physical harm or imminent danger' to employees. . . . Minor complaints will be resolved by registered letter. . . . Murray Seeger, a spokesman for the AFL-CIO, said, 'Fewer inspections mean more danger on the job.'"[63] More recently, Reagan's OSHA has proposed a sharp reduction in "the records that employers have to keep on medical histories of employees and the toxic substances to which they have been exposed. . . . The OSHA proposal would reduce the number of substances on which records must be kept from 39,000 to 3500," and the number of years that medical records must be kept on employees after they have left from 30 to 5.[64] On November 8, 1982, the Health Research Group—an organization founded by Ralph Nader—charged that OSHA has made "a shambles out of worker health and safety protection" since the Reagan administration took office.[65]

An editorial in the January, 1983 issue of the *American Journal of Public Health*, entitled "Can Reagan Be Indicted for Betraying Public Health?," answers the question in its title affirmatively by listing the Reagan administration's attempts to cut back government support for public health programs. On the issue of occupational safety and health, the editorial states:

> The Occupational Safety and Health Administration (OSHA) has delayed the cotton and lead [safe exposure level] standards. It proposes to weaken the generic carcinogen policy, the labeling standard, the access to medical and exposure records standard. Mine fatalities are rising again, but the Mine Safety and Health Administration and OSHA enforcement have been cut back. Research on occupational safety and health has been slashed more than any other research program in the Department of Health and Human Services. The National Institute for Occupational Safety and Health funding in real dollars is lower in 1983 than at any time in the 12-year history of the Institute. Reporting and data requirements have been devastated.[66]

The editorial ends by asking rhetorically, "How can anyone believe that the Reagan Administration wishes to prevent disease or promote health or preserve public health in America?"

*And so it goes on.*

Is a person who kills another in a bar brawl a greater threat to society than a business executive who refuses to cut into his profits in order to make his plant a safe place to work? By any measure of death and suffering the latter is by far a greater danger than the former. But because he wishes his workers no harm, because he is only indirectly responsible for death and disability while pursuing legitimate economic goals, his acts are not called *crimes*. Once we free our imagination from the irrational shackle of the one-on-one model of crime, can there be any doubt that the criminal justice system does *not* protect us from the gravest threats to life and limb? It seeks to protect us when danger comes from a young, lower-class male in the inner city. When a threat comes from an upper-class business executive in an office, the criminal justice system looks the other way. And this in the face of growing evidence that for every American citizen murdered by some thug, two American workers are killed by their bosses.

## Health Care May Be Dangerous to Your Health

Almost 20 years ago, when the annual number of willful homicides in the nation was about 10,000, the President's Commission on Law Enforcement and Administration of Justice reported that

> A recent study of emergency medical care found the quality, numbers, and distribution of ambulances and other emergency services severely deficient, and estimated that as many as 20,000 Americans die unnecessarily each year as a result of improper emergency care. The means necessary for correcting this situation are very clear and would probably yield greater immediate return in reducing death than would expenditures for reducing the incidence of crimes of violence.[67]

On July 15, 1975, Dr. Sidney Wolfe of Ralph Nader's Public Interest Health Research Group testified before the House Commerce Oversight and Investigations Subcommittee that there "were 3.2 million cases of unnecessary surgery performed each year in the United States." These unneeded operations, Dr. Wolfe added, "cost close to $5 billion a year and kill as many as 16,000 Americans."[68] Wolfe's estimates of unnecessary surgery were based on studies comparing the operations performed and surgery recommended by doctors who are paid for the operations they do with those performed and recommended by salaried doctors who receive no extra income from surgery.

The figure accepted by Dr. George A. Silver, professor of public health at the Yale University School of Medicine, is 15,000 deaths a year "attributable to unnecessary surgery."[69] Dr. Silver places the annual cost of excess surgery at $4.8 billion.[70] In an article on an experimental program by Blue Cross and Blue Shield aimed at curbing unnecessary surgery, Newsweek reports that

> a Congressional committee earlier this year [1976] estimated that more than 2 million of the elective operations performed in 1974 were not only unnecessary—but also killed about 12,000 patients and cost nearly $4 billion.[71]

Since the number of surgical operations performed in the United States rose from 20 million in 1975 to 23.8 million in 1979 (from 95.6 per 1000 population to 110.5 per 1000),[72] there is every reason to believe that at least somewhere between 12,000 and 16,000 people a year still die from unnecessary surgery. In 1980, the FBI reported that 4212 murders were committed by a "cutting or stabbing instrument."[73] Obviously, the FBI does not include the scalpel as a cutting or stabbing instrument. If they did, they would have had to report that between 16,212 and 20,212 persons were killed by "cutting or stabbing" in 1980—depending on whether you take *Newsweek's* figure or Dr. Wolfe's. No matter how you slice it, the scalpel may be more dangerous than the switchblade.

While they are at it, the FBI should probably add the hypodermic needle and the prescription to their list of potential murder weapons. Professor Silver points out that these are also death-dealing instruments.

*Of the 6 billion doses of antibiotic medicines administered each year by injection or prescription, it is estimated that 22 percent are unnecessary. Of the doses given, 10,000 result in fatal or near-fatal reactions. Somewhere between 2,000 and 10,000 deaths probably would not have occurred if the drugs, meant for the patient's benefit, had not been given.*[74]

In fact, if someone had the temerity to publish a *Uniform Crime Reports* that really portrayed the way Americans are murdered, the FBI's statistics on the *type of weapon used* in murder would have to be changed, for 1980, from those shown in Table 2a to those shown in Table 2b.

The figures shown in Table 2b would give American citizens a much more honest picture of what threatens them. We are not likely to see it broadcast by the criminal justice system, however, since it would also give American citizens a more honest picture of *who* threatens them.

We should not leave this topic without noting that, aside from the other losses it imposes, unnecessary surgery was estimated to have cost between $4 and $5 billion dollars in 1974. Medical costs have been subject to 76.7 percent inflation between 1974 and 1980.[75] Thus, in 1980 dollars, the cost of unnecessary surgery (if performed at the same rate in 1980 as in 1974) would be between $7 and $8.8 billion dollars. To this we should add the cost of the unnecessary 22 percent of the 6 billion administered doses of antibiotic medicine. Even at the extremely conservative estimate of $2 per dose, this adds $2.6 billion. In short, assuming that earlier trends have continued into the present, there is reason to believe that unnecessary surgery and medication cost the public between $9.6 and $11.4 billion annually, far outstripping the $8.6 billion taken by the thieves that concern the FBI.

### Waging Chemical Warfare Against America

One in four Americans can expect to contract cancer during their lifetimes. The American Cancer Society estimated that 420,000

## TABLE 2a

### How Americans Are Murdered

| Total | Firearms | Knife or Other Cutting Instrument | Other Weapon: Club, Arson, Poison, Strangulation, etc. | Personal Weapon: Hands, Fists, etc. |
|---|---|---|---|---|
| 21,860[a] | 13,650 | 4212 | 2733 | 1265 |

[a]Note that this figure diverges somewhat from the figure of 23,044 murders and nonnegligent manslaughters used elsewhere in the FBI *Uniform Crime Reports*, 1980; see for example, p. 7.

Source: FBI *Uniform Crime Reports*, 1980: "Murder Victims: Weapons Used, 1980."

## TABLE 2b

### How Americans Are (Really) Murdered

| Total | Occupational Hazard | Inadequate Emergency Medical Care | Knife or Other Cutting Instrument Including Scalpel | Firearms | Other Weapon: Club, Poison, Hypodermic, Prescription Drug | Personal Weapon: Hands, Fists, etc. |
|---|---|---|---|---|---|---|
| 93,860 | 38,000 | 20,000 | 16,212[a] | 13,650 | 4733[a] | 1265 |

[a]These figures represent the relevant figures in Table 2a plus the most conservative figures for the relevant categories discussed in the previous pages.

Americans would die of cancer in 1981, up from 412,000 in 1980, and 404,000 in 1979. "A 1978 report issued by the President's Council on Environmental Quality (CEQ) unequivocally states that 'most researchers agree that 70 to 90 percent of cancers are caused by environmental influences and are hence theoretically preventable.'"[76] This means that a concerted national effort could result in saving 300,000 or more lives a year and reducing each individual's chances of getting cancer in his or her lifetime from 1-in-4 to 1-in-12 or less. If you think that this would require a massive effort in terms of money and personnel, you are right. But how much of an effort would the nation make to stop a foreign invader who was killing a thousand people a day and bent on capturing one-quarter of the present population?

In face of this "invasion" that is already underway, the United States government has allocated $1 billion to the National Cancer Institute, and NCI has allocated $124 million to the study of the physical and chemical (i.e., environmental) causes of cancer.[77] Compare this to the $164 billion spent to fight the Vietnam War, in which fewer Americans were killed than are currently killed by cancer every two months! The simple truth is that the government that strove so mightily to protect us against a guerrilla war 10,000 miles from home is doing next to nothing to protect us against the chemical war in our midst. This war is being waged against us on three fronts:

- Air pollution
- Cigarette smoking
- Food additives

Not only are we losing on all three fronts, but it looks like we do not even have the will to fight.

In April, 1976, Dr. Umberto Saffioti, director of the National Cancer Institute's program of research into the chemical causes of cancer, resigned to protest three years' lack of support by NCI leaders.[78] In a letter stating his reasons for stepping down, he said:

> I cannot accept any longer a situation which in fact deprives the regulatory agencies, industry, labor, consumers, and the scientific community of data of urgent public health value: It is people who are now exposed to toxic agents and who are not protected because the necessary support was not provided in time.[79]

Earlier the same year, three lawyers for the Environmental Protection Agency resigned "'because of the continued failure of the EPA to take effective action,' to regulate possible cancer-causing and other toxic chemicals in the air, food supply, drinking water and waterways." In a joint statement, the attorneys said:

> It is clear from recent actions that the agency intends to refrain from vigorous enforcement of available toxic-substances controls and to retrench from the few legal precedents which it has set for evaluating the cancer hazards posed by the chemicals.[80]

In 1976, after extensive hearings, the Senate Subcommittee on Administrative Practices and Procedure, chaired by Senator Edward M. Kennedy, issued a report extremely critical of EPA's enforcement of regulations regarding the use of chemical pesticides.[81] In the report's introduction, Senator Kennedy states:

> I find it incredible that a regulatory agency charged with safeguarding the public health and the environment would be so sluggish to recognize and react to so many warnings over the past 5 years. The EPA was warned and certainly should have known that testing data, submitted by industry as long as 25 years ago, should not be accepted at face value in the re-registration of thousands of pesticide products presently being used on our farms and in our homes. But EPA by and large ignored these warnings.[82]

In testimony before the U.S. Senate Committee on Commerce, Samuel S. Epstein, M.D., Swetland Professor of Environmental Health and Human Ecology, in the Department of Pharmacology of the Case Western Reserve University School of Medicine, said in 1973:

> It is preposterous . . . that [the administration] can recommend a $100 million program for the treatment and prevention of cancer when current FDA [Food and Drug Administration] practice is deliberately allowing an increase in the total burden of carcinogenic elements in our human diet.[83]

The evidence linking air pollution and cancer, as well as other serious and often fatal diseases, has been rapidly accumulating in recent years. During 1975, the epidemiological branch of the National Cancer Institute did a massive county-by-county analysis of cancer in the United States, mapping the "cancer hotspots" in the nation. The result was summed up by Dr. Glenn Paulson, Assistant Commissioner of Science in the New Jersey Department of Environmental Protection: "If you know where the chemical industry is, you know where the cancer hotspots are."[84] What distinguishes these findings from the material on occupational hazards discussed above is that

NCI investigators found higher death rates for *all* those living in the "cancer hotspots"—not just the workers in the offending plants.

For instance, NCI researchers found that Deer Lodge County in Montana ranked ninth out of 3021 United States counties in lung cancer death rates. Deer Lodge County is the home of the Anaconda Company's giant copper-smelting works. The county's death rate was twice the rate expected for a rural county. A study by the Montana Department of Health and Environmental Sciences showed that the county's death rate for emphysema, asthma, and bronchitis are also well above the national average. Another study by two NCI researchers found that in *all* United States counties with smelters, the incidence of lung cancer is above the national average. And "the researchers found high lung cancer death rates not only in men—who are often exposed to arsenic on their jobs inside smelters—but also among women, who generally never went inside smelters and were not previously believed to have been exposed to arsenic." Explanation: "neighborhood air pollution from industrial sources of inorganic arsenic."[85]

New Jersey, however, took the prize for having the highest cancer death rate in the nation. NCI investigators found that "19 of New Jersey's 21 counties rank in the top 10 percent of all counties in the nation for cancer death rates." Salem County, home of E. I. Du Pont de Nemours and Company's Chambers Works, which has been manufacturing chemicals since 1919, "has the highest bladder cancer death rate in the nation—8.7 deaths per 100,000 persons."[86]

In 1970, Lester B. Lave and Eugene P. Seskin reviewed over 50 scientific studies of the relationship between air pollution and morbidity and mortality rates for lung cancer, nonrespiratory tract cancers, cardiovascular disease, bronchitis, and other respiratory diseases. They found in every instance a *positive quantifiable relationship.* Using sophisticated statistical techniques, they concluded that a 50 percent reduction in air pollution in major urban areas would result in:

- A 25 percent reduction in mortality from lung cancer (using 1974 mortality rates, this represents a potential saving of 19,500 lives per year).
- A 25 percent reduction in morbidity and mortality due to respiratory disease (a potential saving of 27,000 lives per year).
- A 20 percent reduction in morbidity and mortality due to cardiovascular disease (a potential saving of 52,000 lives per year.)[87]

In addition, even a 10 percent reduction in air pollution could be expected to "decrease the total death rate by 0.5 percent."[88]

A more recent study, done in 1978 by Robert Mendelsohn of the University of Washington and Guy Orcutt of Yale University, estimates that air pollution causes a total of 142,000 deaths a year.[89] A government study released in February, 1981 indicates that "sulfates and other air pollutants, just from coal-fired power plants, may help cause the deaths of 8000 people a year in Ohio."[90] And this chemical war is not limited to the air. The National Cancer Institute has identified as carcinogens or suspected carcinogens 23 of the chemicals commonly found in our drinking water. The Great Lakes, a source of drinking water for some 24 million Americans, is known to be contaminated by toxic chemicals.[91] Moreover, American industry produces some 57 to 80 million tons of toxic wastes a year. And "the Environmental Protection Agency estimates that only about 10 percent of the hazardous wastes . . . are disposed of in a safe, legal and acceptable manner; 90 percent are dumped illegally or disposed of in a manner that represents a potential threat to humans or the natural environment."[92]

And as with OSHA, the Reagan administration shows every sign of slowing down enforcement of EPA and FDA (Food and Drug Administration) regulations rather than making them more aggressive. "One of President Reagan's first acts upon ontoring office was to rescind an executive order designed to protect American consumers and foreign nations from particularly hazardous products that cause death and disability and are ostensibly banned for sale in the U.S. . . . Each year, hundreds of millions of pounds of pesticides banned for use in the U.S. are shipped abroad. . . . These toxins also end up poisoning American consumers when they reenter the country on imported fruits and vegetables."[93] On the subject of toxic agent control, the *American Journal Public Health* states that the Reagan "Administration has made a determined effort to reverse the progress of the last 10 years. It has rejected a protective carcinogen policy. It has decided against protective action on formaldehyde, despite the evidence from valid animal tests. . . . It has weakened the warning and cut back efforts to identify schools in which building materials expose children to asbestos."[94]

And so the chemical war goes on. No one can deny that we know the enemy. No one can deny that we know the toll it is taking. Indeed, we can compute the number of deaths that result from every day that we refuse to mount an offensive. Yet we still refuse. And thus for the time being the only advice we can offer someone who values his life, is: If you must breathe our air, don't inhale.

The evidence linking *cigarette smoking* and cancer is overwhelming and need not be repeated here. It should be noted, however, that the current U.S Surgeon General, C. Everett Koop, estimates that 30 percent of all cancer deaths are attributable to smoking, and that 1982 will see 129,000 cigarette-related cancer deaths.[95] This is enough to expose the hypocrisy of running a full-scale war against heroin (which produces no degenerative disease) while allowing cigarette sales and advertising to flourish. It should also be enough to underscore the point that once again there are threats to our lives much greater than criminal homicide. And the legal order does not protect us against them. Indeed, not only does our government not protect us against this threat, it subsidizes the the tobacco industry to the extent of nearly $100 million annually in the form of direct assistance programs and indirect support.[96] Moreover, the Administration first supported and then, under intense lobbying pressure from the tobacco industry, withdrew its support for more and stronger warnings on cigarettes.[97]

Having advocated the legalization of heroin in Chapter 1, I do not intend to argue for the criminalization of tobacco in Chapter 2. It should be said, however, that the heroin and cigarette issues are not strictly parallel. Making the sale and possession of cigarettes illegal could save many more lives a year than the whole criminal justice effort, including the "war" on heroin, currently does. I will stand, however, by the age-old liberal principle that in a free society each individual should be allowed to go to hell by a route of his choosing.

However, it is no violation of this principle to use the law to protect people who are endangered by tobacco and who have not freely chosen to subject themselves to that danger. In this light, there is growing evidence of high cancer rates among "passive smokers"— people who are regularly in the vicinity of smokers. U.S. Surgeon General Koop has reported on three studies that show a heightened risk of cancer for "non-smokers exposed to other people's smoking" (only two of the studies are claimed to be statistically significant).[98] As this evidence accumulates there will be increasing justification to protect nonsmokers from smokers by legally mandating smoke-free zones in airplanes, restaurants, offices, and so on. More immediate, however, is the case of the teenage smoker.

The law has regularly been used to protect people from their own "choices" when they are either subject to undue pressure or too young to make a sound choice (i.e., below the "age of consent"). I think both conditions obtain for teenage smokers in the United States. They find themselves in a period of maximum awkwardness, with little support from the adult world they are struggling to enter. They reach out, almost involuntarily, for a crutch, a prop, a mark of *savoir faire.* And magazine advertisements, coupled with television and film images, offer them what they think they need: the cigarette erotically inhaled by healthy, sexy, fashionable men and women or casually drooping (Bogart-style) from the cool, tough hero's lips.

And they take the prop. In fact, in the years since the surgeon general's report officially linked cancer and cigarettes, even in the years since 1970, when cigarette ads were taken off TV and radio, smoking among high school youngsters has been increasing rapidly. One study published in the *American Journal of Public Health* calls the growth of smoking among students in grades 7 through 12 an *epidemic.*[99] And "people who start smoking at age 15 are five times more likely to die of lung cancer than those who start at 25."[100]

Today, more money is being spent advertising cigarettes in newspapers and magazines and on billboards than was spent on *all* cigarette advertising during the last year that television and radio advertising was allowed.[101] And these advertisers are getting their money's worth. Between 1969 and 1976, cigarette sales increased 30 percent. Of the cigarette industry, *Business Week* says, "Increased advertising and an emphasis on new low-tar brands have kept the industry alive, although it is growing at a slower pace." The six major cigarette producers reported sales of 634.5 billion cigarettes in 1982, up from 627.3 billion in 1981.[102] In other words, *a multibillion dollar industry that thrives on hooking people to a known killer is not only allowed to flourish (subsidized at taxpayers' expense) but also to advertise its deadly wares.* Certainly, it is time to forbid *all* advertising of tobacco products and to consider drastically restricting the use of cigarettes in all media presentations. Until that time we are accomplices in yet another massive assault on the lives and well-being of American citizens.

The average American consumes *one pound* of chemical *food additives* per year.[103] Speaking on the floor of the United States Senate in 1972, Senator Gaylord Nelson said:

> *People are finally waking up to the fact that the average American daily diet is substantially adulterated with unnecessary and poisonous chemicals and frequently filled with neutral, nonnutritious substances. We are being chemically medicated against our will and cheated of food value by low nutrition foods.*[104]

A hard look at the chemicals we eat and at the federal agency that is empowered to protect us against eating dangerous chemicals reveals the recklessness with which we are being "medicated against our will."

Beatrice Hunter has taken such a hard look and reports her findings in a book aptly titled *The Mirage of Safety*. Her book is a catalogue of the possible dangers that lurk in the foods we eat. But more than this, it is a description of how the Food and Drug Administration, through a combination of lax enforcement and uncritical acceptance of the results of the food industry's own "scientific" research, has allowed a situation to exist in which the American food-eating public is the real guinea pig for nearly *three thousand* food additives. As a result, we are subjected to chemicals that are strongly suspected of producing cancer,[105] gallbladder ailments,[106] hyperkinesis in children,[107] and allergies[108]; to others that inhibit "mammalian cell growth" and "may adversely affect the rate of DNA, RNA, and protein synthesis"[109]; and to still others that are capable of crossing the placental barrier between mother and fetus and are suspected causes of birth defects and congenital diseases.[110]

The food additives are, of course, only part of the dangerous chemicals that we eat. "Deadly synthetic chemicals are now present in our food, air, water, and even our own bodies—including mother's milk—where they remain and accumulate. By the time many of the dangerous pesticides were banned or restricted as powerful cancer-causing agents, they had contaminated virtually every American and most of our food supply. Dieldrin was being found in the flesh of 99.5 percent of all human tissue samples tested, as well as in 96 percent of all meat, fish and poultry. BHC [benzene hexachloride] had been detected in 99 percent of all Americans tested, and heptachlor in 95 percent, as well as in 70 percent of meat, poultry, fish and dairy products. DDT and PCB's [pentachlorophenols] were turning up in almost all human tissue samples, fresh water fish, meat, and dairy products."[111] A 1976 EPA study of cancer-causing chemicals in the milk of nursing mothers across the U.S. found that virtually all samples contained DDT and PCB's, 81 percent showed levels of dieldrin, and 87 percent had BHC."[112]

To call government and industry practices reckless is mild in view of the fact that "one out of every five to ten people has a major allergy of disabling proportions and consequences"[113] and that between "4 to 7.5 percent of human deliveries yield individuals that have developmental defects that will interfere with survival or result in clinical disease before the end of the first year of life."[114] According "to the March of Dimes Birth defects Foundation, each year some 233,000 infants are born with birth defects."[115] Couple these facts with what we already know about the role of external chemicals in the causation of cancer, and we have a callous policy that subjects the food-eating public to unknown but reasonably suspected risks to their lives and well-being in the name of food industry profits.

Based on the knowledge we have, there can be no doubt that air pollution, tobacco, and food additives amount to a chemical war that makes the crime wave look like a football scrimmage. Quite conservatively, I think we can estimate the death toll in this war as at least a quarter of a million lives a year—*more than ten times the number killed by criminal homicide!*

## Poverty Kills

We are long passed the day when we could believe that poverty was caused by forces outside human control. Poverty is "caused" by lack of money, which means that once a society reaches a level of prosperity at which many enjoy a relatively high standard of living, then poverty can be eliminated or at least significantly reduced by transferring some of what the "haves" have to the "have-nots." In other words, regardless of what caused poverty in the past, what causes it to continue in the present is the refusal of those who have more to share with those who have less. Now you may think these remarks trite or naïve. But they are not offered as an argument of redistribution of income, although I think such a redistribution is long overdue. These remarks are presented to make a much simpler point, which is that poverty exists in a wealthy society like our own *because we allow it to exist.* And, therefore, we[116] share responsibility for poverty and for its consequences.

We are prone to think that the consequences of poverty are fairly straightforward: Less money equals less things. And so poor people have fewer clothes or cars or appliances, go to the theater less often, and live in smaller homes with less or cheaper furniture. And this is true and sad, but perhaps not intolerable. I will argue that one of the things poor people have less of is *good health.* Less money means less nutritious food, less heat in winter, less fresh air in summer, less distance from other sick people, less knowledge about illness or medicine, fewer doctor visits, fewer dental visits, less preventive health care, and above all, less first-quality medical attention when all these other deprivations take their toll and a poor person finds himself seriously ill. What this means is that the poor suffer more from poor health and die earlier than do those who are well off. Poverty robs them of their days while they are alive and then kills them before their time. A prosperous society that allows poverty in its midst is guilty of murder.

William Ryan writes in his book *Blaming the Victim:*

> *Our health problems are concentrated among the poor. In New York City, the central Harlem health district reports an infant mortality rate of 49.5 per thousand while the well-to-do district of Kips Bay-Yorkville has a rate of only 14.7 per thousand. According to the American Public Health Association, poor families suffer from disabling heart disease three times more frequently than others; and from visual impairment, seven times more frequently. A study of Head Start children in Boston revealed that almost one in three had major undiscovered health problems. The statistics can be cited almost indefinitely, and they add up to a formulation that is wearingly familiar—the poor man and the black man suffer and end up with the lowest health status.*[117]

In the 1960s, a study was done in Chicago comparing health in the poor areas of the city with health in the wealthier areas.[118] The study found that

> *the overall mortality rate in poverty areas was 40 percent higher than in nonpoverty areas. With respect to infant mortality rates, the measure used worldwide as a general indicator of community health, poverty areas exceeded nonpoverty areas by 75 percent. In a measure that many students consider to be an even better and more sensitive indicator of community health, the post-neonatal mortality rate (deaths among infants who survive the first month of life) for poverty areas exceeded nonpoverty areas by 100 percent.*[119]

A review of over 30 historical and contemporary studies of the relationship of economic class and life expectancy affirms the obvious conclusion that "class influences one's chances of staying alive. Almost without exception, the evidence shows that classes differ on mortality rates."[120] An article in the July 1976 issue of the *American Journal of Epidemiology* states that a "vast body of evidence has shown consistently that those in the lower classes have higher mortality, morbidity, and disability rates" and that these "are in part due to inadequate medical care services as well as to the impact of a toxic and hazardous physical environment."[121] Supporting this is an article in the September, 1982 issue of *The New England Journal of Medicine*, entitled "National Estimates of Blood Lead Levels: United States, 1976–1980." An editorial in the same issue comments on the findings: "The survey confirms earlier reports that black, inner-city, and poor children are at greater risk. Elevated blood lead levels were found in 2 percent of white children but 12.2 percent of black children, in 2.1 percent of rural children but 11.6 percent of inner-city children, and in 1.2 percent of children from families with an annual income of $15,000 or more but 10.9 percent of those from families with an income under $6,000."[122]

A study of parents' ratings of their childrens' health status found that 69.1 percent of children in families with incomes of $15,000 or more were rated by their parents as in excellent health, compared to 41 percent of children in families with incomes under $5000, 49.7 percent of children in families with incomes from $5000 to $9999, and 60.4 percent of children in families with incomes between $10,000 and $14,999. 1.8 percent of children in families with incomes of $15,000 or more were rated by their parents as in poor health, compared to 6.7 percent in the under $5000 group, 4.1 percent in the $5000–$9999 group, and 2.9 percent in the $10,000–$14,999 group.[123] Another indication of the correlation between low income and poor health is found in statistics on the number of days of reduced activity due to illness or injury suffered by members of different income groups. In 1979, persons from families earning under $5000 a year suffered an average of 37.5 such days, persons from families earning from $5000 to $9999 suffered 26.8 days, persons from families earning between $10,000 and $14,000 suffered 17 4 days, and persons from families earning $15,000 and over suffered 13.6 days of reduced activity.[124]

A 1978 article in *Public Health Reports*, surveying the research on the link between socioeconomic status and mortality rates, concludes that there is not only a strong positive correlation between socioeconomic status and life expectancy, but that this relationship "has changed little, if any, since the 1950s." Their survey of Chicago, Houston, Providence, Hartford, Phoenix, and Tucson, from 1930 to 1970, shows the average annual death rates per 1000 white males in the lowest socioeconomic group to be from 1.3 to 1.86 times greater than the rates for those in the highest socioeconomic group.[125] A study comparing the survival rates of indigent and nonindigent cancer patients in the University of Iowa Hospital from 1940 to 1969, concludes that "The indigents had poorer survival than the private patients for every cancer type for which there was data."[126]

A comparison of the health and mortality of blacks and whites in America yields further insight into the relationship of health and mortality to economic class. In 1981, about 1 out of every 3 blacks lived below the poverty level, as compared to 1 out of every 11 whites. Black unemployment is consistently double that of whites. As of October, 1982, 20.2 percent of blacks were unemployed compared to 9.3. percent of whites. Median income of black families in 1979 was 59 percent (slightly less than *three fifths!*) of the median income of white families—and this too is a relatively stable figure. In 1960, it was 57 percent, in 1975 it rose to 62 percent, and in 1981 it fell to only 56 percent.[127] For these reasons, it is generally a safe bet to assume that data on the lives of blacks in America are also data on the impact of low economic status in America.

In 1978, black mothers died in childbirth at a rate *four times* that of white mothers. Black infant mortality was 23.1 per thousand live births compared to 12.0 for whites.[128] In 1979, the figure for blacks was down to 21.8, and the figure for whites was 11.4.[129] In short, black mothers lose their babies within the first year of life nearly twice as often as white mothers. In the face of this situation, the Reagan administration has reduced funding for maternal and child health programs by more than 25 percent and attempted to reduce support for immunization programs for American children.[130]

Cancer survival statistics show a similar picture. A report entitled *Cancer Patient Survival Experience*, published by the National Institutes of Health in 1980, states that "the survival experience for white [cancer] patients is better than that for black patients." One important cause of this difference is that "white patients tended to have higher percentages of cancers diagnosed while localized,"[131] that is, earlier in their development. This means that the difference is not due to genetic factors, but to such things as better access to medical care, higher levels of education about the early warning signs of cancer, and so on, all of which strongly correlate with higher income levels. Berg, Ross, and Latourette, in their study of cancer survival and economic status referred to earlier, state, "We submit that economic differences could explain most, if not all, the general poor showing of Blacks."[132]

Life expectancy figures paint the most tragic picture of all. In 1979, life expectancy among blacks was 68.3 years, while among whites it was 74.4 years.[133] Now life expectancy figures are averages; some people live longer and some live shorter. And, of course, some blacks live longer than some whites. But however individuals fare, the figures indicate that blacks are cheated out of a considerable number of years of life—enough to average out to six lost years per person. Nor can the difference in life expectancy be wholly attributed to genetic factors, since the difference has steadily shrunk in response to advances in medicine during this century.[134] Indeed, the current difference between white and black life expectancy is the smallest ever.[135] This means that we can assume that the life expectancy of white

Americans is close to the minimum that any American should expect,[136] and thus that the various indignities that go with being black in America are responsible for much if not all the discrepancy between black and white life expectancy rates. Of these various indignities, low economic status is surely the prime cause of poor health and early death, since access to money could undoubtedly do much to overcome the other effects of racism on health.

From this, an inescapable conclusion follows. If we assume that in the absence of poverty, blacks would have about the same life expectancy as whites, then poverty robs every black person of six years of life, on the average. In short *poverty hurts, injures, and kills—just like crime.* And a society that could remedy its poverty but does not is an accomplice in crime.

*   *   *

Once again, our investigations lead to the same result. The criminal justice system does not protect us against the gravest threats to life, limb, or possessions. Its definitions of crime are not simply a reflection of the objective dangers that threaten us. The workplace, the medical profession, the air we breathe, and the poverty we refuse to rectify lead to far more human suffering, far more death and disability, and take far more dollars from our pockets than the murders, aggravated assaults, and thefts reported annually by the FBI. And what is more, this human suffering is preventable. A government really intent on protecting our well-being could enforce work safety regulations, police the medical profession, require that clean air standards be met, and funnel sufficient money to the poor to alleviate the major disabilities of poverty. But it does not. Instead we hear a lot of cant about law and order and a lot of rant about crime in the streets. It is as if our leaders were not only refusing to protect us from the major threats to our well-being but trying to cover up this refusal by diverting our attention to crime—as if this were the only real threat. But as we have seen, the criminal justice system is a carnival mirror that presents a distorted image of what threatens us. And the distortions do not end with the definitions of crime. As we will see in what follows, new distortions enter at every level of the system, so that in the end, when we look in our prisons to see who really threatens us, all we see are poor people. By that time, virtually all the well-to-do people who endanger us have been discreetly weeded out of the system. As we watch this process unfold in the following chapter, we should bear in mind the conclusion of the present chapter: All the mechanisms by which the criminal justice system comes down more frequently and more harshly on the poor criminal than on the well-off criminal take place *after* most of the dangerous acts of the well-to-do have been excluded from the definition of crime itself. The bias against the poor within the criminal justice system is all the more striking when we recognize that the door to that system is shaped in a way that excludes in advance the most dangerous acts of the well-to-do. Demonstrating this has been the purpose of the present chapter.

# 3

# . . . And the Poor Get Prison

> When we come to make an intelligent
> study of the prison at first hand . . . we are
> bound to conclude that after all it is not
> so much crime in its general sense that is
> penalized, but that it is poverty which
> is punished . . .
>
> Take a census of the average prison and
> you will find that a large majority of
> people are there not so much because of
> the particular crime they are alleged to
> have committed, but for the reason that
> they are poor and . . . lacked the money to
> engage the services of first class and
> influential lawyers.
>
> **Eugene V. Debs,** Walls and Bars

## WEEDING OUT THE WEALTHY

*The offender at the end of the road in prison is likely to be a member of the
lowest social and economic groups in the country.*[1]

This statement in the *Report of the President's Commission on Law
Enforcement and Administration of Justice* is as true today as it was
nearly two decades ago when it was written. Our prisons are indeed,
as Ronald Goldfarb has called them, the National Poorhouse.[2] To
most citizens this comes as no surprise—recall the Typical Criminal
and the Typical Crime. Dangerous crimes, they think, are mainly
committed by poor people. And seeing that prison populations are
made up primarily of the poor only makes them surer of this. They

think, in other words, that the criminal justice system gives a true reflection of the dangers that threaten them.

In my view, it also comes as no surprise that our prisons and jails
predominantly confine the poor. But this is not because these are the
individuals who most threaten us. Instead, it is because the criminal
justice system effectively weeds out the well-to-do, so that at *the end
of the road in prison*, the vast majority of those we find there come
from the lower classes. This "weeding out" process starts before the
agents of law enforcement go into action. In the last chapter, I argued that our very definition of crime *excludes* a wide variety of
actions at least as dangerous as those included and often worse. Is it
any accident that the kinds of dangerous actions excluded are the
kinds most likely to be performed by the affluent in America? Even
before we mobilize our troops in the war on crime, we have already
guaranteed that large numbers of upper-class individuals will never
come within their sights.

But this process does not stop at the definition of crime. It continues throughout each level of the criminal justice system. At each
step, from arrest to sentencing, the likelihood of being ignored or released or lightly treated by the system is greater the better off one is
economically. As the late U.S. Senator Philip Hart has written:

> *Justice has two transmission belts, one for the rich and one for the poor. The
> low-income transmission belt is easier to ride without falling off and it gets
> to prison in shorter order.*
>
> *The transmission belt for the affluent is a little slower and it passes innu-
> merable stations where exits are temptingly convenient.*[3]

This means that the criminal justice system functions from start to
finish in a way that makes certain that "the offender at the end of the
road in prison is likely to be a member of the lowest social and economic groups in the country."

*For the same criminal behavior*, the poor are more likely to be arrested; if arrested, they are more likely to be charged; if charged,
more likely to be convicted; if convicted, more likely to be sentenced
to prison; and if sentenced, more likely to be given longer prison
terms than members of the middle and upper classes.[4] In other
words, the image of the criminal population one sees in our nation's
jails and prisons is distorted by the shape of the criminal justice system itself. It is the face of evil reflected in a carnival mirror, but it is
no laughing matter.

The face in the criminal justice carnival mirror is also, as we have
already noted, very frequently a black face. Although blacks do not

comprise the majority of the inmates in our jails and prisons, they make up a proportion that far outstrips their proportion in the population.[5] But here, too, the image we see is distorted by the processes of the criminal justice system itself. Edwin Sutherland and Donald Cressey write, in their widely used textbook, *Criminology*, that

> *numerous studies have shown that African-Americans are more likely to be arrested, indicted, convicted, and committed to an institution than are whites who commit the same offenses, and many other studies have shown that blacks have a poorer chance than whites to receive probation, a suspended sentence, parole, commutation of a death sentence, or pardon.*[6]

There can be little doubt that the criminal justice process is distorted by racism as well as by economic bias.[7] Nevertheless, it does not pay to look at these as two independent forms of bias. It is my view that, at least as far as criminal justice is concerned, racism is simply one powerful form of economic bias. I use evidence on differential treatment of blacks as evidence of differential treatment of members of the lower-classes. There are five reasons:

1. First and foremost, black Americans are disproportionately poor. Nearly *one-third* of all black Americans were below the poverty level in 1980, compared to about *one-eleventh* of white Americans—very much the same as it was in 1974, the year from which the figures in the first edition of this book were taken.

2. Blacks who travel the full route of the criminal justice system and end up in jail or prison are nearly identical in economic condition to whites who do. For example, in 1972, 47 percent of black jail inmates and 43 percent of white jail inmates had pre-arrest annual incomes of less than $2000.[8] In 1978, 53 percent of black jail inmates had pre-arrest incomes below $3000, compared to 44 percent of whites.[9]

3. The factors that are most likely to keep one out of trouble with the law and out of prison, such as a suburban living room instead of a tenement alley to gamble in, or legal counsel able to devote time to one's case instead of an overburdened public defender, are the kinds of things that money can buy regardless of one's race, creed, or national origin.

4. Curiously enough, statistics on differential treatment of races are available in greater abundance than are statistics on differential treatment of economic classes. For instance, although the FBI tabulates arrest rates by race (as well as by sex, age, and geographical area), it omits class or income. Similarly, both the Pres-

ident's Crime Commission Report and Sutherland and Cressey's *Criminology* have index entries for race or racial discrimination but none for class or income of offenders. It would seem that both independent and government data gatherers are more willing to own up to America's racism than to its class bias.

5. Finally, it is my belief that the economic powers-that-be in America have sufficient power to end or drastically reduce racist bias in the criminal justice system. To the extent that they allow it to exist, it is not unreasonable to assume that it furthers their economic interests.

For all these reasons, racism will be treated here as either a form of economic bias or a tool that achieves the same end.

In the remainder of this chapter, I show how the criminal justice system functions to *weed out the wealthy* (meaning both middle- and upper-class offenders) at each stage of the process and thus produces a distorted image of the crime problem. Before entering into this discussion, two provisos should be noted. First, it is not my view that the poor are all innocent victims persecuted by the evil rich. The poor do commit crimes, and my own assumption is that the vast majority of the poor who are confined in our prisons are guilty of the crimes for which they were sentenced. In addition, there is good evidence that the poor do commit a greater portion of the crimes against person and property listed in the FBI Index than the middle and upper classes do, relative to their numbers in the national population. What I have already tried to prove is that the crimes in the FBI Index are not the acts that threaten us most, and what I will try to prove in what follows is that the poor are arrested and punished by the criminal justice system much more frequently than their contribution to the crime problem would warrant—thus the criminals who populate our prisons as well as the public's imagination are disproportionately poor.

The second proviso is this. The following discussion has been divided into three sections that correspond to the major criminal justice decision points and that also correspond to hypotheses two, three, and four that were stated on page 45. As always, such classifications are a bit neater than reality, and so they should not be taken as rigid compartments. Many of the distorting processes oper-. ate at all criminal justice decision points. So, for example, while I will primarily discuss the light-handed treatment of white-collar criminals in the section on sentencing, it is also true that white-collar criminals are less likely to be arrested, or charged, or convicted than are blue-collar criminals. The section in which a given issue will be treated is a reflection of the point in the criminal justice process at which the disparities are most striking. Suffice it to say, however, that the disparities between the treatment of the poor and the non-poor are to be found at all points of the process.

## Arrest

The problem with most official records of who commits crime is that they are really statistics on who gets arrested and convicted. If, as I will show, the police are more likely to arrest some people than others, these official statistics may tell us more about police than about criminals. In any event, they give us little reliable data about those who commit crime and do not get caught. Some social scientists, suspicious of the bias built into official records, have tried to devise other methods of determining who has committed a crime. Most often, these methods involve an interview or questionnaire in which the respondent is assured of anonymity and asked to reveal whether or not he has committed any offenses for which he could be arrested and convicted. Techniques to check reliability of these self-reports have also been devised; however, if their reliability is still in doubt, common sense would dictate that they would understate rather than overstate the number of individuals who have committed crimes and never come to official notice. In light of this, the conclusions of these studies are rather astounding. It would seem that crime is the national pastime.

The President's Crime Commission conducted a survey of 10,000 households and discovered that "91 percent of all Americans have violated laws that could have subjected them to a term of imprisonment at one time in their lives."[10] They also report the findings of a study of 1690 persons (1020 males, 670 females) mostly from the state of New York. Asked which of 49 felonies and misdemeanors (excluding traffic offenses) they had committed:

> Ninety-one percent of the respondents admitted they had committed one or more offenses for which they might have received jail or prison sentences. Thirteen percent of the males admitted to grand larceny, 26 percent to auto theft, and 17 percent to burglary. Sixty-four percent of the males and 27 percent of the females committed at least one felony for which they had not been apprehended.[11]

Keep in mind that a felony is a crime for which an individual can serve one or more years in prison and that many of the individuals now in jail are there only for misdemeanors.

A number of other studies support the conclusion that serious criminal behavior is widespread among middle- and upper-class individuals, although these individuals are rarely, if ever, arrested. Some of the studies show that there are no significant differences between economic classes in the incidence of criminal behavior.[12] Others conclude that while lower-class individuals do commit more than their share of crime, arrest records overstate their share and understate that of the middle and upper classes.[13]

Still other studies suggest that some forms of serious crime—forms usually associated with lower-class youth—show up *more frequently* among higher-class persons than among lower.[14] For instance, Empey and Erikson interviewed 180 white males aged 15 to 17 who were drawn from different economic strata. They found that "virtually all respondents reported having committed not one but a variety of different offenses." Although youngsters from the middle classes constituted 55 percent of the group interviewed, they admitted to 67 percent of the instances of breaking and entering, 70 percent of the instances of property destruction, and an astounding 87 percent of all the armed robberies admitted to by the entire sample.[15] Williams and Gold studied a national sample of 847 males and females between the ages of 13 and 16.[16] Of these, 88 percent admitted to at least one delinquent offense. Eugene Doleschal writes of the Williams-Gold study:

> In support of recent studies, this research found that the relationship between social status and delinquent behavior was weak except that higher-status white boys were more delinquent than lower-status white boys. The greater seriousness of the higher-status boys' delinquent behavior stemmed from their committing proportionally more thefts, joy riding, and (surprisingly) assaults.[17]

Even those who conclude "that more lower status youngsters commit delinquent acts more frequently than do higher status youngsters"[18] also recognize that lower-class youth are significantly overrepresented in official records. Gold writes that "about five times more lowest than highest status boys appear in the official records; if records were complete and unselective, we estimate that the ratio would be closer to 1.5:1."[19] The simple fact is that for the same offense, *a poor person is more likely to be arrested, and if arrested charged, than a middle- or upper-class person.*[20]

This means, first of all, that poor people are more likely to come to the attention of the police. Furthermore, even when apprehended, the police are more likely to formally charge a poor person and release a higher-class person *for the same offense.* Gold writes that

> boys who live in poorer parts of town and are apprehended by police for delinquency are four to five times more likely to appear in some official record than boys from wealthier sections who commit the same kinds of offenses. These same data show that, at each stage in the legal process from charging a boy with an offense to some sort of disposition in court, boys from different socio-economic backgrounds are treated differently, so that those eventually incarcerated in public institutions, that site of most of the research on delinquency, are selectively poorer boys.[21]

Based on a study of self-reported delinquent behavior, Gold finds than when individuals were apprehended, "if the offender came from a higher status family, police were more likely to handle the matter themselves without referring it to the court."[22]

Terence Thornberry reaches a similar conclusion in a more recent study of 3475 delinquent boys in Philadelphia. Thornberry found that among boys arrested *for equally serious offenses* and who had *similar prior offense records*, police were more likely to refer the lower-class youths than the more affluent ones to juvenile court. The police were more likely to deal with the wealthier youngsters informally, for example, by holding them in the station house until their parents came rather than instituting formal procedures. Of those referred to juvenile court, Thornberry found further that for *equally serious offenses* and with *similar prior records*, the poorer youngsters were more likely to be institutionalized than were the affluent ones. The wealthier youths were more likely to receive probation than the poorer ones. As might be expected, Thornberry found the same relationships when comparing the treatment of black and white youths apprehended for equally serious offenses.[23]

Ronald Goldfarb cites a 1966 study in Contra Costa County, California, performed under the auspices of the President's Committee on Juvenile Delinquency and Youth Development, which further supports these conclusions:

> 48.2 percent of juveniles arrested in California were released by the police after some informal handling and without charges being preferred. But in the upper-middle-class suburban community of Lafayette in Contra Costa County, 80 percent were released after arrests. Of the total juveniles arrested in California, 46.5 percent were referred to a juvenile court; in Lafayette,

*17.9 percent. Of those who eventually were institutionalized, the California average was 5.3 percent; in Lafayette County, 1.3 percent.*[24]

If you conclude that these differences are not so important because they are only true of young offenders, it would be wise to keep in mind that this group accounts for much of the "crime problem"— 38.4 percent of all police arrests in the United States in 1980 were of persons under 21 years old, and 56.2 percent were of persons under 25[25]—and many commentators have blamed this group more than others for the rapid increase in crime in recent years. Beyond this, other studies, not limited to the young, bear out the same economic bias.

For example, a study of drunken driving "demonstrated that minority group members, the lower class, males, and youth are consistently more likely to be convicted of driving while intoxicated than are whites, the upper class, and older persons."[26] A study of the treatment of employee theft found that *for the same amount stolen* "more lower status employees (cleaners, servicemen, stock personnel) than higher status ones (executives, salespersons, white collar workers) were prosecuted. A significantly larger proportion of the former (73 percent) than of the latter (50 percent) were prosecuted."[27]

Any number of reasons can be offered to account for these differences in treatment. Some argue that they reflect the fact that the poor have less privacy.[28] What others can do in their living rooms or backyards, the poor do on the street. Others argue that a police officer's decision to book a poor youth and release a middle-class youth reflects either the officer's judgment that the higher-class youngster's family will be more likely and more able to discipline him or her than the lower-class youngster's, or differences in the degree to which poor and middle-class complainants demand arrest. Others argue that police training and police work condition police officers to be suspicious of certain kinds of people, such as lower-class youth, blacks, Mexicans, and so on,[29] and thus more likely to detect their criminality. Still others hold that police mainly arrest those with the least political clout,[30] those who are least able to focus public attention on police practices or bring political influence to bear, and these happen to be the members of the lowest social and economic classes.

Regardless of which view one takes, and probably all have some truth in them, one conclusion is inescapable: One of the reasons that the offender "at the end of the road in prison is likely to be a member of the lowest social and economic groups in the country" is that the police officers who guard the access to the road to prison make sure that more poor people will make the trip than well-to-do people.

The *weeding out of the wealthy* starts at the very entrance to the criminal justice system: The decision about whom to investigate, arrest, or charge is not made simply on the basis of the offense committed or the danger posed. It is a decision that is distorted by a systematic economic bias that works to the disadvantage of the poor.

This economic bias is a two-edged sword. Not only are the poor arrested and charged out of proportion to their numbers for the kinds of crimes poor people generally commit—burglary, robbery, assault, and so forth—but when we reach the kinds of crimes poor people almost never have the opportunity to commit, such as antitrust violations, industrial safety violations, embezzlement, serious tax evasion, the criminal justice system shows an increasingly benign and merciful face. The more likely that a crime is the type committed by middle- and upper-class people, the less likely that it will be treated as a criminal offense. When it comes to crime in the streets, where the perpetrator is apt to be poor, he or she is even more likely to be arrested, formally charged, and so on. When it comes to crime in the suites, where the offender is apt to be affluent, the system is most likely to deal with the crime noncriminally, that is, by civil litigation or informal settlement. Where it does choose to proceed criminally as we will see in the section on sentencing, it rarely goes beyond a slap on the wrist. Not only is the main entry to the road to prison held wide open to the poor, but the access routes for the wealthy are largely sealed off. Once again, we should not be surprised at who we find in our prisons.

Many writers have commented on the extent and seriousness of "white-collar crime," so I will keep my remarks to a minimum. Nevertheless, for those of us trying to understand how the image of crime is created, four points should be noted.

1.  White-collar crime is costly; it takes far more dollars from our pockets than all the FBI Index Crimes combined.
2.  White-collar crime is widespread, probably much more so than the crimes of the poor.
3.  White-collar criminals are rarely arrested or charged; the system has developed kindlier ways of dealing with the more delicate sensibilities of its higher-class clientele.
4.  When the white-collar criminals are prosecuted and convicted, their sentences are either suspended or very light when judged by the cost their crimes have imposed on society.

The first three points will be discussed here, and the fourth will be presented in the section on sentencing below.

There is considerable disagreement about the magnitude of the cost of white-collar crime, except that all experts agree that it is enormous! Speaking before the Executive Club of Chicago, on November 14, 1980, Herschell Britton, executive vice president of Burns International Security Services, stated, "White-collar crime . . . currently costs the country nearly $70 billion a year!"[31] "The [Senate] Judiciary Subcommittee on Antitrust and Monopoly, headed by the late Senator Philip Hart, estimated that faulty goods, monopolistic practices, and other violations annually cost consumers between $174 and $231 billion."[32] A 1979 article on white-collar crime in *Newsweek* reports that estimates "of the total cost to the nation vary widely—from $50 billion to $200 billion a year."[33] A 1982 article on corporate crime in *U.S. News and World Report* states that "Corporate crime exacts a hefty toll from the nation—as much as 200 billion dollars a year, say consumer advocates—in inflated prices; poisoned air, land and water; corruption of public officials; and evaded taxes. Price fixing alone is believed to cost consumers perhaps 60 billion dollars a year."[34]

Fortunately, all we need is a rough estimate of the cost of white-collar crime so that we can compare its impact with that of the crimes reported on by the FBI. For this purpose, we can use the conservative estimates in the U.S. Chamber of Commerce's *Handbook on White-Collar Crime*.[35] Since the Handbook was issued in 1974, we will have to adjust its figures to take into account both inflation and growth in population, so that we can compare these figures with losses reported for 1980 by the FBI. Between 1974 and 1980, the population of the United States increased 7 percent, and the consumer price index increased 67 percent. Assuming that the rate of white-collar crime relative to the population has remained constant from 1974 to 1980, and assuming that its real dollar value has remained constant as well (two conservative assumptions in light of the judgments just cited that white-collar crime is on the rise), we can bring the Chamber of Commerce's figures up-to-date by multiplying them by 1.8 (1.07 × 1.67 = 1.7869). The Chamber of Commerce estimated the total cost of white-collar crime in 1974 to be $41.78 billion. In 1980, this means that white-collar crimes cost *over $75 billion*. (See Table 3, for the breakdown into costs per category of white-collar crime.) This is certainly a conservative estimate in light of the estimates quoted earlier, but large enough for our purposes. For example, it is over *3000 times* larger than the total amount taken in all bank robberies in the United States in 1980, and nearly *nine times* the total amount taken in all thefts reported in the FBI *Uniform Crime Reports* for that year.[36]

**TABLE 3**

The Cost of White-Color Crime (in Billions of Dollars)

| | | |
|---|---|---|
| Bankruptcy fraud | | $ 0.14 |
| Bribery, kickbacks, and payoffs | | 5.40 |
| Computer-related crime | | 0.18 |
| Consumer fraud, illegal competition, deceptive practices | | 37.80 |
| Consumer victims | $ 9.9 | |
| Business victims | 6.3 | |
| Government revenue loss | 21.6 | |
| Credit card and check fraud | | 1.98 |
| Credit card | 0.18 | |
| Check | 1.80 | |
| Embezzlement and pilferage | | 12.60 |
| Embezzlement (cash, goods, services) | 5.4 | |
| Pilferage | 7.2 | |
| Insurance fraud | | 3.60 |
| Insurer victims | 2.7 | |
| Policyholder victims | 0.9 | |
| Receiving stolen property | | 6.30 |
| Securities thefts and frauds | | 7.20 |
| | Total (billions) | $75.20 |

Source: Chamber of Commerce of the United States, A Handbook on White-Collar Crime, 1974 (figures adjusted for inflation through 1980).

Almost two decades ago, the President's Crime Commission reported that

> estimates of the amount of reportable income that goes unreported each year range from $25 to $40 billion. Some of this is inadvertent, but undoubtedly a sizable amount is deliberate, criminal evasion. The financial loss to the public caused by a single conspiracy in restraint of trade may be untold millions in extra costs paid ultimately by the buying public. It is estimated that the cost to the public annually of securities frauds, while impossible to quantify with any certainty, is probably in the $500 million to $1 billion range. A conservative estimate is that nearly $500 million is spent annually on worthless or extravagantly misrepresented drugs and therapeutic devices. Fraudulent and deceptive practices in the home repair and improvement field are said to result in $500 million to $1 billion losses annually; and in the automobile repair field alone, fraudulent practices have been estimated to cost $100 million annually.[37]

Another observer claims that unreported taxable income may cost "the national treasury $4 to $5 billion annually."[38] In any event, it should be kept in mind that all of these actions are thefts just as much as the most commonly recognized forms. If taxable income goes unreported, others must pay more taxes to make up the difference. If corporations engage in price-fixing, then consumers must pay higher prices than they would under free competition. If businesses lose money to embezzlers, they pass the costs (including the costs of higher insurance premiums) on to the consumer in the form of higher prices. In all these cases, individuals may not "feel" victimized, but the impact on them is in every other respect the same as if they had been held up at gunpoint: They have fewer dollars in their pockets than they would otherwise have.

In addition to fraud and tax evasion by individuals, corporate crime is also rampant. Sutherland, in a study published in 1949 that has become a classic, analyzed the "behavior" of 70 of the largest 200 U.S. corporations over a period of some 40 years:

> The records reveal that every one of the seventy corporations had violated one or more of the laws, with an average of about thirteen adverse decisions per corporation and a range of from one to fifty adverse decisions per corporation. The corporations had a total of 307 adverse decisions on charges of restraint of trade, 222 adverse decisions on charges of infringements [of patents, trademarks, and copyrights], 158 adverse decisions under the National Labor Relations Act, 97 adverse decisions under the laws regulating advertising, and 196 adverse decisions on charges of violating other laws. Thus, generally, the official records reveal that these corporations violated the trade regulations with great frequency. The "habitual criminal" laws of some states impose severe penalties on criminals convicted the third or fourth time. If this criterion were used here, about 90 percent of the large corporations studied would be considered habitual white-collar criminals.[39]

Nevertheless, corporate executives almost never end up in jail, where they would find themselves sharing cells with poorer persons who had stolen less from their fellow citizens.

Recently, Marshall Clinard and Peter Yeager attempted to replicate Sutherland's pioneering work by studying legal violations and enforcement actions for the 582 largest manufacturing, wholesale, retail, and service establishments during a two year period, 1975 to 1976. They found that little had changed: "A total of 1,553 federal cases were begun against all 582 corporations during 1975 and 1976, or an average of 2.7 federal cases of violation each. Of the 582 corporations, 350 (60.1 percent) had at least one federal action brought against them, and for those firms that had at least one action brought against them, the average was 4.4 cases."[40] And the vast majority of these were treated lightly, either by administrative action or civil penalty. Of the 1553 cases, only 39 were dealt with criminally, and normally this meant a small fine.[41]

There are many reasons for this. Perhaps most important is the fact that with many of these law violations, the government has the choice to proceed criminally *or* civilly and usually chooses the latter. That is, with upper-class lawbreakers, the authorities prefer to sue in civil court for damages or for an injunction rather than treat the wealthy as common criminals. Judges have on occasion stated in open court that they "would not make criminals of reputable businessmen."[42] One would think that it would be up to the businessmen to make criminals of themselves by their actions, but alas, *this* right is reserved for the lower classes.

Another tool that the government uses to spare the corporate executive the trials of criminality is the consent decree. Senator Philip Hart said of the consent decree that it "is a negotiated instrument whereby a firm, in effect, says it has done nothing wrong and promises never to do it again. The agreement is filed in court and that's the end of it, unless the firm is caught doing it again."[43] Imagine if this were available to burglars. Instead of arresting them and giving them a criminal record, the police would ask them to sign a statement promising never to do it again and file it in court. This alternative, however, is reserved for a higher class of thief.

Examples of reluctance to use the full force of the criminal process for crimes not generally committed by the poor can be multiplied ad infinitum. Let me close with one final example that typifies this particular distortion of criminal justice policy.

Embezzlement is the crime of misappropriating money or property entrusted to one's care, custody, or control. Since the poor are rarely entrusted with tempting sums of money or valuable property, this is predominantly a crime of the middle and upper classes. The U.S. Chamber of Commerce estimates the annual economic cost of embezzlement (adjusted for 1980) at $5.4 billion, nearly two-thirds the total value of all the property and money stolen in all FBI Index property crimes in 1980. Thus it is fair to conclude that embezzlement imposes a cost on society comparable to that imposed by the Index property crimes. Nevertheless, the FBI reports that in 1980, when there were 1,863,300 arrests for Index property crimes, there were 8500 arrests for embezzlement nationwide.[44] Although their cost to society is comparable, the number of arrests for property crimes was *219 times greater* than the number of arrests for embezzlement. Roughly, this means that there was one property crime arrest for every $4600 stolen, and one embezzlement arrest for every $635,000 "misappropriated." Note that even the language becomes more delicate as we deal with a "better class" of crook.

The clientele of the criminal justice system form an exclusive club. Entry is largely a privilege of the poor. The crimes they commit are the crimes that qualify one for admission—and they are admitted in greater proportion than their share of those crimes. Curiously enough, the crimes the affluent commit are not the kind that easily qualify one for membership in the club.

## Conviction

Between arrest and imprisonment lies the crucial process that determines guilt or innocence. Studies of individuals accused of similar offenses and with similar prior records show that the poor defendant is more likely to be adjudicated guilty than is the wealthier defendant.[45] In the adjudication process the only thing that *should* count is whether the accused is guilty and whether the prosecution can prove it beyond a reasonable doubt. Unfortunately, at least two other factors that are irrelevant to the question of guilt or innocence significantly affect the outcome: One is the ability of the accused to be free on bail prior to trial, and the second is access to legal counsel able to devote adequate time and energy to the case. Since both bail and high-quality legal counsel cost money, it should come as no surprise that here as elsewhere the poor do poorly. "A defendant in a criminal court," writes Abraham Blumberg, "is really beaten by the deprivations and limitations imposed by his social class, race and ethnicity. These in turn preclude such services as bail, legal counsel, psychiatric services, expert witnesses, and investigatory assistance. In essence the concomitants of poverty are responsible for the fact that due process sometimes produces greatly disparate results in an ill-matched struggle."[46]

Being released on bail is important in several respects. First and foremost, of course, is the fact that those who are not released on bail are kept in jail like individuals who have been found guilty. They are thus punished while they are still legally innocent. In 1972, 51,000 (out of a total of 142,000) inmates of local jails were confined while awaiting trial. Their average pretrial or presentence confinement was three months, and 60 percent of the nation's jails do not separate pretrial defendants from convicted offenders. In 1978, out of 158,000 inmates of local jails, 67,000 had not yet been convicted.[47] Beyond the obvious ugliness of punishing people before they are found guilty, confined defendants suffer from other disabilities. Specifically, they cannot actively aid in their own defense by seeking out witnesses and evidence. Several studies have shown that among defendants accused of the same offenses, those who make bail are more likely to be acquitted than those who do not.[48]

Furthermore, since the time spent in jail prior to adjudication of guilt may count as part of the sentence if one is found guilty, the accused are often placed in a ticklish position. Let us say the accused believes that he or she is innocent or at least that the state cannot prove guilt, and let us say also that he or she has been in the slammer for two months awaiting trial. Along comes the prosecutor to offer a deal: If you plead guilty to such-and-such (usually a lesser offense than has been charged, e.g., possession of burglar's tools instead of burglary), the prosecutor promises to ask the judge to sentence you to two months. In other words, plead guilty and walk out of jail today—or maintain your innocence, stay in jail until trial, and then be tried for the full charge instead of the lesser offense! Plea-bargaining is an everyday occurrence in the criminal justice system. Contrary to the Perry Mason image, the vast majority of criminal convictions in the United States are reached without a trial. It is estimated that between 70 and 95 percent of convictions are the result of a negotiated plea,[49] that is, a bargain in which the accused agrees to plead guilty (usually to a lesser offense than he or she is charged with or to one offense out of many he or she is charged with) in return for an informal promise of leniency from the prosecutor with the tacit consent of the judge. If you were the jailed defendant offered a deal like this, how would you choose? Suppose you were a poor black man not likely to be able to retain F. Lee Bailey or Edward Bennett Williams for your defense?

The advantages of access to adequate legal counsel during the adjudicative process are obvious but still worthy of mention. In 1963, the U.S. Supreme Court handed down the landmark *Gideon v. Wainwright* decision, holding that the states must provide legal counsel to the indigent in all felony cases. As a result, no person accused of a serious crime need face their accusers without a lawyer. However, the Supreme Court has not held that the Constitution requires that individuals are entitled to lawyers able to devote equal time and resources to their cases. Even though *Gideon* represents significant progress in making good on the constitutional promise of equal treatment before the law, we still are left with two transmission belts of justice: one for the poor and one for the affluent. There is, to be sure, an emerging body of case law on the right to effective assistance of counsel;[50] however, this is yet to have any serious impact on the assembly-line legal aid handed out to the poor.

Indigent defendants, those who cannot afford to retain their own lawyers, will be defended either by a public defender or by a private attorney assigned by the court. Since the public defender is a salaried attorney with a case load much larger than that of a private criminal lawyer,[51] and since court-assigned private attorneys are paid a fixed fee that is much lower than they charge their regular clients, neither is able or motivated to devote much time to the indigent defendant's defense. Both are strongly motivated to bring their cases to a close quickly by negotiating a plea of guilty. Since the public defender works in day-to-day contact with the prosecutor and the judge, the pressures on him or her to negotiate a plea as quickly as possible, instead of rocking the boat by threatening to go to trial,[52] are even greater than those that work on court-assigned counsel. In an essay, aptly entitled "Did You Have a Lawyer When You Went to Court? No, I Had a Public Defender," Jonathan Casper reports the perceptions of this process from the standpoint of the defendants:

> Most of the men spent very little time with their public defender. In the court in which they eventually plead guilty, they typically reported spending on the order of five to ten minutes with their public defender. These conversations usually took place in the bull-pen of the courthouse or in the hallway.
>
> The brief conversations usually did not involve much discussion of the details surrounding the alleged crime, mitigating circumstances or the defendants' motives or backgrounds. Instead, they focused on the deal, the offer the prosecution was likely to make or had made in return for a cop out. Often the defendants reported that the first words the public defender spoke (or at least the first words the defendants recalled) were, "I can get you . . ., if you plead guilty."[53]

Abraham S. Blumberg studied 724 male felony defendants who pleaded guilty in a large metropolitan court. He found that in the majority of cases it was the defense counsel who first suggested a guilty plea and who most influenced the defendant's decision to plead guilty. More striking still, however, was the finding that public defenders and court-assigned lawyers suggested the plea of guilty earlier than privately retained attorneys. On this, Blumberg comments, "Legal-aid and assigned counsel are apparently more likely to suggest the plea in the initial interview, perhaps as a response to the pressures of time and, in the case of the assigned counsel, the strong possibility that there is no fee involved."[54] Privately retained counsel suggested the plea in the initial meeting in 35 percent of their cases, public defenders in 49 percent, and assigned counsel in 60 percent.[55] It should be noted that Blumberg concludes that these differences have little impact on the eventual outcome. Other findings point to a different conclusion.

As might be expected, with less time and resources to devote to the cause, public defenders and assigned lawyers cannot devote as much time and research to preparing the crucial pretrial motions that can often lead to dismissal of charges against the accused. One study shows that public defenders got dismissals in 8 percent of their cases, assigned lawyers in 6 percent, and privately retained counsel in *29 percent of their cases.*[56] And, as also might be expected, the overall acquittal rate for privately retained counsel is considerably better than that for public defenders and assigned counsel. The same study shows that public defenders achieved either dismissal of charges or a finding of not guilty in 17 percent of the indictments they handled, assigned counsel did the same in 18 percent, and privately retained counsel got their clients off the hook in *36 percent of their indictments.* The picture that emerges from the federal courts is not much different.[57]

The problem of adequate legal representation may be particularly acute in capital cases. According to Robert Johnson, "Most attorneys in capital cases are provided by the state. Defendants, as good capitalists, routinely assume that they will get what they pay for: next to nothing." Their perceptions, he concludes, "may not be far from wrong." Indeed, Stephen Gettinger maintains that an inadequate defense was "the single outstanding characteristic" of the condemned persons he studied. The result: Capital defendants appeared in court as "creatures beyond comprehension, virtually gagged and masked in preparation for the execution chamber."[58]

Needless to say, the distinct legal advantages that money can buy become even more salient when we enter the realm of corporate and other white-collar crime. Indeed, it is often precisely the time and cost involved in bringing to court a large corporation with its army of legal eagles that is offered as an excuse for the less formal and more genteel treatment accorded to corporate crooks. This excuse is, of course, not equitably distributed to all economic classes, anymore than quality legal service is. What this means in simple terms is that regardless of actual innocence or guilt, one's chances of beating the rap increase as one's income increases. Regardless of what fraction of crimes are committed by the poor, the criminal justice system is distorted so that an even greater fraction of those convicted will be poor. And with conviction comes sentencing.

## Sentencing

*He had a businessman's suit and a businessman's tan, but Jack L. Clark no longer had a business. His nursing home construction company had collapsed in a gigantic stock fraud, leaving shareholders out $200 million and leaving Clark in a federal courthouse, awaiting sentence for stock manipulation. Ten million of the swindled dollars had allegedly gone for Clark's personal use, and prosecutors accused him of stashing away 4 million unrecovered dollars in a retirement nest egg. Out of an original indictment of 65 counts, Clark had pleaded guilty to one charge. He faced a maximum penalty of a $10,000 fine and five years in prison. But the judge, before passing sentence, remembered the "marked improvement" in care for the elderly that Clark's nursing homes had provided . . . He considered that Clark was a 46-year-old family man who coached little kids in baseball and football. Then he passed sentence. No fine. One year in prison. Eligible for parole after four months.*

*In another federal courtroom stood Matthew Corelli (not his real name), a 45-year-old, $125-a-week laborer who lived with his wife and kids in a $126-a-month apartment. Along with three other men, Corelli had been convicted of possessing $5,000 of stolen drugstore goods that government prosecutors identified as part of a $63,000 shipment. The judge considered Corelli's impoverished circumstances, his number of dependents, the nature of his crime, and then passed sentence: four years in prison. Or in other words, four times the punishment Clark received for a fraction of the crime.[59]*

*Jack Greenberg took $15 from a post office; last May in Federal Court in Manhattan he drew six months in jail. Howard Lazell "misapplied" $150,000 from a bank; in the same month in the same courthouse he drew probation.[60]*

The first quotation is the opening passage of a magazine article on white-collar crime, aptly titled "America's Most Coddled Criminals." The second quotation is the opening paragraph of a *New York Times* article, more prosaically titled "Wide Disparities Mark Sentences Here." Both, however, are testimony to the fact that the criminal justice system reserves its harshest penalties for its lower-class clients and puts on kid gloves when confronted with a better class of crook.

The system is doubly biased against the poor. First, there is the class bias *between* crimes that we have just seen. The crimes that poor people are likely to commit carry harsher sentences than the "crimes in the suites" committed by well-to-do people. Second, for *all* crimes, the poor receive less probation and more years of confinement than well-off defendants *convicted of the same offense,* assuring us once again that the vast majority of those who are put behind bars are from the lowest social and economic classes in the nation.

The *New York Times* article referred to above reports the results of a study done by the *New York Times* on sentencing in state and federal courts. The *Times* states that "crimes that tend to be committed by the poor get tougher sentences than those committed by the well-to-do," that federal "defendants who could not afford private counsel were sentenced nearly twice as severely as defendants with private or no counsel," and that a "study by the Vera Institute of Justice of courts in the Bronx indicates a similar pattern in the state courts."[61]

Looking at federal and state courts, Stuart Nagel concludes that

> not only are the indigent found guilty more often, but they are much less likely to be recommended for probation by the probation officer, or to be granted probation or suspended sentences by the judge.

And, further, that

> the federal data show that this is true also of those with no prior record: 27 percent of the indigent with no prior record were not recommended for probation against 16 percent of the non-indigent; 23 percent indigent did not receive suspended sentences or probation against 15 percent non-indigent. Among those of both groups with "some" prior record the spread is even greater.[62]

Eugene Doleschal and Nora Klapmuts report as "typical of American studies," Thornberry's analysis of "3,475 Philadelphia delinquents that found that blacks and members of lower socioeconomic groups were likely to receive more severe dispositions than whites and the more affluent even when the appropriate legal variables [i.e., offense, prior record, etc.] were held constant.[63] More recently, applying more sophisticated statistical techniques to the data upon which his Philadelphia study was based, Thornberry concludes, "When seriousness, prior record and SES [socioeconomic strata] were held constant, blacks were significantly more likely than whites to receive more severe dispositions." Although he finds the effect of socioeconomic status weaker than in the earlier study, Thornberry writes, "When the variable of race was suppressed . . . , SES was found to be significantly related to dispositions such that lower SES subjects were treated more severely than their high SES counter-parts."[64]

Studying the experiences of 798 burglary and larceny defendants in North Carolina, Clarke and Koch find that "other things being equal, the low-income defendant had a greater chance than the higher-income defendant of emerging from the criminal court with an active prison sentence. . . . Our tentative conclusion is that most of the influence of income on the likelihood of imprisonment among the defendants studied is explained by the poorer opportunity of the low-income defendant for [release on] bail and his greater likelihood of having a court-assigned rather than a privately retained, attor-ney."[65] Analyzing data from Chicago trial courts, Lizotte finds that, other things being equal, "laborers and non-whites are . . . twice as likely as proprietors to stay incarcerated between arrest and final dis-position [i.e., not be released on bail]. Further, other factors being equal, laborers and non-whites are given longer prison sentences than higher SES groups."[66]

As usual, data on racial discrimination in sentencing exist in much greater abundance than data on class discrimination, but they tell the same story of the treatment of those who cannot afford the going price of justice. Most striking perhaps is the fact that over 44 percent of the inmates of all correctional facilities in the United States—state and federal prisons as well as local jails—are black, while blacks ac-count for a little under one-quarter of all arrests in the nation. Even when we compare the percentage of blacks arrested for serious (i.e., FBI Index) crimes with the percentage of blacks in federal and state prisons (where presumably those convicted of such offenses would be sent), blacks still make up over 46 percent of the inmates but only about 33 percent of the arrestees, which is still a considerable dispar-ity. Furthermore, when we look at federal prisons, where there is rea-son to believe racial and economic discrimination is less prevalent than in state institutions, we find that the average sentence for a white inmate in 1979 was 98.9 months, as compared to 130.2 months (over 2½ years more!) for nonwhite inmates. The nonwhite inmate serves, on the average, 20 more months for a drug law violation than the white inmate, and almost twice as long for income tax evasion.[67]

Studies have confirmed that black burglars receive longer sen-tences than do white burglars. And blacks who plead guilty receive harsher sentences than whites who do, although by an act of dubious mercy of which Americans ought hardly be proud, blacks often re-ceive lighter sentences for murder and rape than whites as long as the victim was black as well.[68] According to a recent four-state study of capital sentencing, this dubious mercy extends to the death penalty. In Florida, for example, blacks "who kill whites are nearly forty times more likely to be sentenced to death than those who kill blacks." Moreover, among "killers of whites, blacks are five times more likely than whites to be sentenced to death." This pattern of double discrimination was also evidenced, though less pronouncedly, in Texas, Ohio, and Georgia, the other states surveyed. Together, these four states "accounted for approximately 70 percent of the nation's death sentences" between 1972 and 1977.[69] Note that these discriminatory sentences were rendered under statutes that had passed constitutional muster and were therefore presumed free of the biases that led the Supreme Court to invalidate death penalty statutes in *Furman v. Georgia* in 1972.

Mary Owen Cameron studied the sentencing practices of judges in the Chicago Women's Court during a three-year period. Her findings were as follows:

> Judges found sixteen percent of the white women brought before them on charges of shoplifting to be "not guilty," but only four percent of the black women were found innocent. In addition, twenty two percent of the black women as compared to four percent of the white women were sent to jail. Finally, of the twenty-one white women sentenced to jail, only two (ten percent) were to be jailed for thirty days or more; of the seventy-six black women sentenced to jail twenty (twenty-six percent) were to be jailed for thirty days or more.[70]

An extensive study by the *Boston Globe* of 4500 cases of armed robbery, aggravated assault, and rape, found that "blacks convicted in the superior courts of Massachusetts receive harsher penalties than whites for the same crimes. . . . The median time served by blacks is nine weeks longer than that served by whites for armed robbery, 13½ months longer for rape and about equal for aggravated assault. . . . The typical minimum sentence for blacks . . . on all three crimes combined is more than a year longer than for whites."[71] The authors of a study of almost 1200 males sentenced to prison for armed robbery in a southeastern state found that "in 1977 whites incarcerated for armed robbery had a greater than average chance of receiving the least severe sentence, while nonwhites had a greater than average chance of receiving a moderately severe sentence."[72] A study of 229 adjudicated cases in a Florida judicial district yielded the finding that "whites have an 18 percent greater chance in the predicted probability of receiving probation than blacks when all other things are equal."[73]

Another study has shown that among blacks and whites on death row, whites are more likely to have their sentences commuted. And blacks or whites who have private counsel are more likely to have their execution commuted than condemned persons defended by court-appointed attorneys.[74]

As I have already pointed out, justice is increasingly tempered with mercy as we deal with a better class of crime. The Sherman Antitrust Act is a criminal law. It was passed in recognition of the fact that one virtue of a free enterprise economy is that competition tends to drive consumer prices down, so agreements by competing firms to refrain from price competition is the equivalent of stealing money from the consumer's pocket. Nevertheless, although such conspiracies cost consumers far more than lower-class theft, price-fixing was a misdemeanor until 1974.[75] In practice, few conspirators end up in prison, and when they do, the sentence is a mere token, well below the maximum provided in the law. Thus, based on the government's track record, there is little reason to expect things to change significantly now that price-fixing is a felony.

In the historic *Electrical Equipment* cases in the early 1960s, executives of several major firms secretly met to fix prices on electrical equipment to a degree that is estimated to have cost the buying public well over a billion dollars. The executives involved knew they were violating the law. They used plain envelopes for their communications, called their meetings "choir practice," and referred to the list of executives in attendance as the "Christmas card list." This case is rare and famous because it was one in which the criminal sanction was actually imposed. Seven executives received and served jail sentences. But in light of the amount of money they had stolen from the American public, their sentences were more an indictment of the government than of themselves: *30 days in jail!*

Speaking about the record of federal antitrust prosecution, Clinard and Yeager write that "even in the most widespread and flagrant price conspiracy cases, few corporate executives are ever imprisoned; of the total 231 cases with individual defendants from 1955 to 1975, prison sentences were given in only 19 cases. Of a total of 1027 individual defendants, only 49 were sentenced to prison."[76] There is some (slight) indication of a toughening in the sentences since antitrust violations were made a felony in 1974, and penalties were increased. "In felony cases prosecuted under the new penalties through March 1978, 15 of 21 sentenced individuals (71 percent) were given terms averaging 192 days each."[77] Nevertheless, when the cost to society is reckoned, even such penalties as these are hardly severe.

Indeed, Clinard and Yeager maintain that "There is even more leniency for corporate than for other white-collar offenders. Few members of corporate management ever go to prison, even if convicted; generally they are placed on probation."[78] In their study of 56 corporate executives who were convicted of criminal offenses, 40 either received probation or a suspended sentence. Only 16 were actually sent to prison. These 16 "were sentenced to a total of 594 days of actual imprisonment (an average of 37.1 days each). Of the total days of imprisonment, 360 (60.6 percent) were accounted for by two officers, who received six months each in the same case."[79] The remaining 14 served an average of 16.7 days each.

In general the crimes of the poor receive stiffer sentences than the crimes of the well-to-do. For instance, Marvin Frankel points out, in his book *Criminal Sentences: Law Without Order*, that "of 502 defendants convicted for income tax fraud 95, or 19 percent, received prison terms, the average being three months. Of 3,791 defendants sentenced for auto theft, 2,373, or 63 percent, went to prison, the average term being 7.6 months."[80] More recent figures fit this pattern. A statistical report of the Federal Bureau of Prisons yields information about the average sentences received by inmates of federal institutions and the average time served until parole (see Table 4).

**TABLE 4**

*Sentences for Different Classes of Crime*

|  | Average Sentence (in months) | Average Time Served Until First Release (in months) |
|---|---|---|
| Crimes of the poor |  |  |
| Robbery | 131.3 | 44.4 |
| Burglary | 63.4 | 31.6 |
| Larceny/theft | 31.0 | 17.1 |
| Crimes of the affluent |  |  |
| Embezzlement | 18.8 | 10.3 |
| Fraud | 22.0 | 11.0 |
| Income tax evasion | 15.5 | 7.9 |

Source: Federal Bureau of Prisons—Statistical Report, Fiscal Year 1976.

Keep in mind while looking at these figures that *each* of the "crimes of the affluent" costs the public more than *all* of the "crimes of the poor" put together.

A study of sentencing practices in the Southern District of New York, optimistically entitled *Justice in Sentencing*, found

> plain indications that white collar defendants, predominantly white, receive more lenient treatment as a general rule, while defendants charged with common crimes, largely committed by the unemployed and undereducated, a group which embraces large numbers of blacks in today's society, are more likely to be sent to prison. If these indications are correct, then one may conclude that poor persons receive harsher treatment in the Federal Courts than do well-to-do defendants charged with more sophisticated crimes.

Specifically, the study reports that "during the six-month period covered by the Southern District of New York sentencing study, *defendants convicted of white collar crimes stood a 36% chance of going to prison; defendants convicted of nonviolent common crimes stood a 53% chance of going to prison; and defendants convicted of violent crimes stood an 80% chance of going to prison.*"[81] Several things are worthy of note here. First, the study carries forth the distorted conventional wisdom about crime by distinguishing between "white-collar" and "common" crime, when, as we have found, there is every reason to believe that white-collar crime is just as common as the so-called common crimes of the poor. Second, the disparities reported refer only to likelihood of imprisonment *for any length of time*, and so they really understate the disparities in treatment, since the so-called common crimes also receive *longer* prison sentences than the white-collar crimes. But third, and most importantly, the disparities cannot be explained by the greater danger of lower-class criminals because even the perpetrators of *nonviolent* "*common*" crimes stand a 50 percent greater chance of going to prison than do white-collar crooks.

A graphic illustration of the way the criminal justice system treats the wealthy is provided by Fleetwood and Lubow in their article "America's Most Coddled Criminals." They put together their pick of ten convicted white-collar criminals, comparing their sentences with the crimes they committed. The chart speaks for itself (see Table 5).

Equally eloquent testimony to the merciful face that the criminal justice system turns toward upper-class crooks is found in a *New York Times* report on the fate of 21 business executives found guilty of making illegal campaign contributions during the Watergate scandal:

> Most of the 21 business executives who admitted their guilt to the Watergate Special Prosecutor in 1973 and 1974—especially those from large corporations—are still presiding over their companies. . . .
> Only two went to jail. They served a few months and were freed. . . .
> Furthermore, the fines of $1,000 or $2,000 that most of the contributors of illegal funds had to pay have not made much of a dent in their style of living. . . .
> An investigation into the whereabouts and financial status of the 21 executives involved in illegal contributions leads to a conclusion that the higher the position the more cushioned the fall—if indeed there was a fall.[82]

The *Times* report also includes a chart illustrating the fate of these upper-class criminals, who were found guilty of nothing less than participating in schemes that undermine the independence of the electoral process—guilty, that is, of contaminating the very lifeblood of democratic government. Here, again, the chart speaks for itself (see Table 6). As for the government officials themselves (and their hirelings) who were directly responsible for the Watergate crimes, their treatment has also been relatively gentle (see Table 7).

On either side of the law, the rich get richer . . .

## . . . AND THE POOR GET PRISON

At 9:05 A.M. on the morning of Thursday, September 9, 1971, a group of inmates forced their way through a gate at the center of the prison, fatally injured a guard named William Quinn, and took 50 hostages. The Attica uprising had begun. It lasted almost exactly four days, until 9:43 A.M. on the morning of Monday, September 13, when corrections officers and state troopers stormed the prison and killed 10 hostages and 29 inmates.[83] During those four days the nation saw the faces of its captives on television—the hard black faces of young men who had grown up on the streets of Harlem and other urban ghettos. Theirs were the faces of crime in America. The television viewers who saw them were not surprised. Here were the faces of dangerous men who should be locked up. Nor were people outraged when the state launched its murderous attack on the prison, killing many more inmates and guards than did the prisoners themselves. Maybe they

**TABLE 5**

*Ten Bandits: What They Did and What They Got*

This isn't the Chamber of Commerce list of brightest young businessmen, and it's not the ten best-dressed list. It's a list of ten very respectable criminals. Have any favorites you don't see here? Send them in.

| Criminal | Crime | Sentence |
|---|---|---|
| Jack L. Clark | President and chairman of Four Seasons Nursing Centers, Clark finagled financial reports and earnings projections to inflate his stock artificially. Shareholders lost $200 million. | One year in prison. |
| John Peter Galanis | As portfolio manager of two mutual funds, Galanis bilked investors out of nearly $10 million. | Six months in prison and five years probation. |
| Virgil A. McGowen | As manager of the Bank of America branch in San Francisco, McGowen siphoned off $591,921 in clandestine loans to friends. Almost none of the money was recovered. | Six months in prison, five years probation and a $3,600 fine. |
| Valdemar H. Madis | A wealthy drug manufacturer, Madis diluted an antidote for poisoned children with a worthless, look-alike substance. | One year probation and a $10,000 fine. |

| | | |
|---|---|---|
| John Morgan | President of Jet Craft Ltd, John Morgan illegally sold about $2 million in unregistered securities. | One year in prison and a $10,000 fine. |
| Irving Projansky | The former chairman of the First National Bank of Lincolnwood, Ill., Projansky raised stock prices artifically and then dumped the shares, costing the public an estimated $4 million. | One year in prison and two years probation. |
| David Ratliff | Ratliff spent his 21 years as a Texas state senator embezzling state funds. | Ten years probation. |
| Walter J. Rauscher | An executive vice-president of American Airlines, Rauscher accepted about $200,000 in kickbacks from businessmen bidding for contracts. | Six months in prison and two years probation. |
| Frank W. Sharp | The multimillion-dollar swindles of Sharp, a Houston banker, shook the Texas state government and forced the resignation of the head of the Criminal Division of the Justice Dept. | Three years probation and a $5,000 fine. |
| Seymour R. Thaler | Soon after his election to the New York State Supreme Court, Thaler was convicted of receiving and transporting $800,000 in stolen U.S. Treasury bills. | One year in prison and a fine of $10,000. |

*Source:* Blake Fleetwood and Arthur Lubow, "America's Most Coddled Criminals," *New Times Magazine*, September 19, 1975.

## TABLE 6

### Convicted Watergate Campaign Contributors

| Company | Name | Fine/Prison | Current Status |
|---|---|---|---|
| American Ship Building | George M. Steinbrenner | $15,000 | Still chairman at $50,000/year |
| | John H. Melcher, Jr. | $ 2,500 | Discharged; practicing law in Cleveland |
| Ashland Oil | Orin E. Atkins[a] | $ 1,000 | Still chairman at $314,000/year |
| Associated Milk Producers | Harold S. Nelson | 4 months prison $10,000 | Resigned; now in commodities exports |
| | David L. Parr | 4 months prison $10,000 | Resigned |
| | Stuart H. Russell | 2 years prison[b] | Resigned; now in private law practice |
| Braniff International | Harding L. Lawrence | $ 1,000 | Still chairman at $335,000/year |
| Carnation | H. Everett Olson | $ 1,000 | Still chairman at $212,500/year |
| Diamond International | Ray Dubrowin | $ 1,000 | Still V.P. for public affairs |
| Goodyear Tire and Rubber | Russell DeYoung | $ 1,000 | Still chairman of 2 committees at $306,000/year and pension $144,000/year |

| | | | |
|---|---|---|---|
| Gulf Oil | Claude C. Wild, Jr. | $ 1,000 | Consultant in Washington, D.C. |
| HMS Electric | Charles H. Huseman | $ 1,000 | Still president |
| LBC&W Inc. | William G. Lyles, Sr. | $ 2,000 | Still chairman |
| Lehigh Valley Cooperative Farmers | Richard L. Allison | $ 1,000 (suspended) | Discharged |
| 3M | Harry Heltzer | $ 500 | Retired as chairman, does special projects at $100,000/year |
| Northrop | Thomas V. Jones | $ 5,000 | Still chief executive at $286,000/year |
| | James Allen | $ 1,000 | Retired as V.P. with pension est. at $36,000/year |
| Phillips Petroleum | William W. Keeler | $ 1,000 | Retired, with pension est. at $201,742/year |
| Ratrie, Robbins and Schweitzer | Harry Ratrie | 1 month probation | Still president |
| | Augustus Robbins III | 1 month probation | Still executive V.P. |
| Time Oil | Raymond Abendroth | $ 2,000 | Still president |

Source: Michael C. Jensen, "Watergate Donors Still Riding High," *The New York Times*, August 24, 1975.
[a]Pleaded no contest.
[b]Under appeal.

# TABLE 7

## The Watergate Roster

| Name | Charge/Conviction | Sentence | Time Served |
|---|---|---|---|
| Richard M. Nixon | Unindicted co-conspirator | Pardoned | |
| Dwight L. Chapin | Convicted of lying to a grand jury | Sentenced to serve 10 to 30 months | Served 8 months |
| Charles W. Colson | Pleaded guilty to obstruction of justice | Sentenced to serve 1 to 3 years and fined $5,000 | Served 7 months |
| John W. Dean III | Pleaded guilty to conspiracy to obstruct justice | Sentenced to serve 1 to 4 years | Served 4 months. |
| John D. Ehrlichman | Convicted of conspiracy to obstruct justice, conspiracy to violate civil rights and perjury | Sentenced to serve concurrent terms of 20 months to 8 years | Served 18 months |
| H.R. Haldeman | Convicted of conspiracy to obstruct justice and perjury | Sentenced to serve 2½ years to 8 years | Served 18 months |
| E. Howard Hunt | Pleaded guilty to conspiracy, burglary and wiretapping | Sentenced to serve 30 months to 8 years and fined $10,000 | Served 33 months |
| Herbert W. Kalmbach | Pleaded guilty to violation of the Federal Corrupt Practices Act and promising federal employment as a reward for political activity | Sentenced to serve 6 to 18 months and fined $10,000 | Served 6 months |
| Richard G. Kleindienst | Pleaded guilty to refusal to answer pertinent questions before a Senate committee | Sentenced to 30 days and fined $100 | Sentence suspended |
| Egil Krogh Jr. | Pleaded guilty to conspiracy to violate civil rights | Sentenced to serve 2 to 6 years (all but 6 months were suspended) | Served 4½ months |
| Frederick C. LaRue | Pleaded guilty to conspiracy to obstruct justice | Sentenced to serve 1 to 3 years (all but 6 months were suspended) | Served 5½ months |

| Name | Charge | Sentence | Time Served |
|------|--------|----------|-------------|
| G. Gordon Liddy | Convicted of conspiracy, conspiracy to violate civil rights, burglary and wiretapping | Sentenced to serve 6 years and 8 months to 20 years and fined $40,000 | Served 52 months |
| Jeb S. Magruder | Pleaded guilty to conspiracy to obstruct justice, wiretapping and fraud | Sentenced to serve 10 months to 4 years | Served 7 months |
| John N. Mitchell | Convicted of conspiracy to obstruct justice and perjury | Sentenced to serve 2½ years to 8 years | Served 19 months |
| Donald H. Segretti | Pleaded guilty to campaign violations and conspiracy | Sentenced to serve 6 months | Served 4½ months |
| Maurice H. Stans | Pleaded guilty to five misdemeanor violations of the Federal Elections Campaign Act | Fined $5,000 | |
| James W. McCord Jr. | Convicted of conspiracy, burglary, wiretapping and unlawful possession of intercepting devices | Sentenced to serve 1 to 5 years | Served 4 months |
| Bernard L. Barker | Pleaded guilty to conspiracy, burglary, wiretapping and unlawful possession of intercepting devices | Sentenced to serve 18 months to 6 years | Served 12 months |
| Virgilio R. Gonzalez | Pleaded guilty to conspiracy, burglary, wiretapping and unlawful possession of intercepting devices | Sentenced to serve 1 to 4 years | Served 15 months |
| Eugenio R. Martinez | Pleaded guilty to conspiracy, burglary, wiretapping and unlawful possession of intercepting devices | Sentenced to serve 1 to 4 years | Served 15 months |
| Frank A. Sturgis | Pleaded guilty to conspiracy, burglary, wiretapping and unlawful possession of intercepting devices | Sentenced to serve 1 to 4 years | Served 13 months |

Source: The Washington Post, June 17, 1982.

were shocked—but not outraged. Neither were they outraged when two grand juries refused to indict any of the attackers, nor when the mastermind of the attack, then-Governor Nelson Rockefeller, was named to be Vice President of the United States three years after the uprising and massacre.[84]

They were not outraged because the faces they saw on the TV screens fit and confirmed their beliefs about who is a deadly threat to American society—and a deadly threat must be met with deadly force. But how did those men get to Attica? And how did Americans get their beliefs about who is a dangerous person? Obviously, these questions are interwoven. People get their notions about who is a criminal at least in part from the occasional television or newspaper picture of who is inside our prisons. And the individuals they see there have been put in prison because people believe that certain kinds of individuals are dangerous and should be locked up.

I have argued in this chapter that this is not a simple process of selecting the dangerous and the criminal from among the peace-loving and the law-abiding. It is also a process of *weeding out the wealthy* at every stage, so that the final picture—a picture like that which appeared on the TV screen on September 9, 1971—is not a true reflection of the real dangers in our society but a distorted image, the kind reflected in a carnival mirror.

It is not my view that the inmates in Attica were innocent of the crimes that sent them there. I am willing to assume that they and just about all the individuals in prisons in America are probably guilty of the crime for which they were sentenced and maybe more. My point is that people who are equally or more dangerous, equally or more criminal, are not there; that the criminal justice system works systematically, not to punish and confine the dangerous and the criminal, *but to punish and confine the poor who are dangerous and criminal.*

And it is successful at all levels. Of the 7724 inmates of *federal* prisons and reformatories in 1970 who had an income in 1969, 4491 (nearly 60 percent) reported an annual income of under $2000.[85] Of 141,600 persons confined in *local* jails throughout the nation in mid-1972, 61,800 (44 percent) had a pre-arrest annual income of less than $2000—only 11 percent reported a pre-arrest income of $7500 or more. "The 1972 U.S. median income of $9255 was exceeded by roughly 10 percent of the inmates. Only 6 percent had pre-arrest incomes of more than $10,000."[86] The U.S. Bureau of the Census conducted a nationwide survey of inmates of *state* correctional facilities for the Law Enforcement Assistance Administration in January

1974. They found 191,400 persons confined in state institutions; of these, 98 percent (187,500) were serving sentences—the remainder was made up of persons awaiting trial or drug addicts who "voluntarily" had submitted to treatment in lieu of being sentenced and so on. Sixty-one percent of the sentenced inmates had less than a high school education, as compared with 48 percent of the males age 18 and over in the general population. Of 168,300 state inmates who had held a full-time job after December 1968 or who had been employed during most of the month prior to their arrest, 40,000 (24 percent) reported income of less than $2000 for the year prior to arrest. Sixty percent reported income of under $6000 for the year prior to arrest. The median annual pre-arrest income of these 168,300 state inmates was $4639. About 69 percent of them "had worked most recently as non-farm laborers, operatives, or craftsmen," as compared to 47 percent of employed males age 16 and over in the general population. Of the inmates who were supporting some dependents prior to arrest, 33,300 (38 percent) "reported at the time of the survey that their dependents were on welfare." And finally, of 187,500 sentenced inmates, 179,400 had been represented by legal counsel. Of these, 127,000 (more than 70 percent) had been defended by a court-appointed lawyer or public defender or legal aid attorney. Less than 30 percent could afford to retain their own lawyer.[87]

Since the early 1970s, the period from which these figures are taken, there has been an unprecedented growth in the number of persons in state and federal prisons. In 1973, there were 204,211 individuals in state and federal prisons, or 96 prisoners for every 100,000 individuals in the general population. By 1979, state and federal inmates numbered 301,470, or 133 per 100,000. In 1981, the number had grown to 353,167—153 prisoners for every 100,000 Americans. And this does not include another 15,605 who are in prisons because they are either awaiting sentencing or have received sentences of under one year.[88] To this, add the 158,394 who were in local jails as of 1978, and we have well over half a million people locked up! They are, of course, still predominantly people from the bottom of society. The median pre-arrest annual income of the 158,394 in local jails was $3714. For those on whom we have the information, 10,659 had no pre-arrest income, 55,118—over a third—had pre-arrest incomes under $2000. Only 21,393 (about 14 percent) had incomes of $10,000 or more.[89] Of the 274,564 inmates in state institutions as of November 1979, 81,000 were not employed prior to arrest and 27,000 were employed part-time. Of these state inmates, 25,940 were admitted after November 1977. In this group, 5768 (nearly a quarter) had no pre-arrest income. 10,750 (40 percent) had pre-arrest incomes under $3000. And 6457 (a quarter) had incomes of $10,000 or more.[90]

The criminal justice system is sometimes thought of as a kind of sieve in which the innocent are progressively sifted out from the guilty, who end up behind bars. I have tried to show that the sieve works another way as well. It sifts the affluent out from the poor, so it is not merely the guilty who end up behind bars, but the *guilty poor*.

With this I think I have proven the hypotheses set forth in Chapter 2, in the section entitled *Criminal Justice as Creative Art*. The criminal justice system does not simply weed the peace-loving from the dangerous, the law-abiding from the criminal. At every stage, starting with the very definitions of crime and progressing through the stages of investigation, arrest, charging, conviction, and sentencing, the system *weeds out the wealthy*. It refuses to define as "crimes" or as serious crimes the dangerous and predatory acts of the well-to-do—acts that, as we have seen, result in the loss of hundreds of thousands of lives and billions of dollars. Instead, the system focuses its attention on those crimes likely to be committed by members of the lower classes. Among those acts defined as "crimes," the system is more likely to investigate and detect, arrest and charge, convict and sentence a lower-class individual than a middle- or upper-class individual who has committed *the same offense, if not a worse one!*

The people we see in jails and prisons may well be dangerous to society. But they are not *the* danger to society, not *the gravest* danger to society. Individuals who pose equal or greater threats to our well-being walk the streets with impunity. The criminal justice system is a mirror that hides as much as it reveals. It is a carnival mirror that throws back a distorted image of the dangers that lurk in our midst—and conveys the impression that those dangers are the work of the poor.

In Chapter 1, I argued that the criminal justice system was rigged to fail in the fight against crime. In this chapter and in the previous one, I have argued that the system is rigged to make crime appear to be the monopoly of the poor. *The joint effect of this two-way rigging is to maintain a real threat of crime that the vast majority of Americans believes is a threat from the poor.* In Chapter 4, I suggest who benefits from this illusion and how.

# 4

# To the Vanquished Belong the Spoils: Who Is Winning the Losing War Against Crime?

> In every case the laws are made by the
> ruling party in its own interest; a
> democracy makes democratic laws, a
> despot autocratic ones, and so on. By
> making these laws they define as "just"
> for their subjects whatever is for their own
> interest, and they call anyone who breaks
> them a "wrongdoer" and punish him
> accordingly.
>
> **Thrasymachus,** in **Plato's** Republic

## WHY IS THE CRIMINAL JUSTICE SYSTEM FAILING?

The streams of my argument flow together at this point in a question: *Why is it happening?* I have shown how it is no accident that "the offender at the end of the road in prison is likely to be a member of the lowest social and economic groups in the country."[1] I have shown that this is not an accurate group portrait of who threatens society—

it is a picture of whom the criminal justice system *selects* for arrest and imprisonment from among those who threaten society. It is an image distorted by the shape of the criminal justice carnival mirror. This much we have seen and now we want to know why: *Why is the criminal justice system allowed to function in a fashion that neither protects society nor achieves justice? Why is the criminal justice system failing?*

My answer to this question will require looking at who benefits from this failure and who suffers from it. More particularly, I will argue that the rich and powerful in America, those who derive the greatest advantage from the persistence of the social and economic system as it is currently organized, reap benefits from the failure of criminal justice that has been documented in this book. But—as I cautioned early on—this should not lead the reader to think that my explanation for the current shape of the criminal justice system is a "conspiracy theory."

A conspiracy theory would argue that the rich and the powerful, seeing the benefits to be derived from the failure of criminal justice, consciously set out to use their wealth and power to make it fail. There are many problems with such a theory. First, it is virtually impossible to prove. If the conspiracy succeeds, then this is only possible to the extent that it is kept secret. Thus evidence for a conspiracy would be as difficult to obtain as the conspiracy was successful. Second, conspiracy theories strain credibility precisely because the degree of secrecy they would require seems virtually impossible in a society as open and fractious as our own. If there is a "ruling elite" in the United States that is comprised of a group as small as the richest *one thousandth of one percent* of the population, it would still be made up of over 2000 people. To think that a conspiracy to make the criminal justice system fail in the way that it does could be kept secret among this number of people in a country like ours is just unbelievable. Third, conspiracy theories are not plausible because they do not correspond to the way most people act most of the time. Though there is no paucity of conscious mendacity and manipulation in our politics, most people most of the time seem sincerely to believe that what they are doing is right. Whether this is a tribute to human beings' creative capacities to rationalize what they do or just a matter of shortsightedness, it seems a fact. For all these reasons it is not plausible that so fateful and harmful a policy as the failure of criminal justice could be purposely maintained by the rich and powerful. Rather, we need an explanation that is compatible with believing that policymakers, in general, are simply doing what they sincerely believe is right.

To understand how the Pyrrhic defeat theory explains the current shape of our failing criminal justice policy, note that this failure is really *three* failures that work together. First, there is the failure to identify as crimes the harmful acts of the rich and powerful. (This is the first of the hypotheses listed on page 45, and it is confirmed by the evidence presented in Chapter 2.) Second, there is the failure to implement policies that stand a good chance of reducing crime and the harm it causes. (This was argued in Chapter 1.) Third, there is the failure to eliminate economic bias in the criminal justice system, so that the poor continue to have a substantially greater chance than better-off people of being arrested, charged, convicted, and penalized for committing the acts that are treated as crimes. (This corresponds to the second through fourth hypotheses listed on page 45, and is confirmed by the evidence presented in Chapter 3.) The effect of the first failure is that the acts that are identified as crimes are acts predominantly done by the poor. The effect of the second failure is that there remains a large amount of crime—even if crime rates occasionally dip as a result of factors outside the control of the criminal justice system, such as the decline in the number of 15- to 24-year-olds. The effect of the third failure is that the individuals who are arrested and convicted for crimes are predominantly poor people. The effect of the three failures working together is that we are largely unprotected against the harmful acts of the well-off, while, at the same time, we are confronted on the streets and in our homes with a real and large threat of crime, and in the courts and prisons with a large and visible population of poor criminals. In short, the effect of current criminal justice policy is at once to narrow the public's conception of what is dangerous to acts of the poor *and* to present a convincing embodiment of this danger.

Note that the Pyrhhic defeat theory aims to explain the *persistence* of this failing criminal justice policy, rather than its origins. The criminal justice system we have originated as a result of complex historical factors that have to do with the development of the common law tradition in England, the particular form in which this was transplanted on American soil, and the zigzagging course of reform and reaction that has marked our history since the English colonies were transformed into an independent American nation. The study of these factors would surely require another book longer than this one—but, more important, for our purposes it would be unnecessary. This is because it is not the origin of criminal justice policy and practices that is puzzling. The focus on one-on-one harm reflects the main ways in which people harmed each other in the days before large-scale industrialization; the refusal to implement policies that might reduce crime (such as gun control, or legalization of heroin, or amelioration of poverty) reflects a defensive and punitive response to crime that is natural and understandable, if not noble and farsighted; and the existence of economic bias in the criminal justice system reflects the real economic and political inequalities that characterize the society in which that system is embedded. What is puzzling, then, is not how these policies came to be what they are, but why they persist in the face of their failure to achieve either security or justice. The explanation that I shall offer for this persistence, I call the "historical inertia" explanation. Later, I will supplement it with a "structural" explanation of the identification of crimes with one-on-one harms. But the historical inertia explanation stands without this supplement.

Put briefly, the historical inertia explanation argues that current criminal justice policy persists because it fails in a way that does not tend to give rise to an effective demand for change. This is due to two facts. First, this failing system provides benefits for those with the power to make changes, while it imposes costs on those without such power. And, second, since the criminal justice system shapes the public's conception of what is dangerous, it creates the impression that the harms it is fighting are the *real* threats to society—thus, even when people see that the system is less than a roaring success, they generally do no more than demand more of the same: more prisons, more prison sentences, and so on.

Consider first the benefits that the system provides for those with wealth and power. I have argued that the triple failure of criminal justice policy diverts attention from the harmful (noncriminal) acts of the well-off and confronts us in our homes and on our streets with a real and substantial threat of crime, and in the courts and prisons with a large and visible population of poor criminals. This in turn has the effect of conveying a vivid image to the American people, namely, that *there is a real threat to our lives and limbs, and it is a threat from the poor.* This image provides benefits to the rich and powerful in America. It carries an *ideological message* that serves to protect their wealth and privilege. Crudely put, the message is this:

- *The threat to "law-abiding middle America" comes from below them on the economic ladder, not above them.*
- *The poor are morally defective, and thus their poverty is their own fault, not a symptom of social or economic injustice.*

The effect of this message is to funnel the discontent of middle Americans into hostility toward, and fear of, the poor. It leads Americans to ignore the ways in which they are injured and robbed by the acts of the affluent (as catalogued in Chapter 2) and leads them to demand harsher doses of "law and order" aimed mainly at the lower classes. Most importantly, it nudges middle America toward a *conservative* defense of American society with its vast disparities of wealth, power, and opportunity—and nudges them away from a progressive demand for equality and an equitable distribution of wealth and power.

On the other hand, but equally important, is the fact that those who are mainly victimized by the "failure" to reduce crime are by and large the poor themselves. That is, those people who are most hurt by the failure of the criminal justice system are those with the least power to change the system. The Department of Justice's *Criminal Victimization in the United States, 1979* states that "in 1979, as in prior years, members of families in the lower income bracket (less than $3,000 per year) had the highest overall rates [of victimization] for crimes of violence."[2] And "the unemployed had an overall violent crime [victimization] rate that was about twice that for employed persons."[3] Individuals from families earning under $3000 annually were victims of robbery with injury at a rate (per 1000 persons) nearly four times the rate for persons from families with annual incomes of $25,000 or more. And the former were victims of aggravated assault with injury at a rate more than five times that for the latter.[4] Even for burglary, where victimization rates are much closer among the different income groups, households with incomes under $3000 were burglarized 10 percent more frequently than households with incomes over $25,000, and 30 percent more frequently than households with incomes between $15,000 and $24,999.[5] The greater similarity of rates of property crime victimization between rich and poor understates the difference in the harms that result. The poor are far less likely than the affluent to have insurance against theft, and, since they have little to start with, what they lose to theft takes a much deeper bite into their ability to meet their basic needs. Needless to add, the various noncriminal harms documented in Chapter 2 (occupational hazards, pollution, poverty, etc.) also fall more harshly on workers and those at the bottom of society than on those at the top.

To summarize, those who suffer most from the failure to reduce crime (and the failure to treat noncriminal harms as crimes) are not in a position to change criminal justice policy. Those who are in a position to change the policy are not seriously harmed by its failure— indeed, there are actual benefits to them from that failure. Note that I do not maintain that criminal justice policy is created in order to achieve this distribution of benefits and burdens. Instead, my claim is that because current criminal justice policy happens to produce this distribution, nothing in the society generates forces with both an inclination to change the criminal justice system and the power to do so. Moreover, since the criminal justice system shapes the public's conception of what is dangerous, it effectively limits their conception of how to protect itself to more of the same. Thus, though it fails, the system persists.

My argument in the remainder of this chapter takes the following form. In the section entitled *The Poverty of Criminals and the Crime of Poverty*, I spell out the content of the ideological message broadcast by the failure of the criminal justice system. In the section entitled *Ideology, or How to Fool Enough of the People Enough of the Time*, I discuss the *nature* of ideology in general and the *need* for it in America. For those who doubt that our legal system could function in such questionable ways, I also present evidence on how the criminal justice system has been used in the past to protect the rich and powerful against those who would challenge their privileges or their policies. These sections, then, flesh out the historical inertia explanation of the failure of criminal justice by showing the ideological benefits that that failure yields and to whom. In the last section, *A Structural Explanation of Criminal Justice in America*, I briefly sketch a Marxian answer to the question of why the American criminal justice system focuses on one-on-one harms and fails to protect against the harmful acts of the well off.

Ultimately, the test of the argument in this chapter is whether or not it provides a plausible explanation of the failure of criminal justice and draws the arguments of the previous chapters together into a coherent theory of contemporary criminal justice policy and practice.

## THE POVERTY OF CRIMINALS AND THE CRIME OF POVERTY

Criminal justice is a very visible part of the American scene. As fact and fiction, countless images of crime and the struggle against it assail our senses daily, even hourly. In every newspaper, in every TV or radio newscast, there is at least one criminal justice story and often more. It is as if we live in an embattled city, besieged by the forces of crime and bravely defended by the forces of the law, and as we go about our daily tasks, we are always conscious of the war raging not very far away; newspapers bring us daily and newscasts bring us hourly reports from the "front." Between reports, we are vividly reminded of the stakes and the desperateness of the battle by fictionalized portrayals of the struggle between the forces of the law and the breakers of the law. There is scarcely an hour on television without some dramatization of the struggle against crime (In the *TV Guide* for the week of February 19 through February 25, 1983, I counted *125 hours* of programming in which the struggle against crime is featured. Keep in mind that there are only 168 hours in a week, and TV stations do not broadcast all around the clock. Also I counted only the regular channels serving the metropolitan Washington, D.C. area and did not include cable or other limited access channels. Remember, too, that 98 percent of American homes have televisions, and it is estimated that they are on an average of six hours a day!)[6] If we add to this the news accounts, the panel discussions, and the political speeches about crime, there can be no doubt that as fact or fantasy or both, criminal justice is vividly present in the imaginations of most Americans.

This is no accident. Everyone can relate to criminal justice in personal and emotional terms. Everyone has some fear of crime, and, as we saw in Chapter 3, just about everyone has committed some. And everyone knows the primitive satisfaction of seeing justice done and the evildoers served up their just deserts. Furthermore, in reality or in fiction, criminal justice is naturally dramatic. It contains the acts of courage and cunning, the high risks and high stakes, and the life-and-death struggle between good and evil that are missing from the routine lives so many of us lead. To identify with the struggle against crime is to expand one's experience vicariously to include the danger, the suspense, the triumphs, the meaningfulness—in a word, the drama—often missing in ordinary life. How else can we explain the seemingly bottomless appetite Americans have for the endless repetition, in only slightly altered form, of the same theme: the struggle of the forces of law against the forces of crime? Criminal justice has a firm grip on the imaginations of Americans and is thus in a unique position to convey a message to Americans and to convey it with drama and with conviction.

Let us now look at this message in detail. Our task falls naturally into two parts. There is an ideological message, a message supportive of the status quo, built into *any* criminal justice system by its very nature. Even if the criminal justice system were not failing, even if it were not biased against the poor, it would still—by its very nature—broadcast a message supportive of established institutions. This is *the implicit ideology of criminal justice.* Beyond this, there is an additional ideological message conveyed by the *failure* of the system and by its *biased* concentration on the poor. I call this the *bonus of bias*.

## The Implicit Ideology of Criminal Justice

Any criminal justice system like ours conveys a subtle, yet powerful message in support of established institutions. It does this for two interconnected reasons: first, because it concentrates on *individual* wrongdoers. This means that *it diverts our attention away from our institutions, away from consideration of whether our institutions themselves are wrong or unjust or indeed "criminal."*

Second, the criminal law is put forth as the *minimum neutral ground rules* for any social living. We are taught that no society can exist without rules against theft and violence, and thus the criminal law is put forth as politically neutral, as the minimum requirements for *any* society, as the minimum obligations that any individual owes his fellows to make social life of any decent sort possible. Thus, it not only diverts our attention away from the possible injustice of our social institutions, but *the criminal law bestows upon those institutions the mantle of its own neutrality.* Since the criminal law protects the established institutions (e.g., the prevailing economic arrangements are protected by laws against theft, etc.), attacks on those established institutions become equivalent to violations of the minimum requirements for any social life at all. In effect, the criminal law enshrines the established institutions as equivalent to the minimum requirements for *any* decent social existence—and it brands the individual who attacks those institutions as one who has declared war on *all* organized society and who must therefore be met with the weapons of war.

This is the powerful magic of criminal justice. By virtue of its focus on *individual* criminals, it diverts us from the evils of the *social* order. By virtue of its presumed neutrality, it transforms the established social (and economic) order from being merely *one* form of society open to critical comparison with others into *the* conditions of *any* social order and thus immune from criticism. Let us look more closely at this process.

What is the effect of focusing on individual guilt? Not only does this divert our attention from the possible evils in our institutions, but it puts forth half the problem of justice as if it were the *whole* problem. To focus on individual guilt is to ask whether or not the individual citizen has fulfilled his obligations to his fellow citizens. *It is to look away from the issue of whether his fellow citizens have fulfilled their obligations to him.* To look only at individual responsibility is to look away from social responsibility. To look only at individual criminality is to close one's eyes to social injustice and to close one's ears to the question of whether our social institutions have exploited or violated the individual. *Justice is a two-way street—but criminal justice is a one-way street.* Individuals owe obligations to their fellow citizens because their fellow citizens owe obligations to them. Criminal justice focuses on the first and looks away from the second. *Thus, by focusing on individual responsibility for crime, the criminal justice system literally acquits the existing social order of any charge of injustice!*

This is an extremely important bit of ideological alchemy. It stems from the fact that the same act can be criminal or not, unjust or just, depending on the conditions in which it takes place. Killing someone is ordinarily a crime. But if it is in self-defense or to stop a deadly crime, it is not. Taking property by force is usually a crime. But if the taking is just retrieving what has been stolen, then no crime has been committed. Acts of violence are ordinarily crimes. But if the violence is provoked by the threat of violence or by oppressive conditions, then, like the Boston Tea Party, what might ordinarily be called criminal is celebrated as just. This means that when we call an act a crime *we are also making an implicit judgment about the conditions in response to which it takes place.* When we call an act a crime, we are saying that the conditions in which it occurs are not themselves criminal or deadly or oppressive or so unjust as to make an extreme response reasonable or justified, that is, to make such a response noncriminal. This means that when the system holds an individual responsible for a crime, *it implicitly conveys the message that the social conditions in which the crime occurred are not responsible for the crime,* that they are not so unjust as to make a violent response to them excusable.

Judges are prone to hold that an individual's responsibility for a violent crime is diminished if it was provoked by something that might lead a "reasonable man" to respond violently and that criminal responsibility is eliminated if the act was in response to conditions so intolerable that any "reasonable man" would have been likely to respond in the same way. In this vein, the law acquits those who kill or injure in self-defense and treats lightly those who commit a crime when confronted with extreme provocation. The law treats leniently the man who kills his wife's lover and the woman who kills her brutal husband, even when neither has acted directly in self-defense. By this logic, when we hold an individual completely responsible for a crime, we are saying that the conditions in which it occurred are such that a "reasonable man" should find them tolerable. In other words, by focusing on individual responsibility for crimes, *the criminal justice system broadcasts the message that the social order itself is reasonable and not intolerably unjust.*

Thus the criminal justice system focuses moral condemnation on individuals and deflects it away from the social order that may have either violated the individual's rights or dignity or literally pushed him or her to the brink of crime. This not only serves to carry the message that our social institutions are not in need of fundamental questioning, but it further suggests that the justice of our institutions is obvious, not to be doubted. Indeed, since it is deviations from these institutions that are crimes, the established institutions become the implicit standard of justice from which criminal deviations are measured.

This leads to the second way in which a criminal justice system always conveys an implicit ideology. It arises from the presumption that the criminal law is nothing but the politically neutral minimum requirements of any decent social life. What is the consequence of this?

Obviously, as already suggested, this presumption transforms the prevailing social order into justice incarnate and all violations of the prevailing order into injustice incarnate. This process is so obvious that it may be easily missed.

Consider, for example, the law against theft. It does indeed seem to be one of the minimum requirements of social living. As long as there is scarcity, any society—capitalist or socialist—will need rules preventing individuals from taking what does not belong to them. But the law against theft is more: It is a law against stealing what individuals *presently* own. *Such a law has the effect of making present property relations a part of the criminal law.*

Since stealing is a violation of law, this means that present property relations become the implicit standard of justice against which criminal deviations are measured. Since criminal law is thought of as the minimum requirements of any social life, this means that present property relations become equivalent to the minimum requirements of *any* social life. And the criminal who would alter the present property relations becomes nothing less than someone who is declaring war on all organized society. The question of whether this "war" is provoked by the injustice or brutality of the society is swept aside. Indeed, this suggests yet another way in which the criminal justice system conveys an ideological message in support of the established society.

Not only does the criminal justice system acquit the social order of any charge of injustice, it specifically cloaks the society's own crime-producing tendencies. I have already observed that by blaming the individual for a crime, the society is acquitted of the charge of injustice. I would like to go further now and argue that by blaming the individual for a crime, the society is acquitted of the charge of *complicity* in that crime. This is a point worth developing, since many observers have maintained that modern competitive societies such as our own have structural features that tend to generate crime. Thus, holding the individual responsible for his or her crime serves the function of taking the rest of society off the hook for their role in sustaining and benefiting from social arrangements that produce crime. Let us take a brief detour to look more closely at this process.

Cloward and Ohlin argue in their book *Delinquency and Opportunity*[7] that much crime is the result of the discrepancy between social goals and the legitimate opportunities available for achieving them. Simply put, in our society everyone is encouraged to be a success, but the avenues to success are open only to some. The conventional wisdom of our free enterprise democracy is that anyone can be a success if he or she has the talent and the ambition. Thus, if one is not a success, it is because of one's own shortcomings: laziness or lack of ability or both. On the other hand, opportunities to achieve success are not equally open to all. Access to the best schools and the best jobs is effectively closed to all but a few of the poor and becomes more available only as one goes up the economic ladder. The result is that many are called but few are chosen. And many who have taken the bait and accepted the belief in the importance of success and the belief that achieving success is a result of individual ability must cope with the feelings of frustration and failure that result when they find the avenues to success closed. Cloward and Ohlin argue that one method of coping with these stresses is to develop alternative avenues to success. Crime is such an alternative avenue. Crime is a means by which people who believe in the American dream pursue it when they find the traditional routes barred. Indeed, it is plain to see that the goals pursued by most criminals are as American as apple pie. I suspect that one of the reasons that American moviegoers enjoy gangster films—movies in which gangsters such as Al Capone, Bonnie and Clyde, or Butch Cassidy and the Sundance Kid are the heroes, as distinct from police and detective films whose heroes are defenders of the law—is that even where they deplore the hero's methods, they identify with his or her notion of success, since it is theirs as well, and respect the courage and cunning displayed in achieving that success.

It is important to note that the discrepancy between success goals and legitimate opportunities in America is not an aberration. It is a structural feature of modern competitive industrialized society, a feature from which many benefits flow. Cloward and Ohlin write that

> a crucial problem in the industrial world . . . is to locate and train the most talented persons in every generation, irrespective of the vicissitudes of birth, to occupy technical work roles. . . . Since we cannot know in advance who can best fulfill the requirements of the various occupational roles, the matter is presumably settled through the process of competition. But how can men throughout the social order be motivated to participate in this competition? . . .
>
> One of the ways in which the industrial society attempts to solve this problem is by defining success-goals as potentially accessible to all, regardless of race, creed, or socioeconomic position.[8]

But since these universal goals are urged to encourage a competition to weed out the best, there are necessarily fewer openings than seekers. And since those who achieve success are in a particularly good position to exploit their success to make access for their own children easier, the competition is rigged to work in favor of the middle and upper classes. As a result, "many lower-class persons . . . are the victims of a contradiction between the goals toward which they have been led to orient themselves and socially structured means of striving for these goals."[9]

> [The poor] experience desperation born of the certainty that their position in the economic structure is relatively fixed and immutable—a desperation made all the more poignant by their exposure to a cultural ideology in which failure to orient oneself upward is regarded as a moral defect and failure to become mobile as proof of it.[10]

The outcome is predictable. "Under these conditions, there is an acute pressure to depart from institutional norms and to adopt illegitimate alternatives."[11]

In brief, this means that the very way in which our society is structured to draw out the talents and energies that go into producing our high standard of living has a costly side effect: It produces crime. But by holding individuals responsible for this crime, those who enjoy that high standard of living can have their cake and eat it. They can reap the benefits of the competition for success and escape the responsibility of paying for the costs of that competition. By holding the poor crook legally and morally guilty, the rest of society not only passes the costs of competition on to the poor, but they effectively deny that they (the affluent) are the beneficiaries of an economic system that exacts such a high toll in frustration and suffering.

Willem Bonger, the Dutch Marxist criminologist, maintained that competitive capitalism produces egotistic motives and undermines compassion for the misfortunes of others and thus makes human beings literally *more capable of crime*—more capable of preying on their fellows without moral inhibition or remorse—than earlier cultures that emphasized cooperation rather than competition.[12] Here again, the criminal justice system relieves those who benefit from the American economic system of the costs of that system. By holding criminals morally and individually responsible for their crimes, we can forget that the motives that lead to crime—the drive for success at any cost, linked with the beliefs that success means outdoing others and that violence is an acceptable way of achieving one's goals—are the *same motives* that powered the drive across the American continent and that continue to fuel the engine of America's prosperity.

David Gordon, a contemporary political economist, maintains "that nearly all crimes in capitalist societies represent perfectly *rational* responses to the structure of institutions upon which capitalist societies are based."[13] That is, like Bonger, Gordon believes that capitalism tends to provoke crime in all economic strata. This is so because most crime is motivated by a desire for property or money and is an understandable way of coping with the pressures of inequality, competition, and insecurity, all of which are essential ingredients of capitalism. Capitalism depends, Gordon writes,

> on basically competitive forms of social and economic interaction and upon substantial inequalities in the allocation of social resources. Without inequalities, it would be much more difficult to induce workers to work in alienating environments. Without competition and a competitive ideology, workers might not be inclined to struggle to improve their relative income and status in society by working harder. Finally, although rights of property are protected, capitalist societies do not guarantee economic security to most of their individual members. Individuals must fend for themselves, finding the best available opportunities to provide for themselves and their families. . . . Driven by the fear of economic insecurity and by a competitive desire to gain some of the goods unequally distributed throughout the society, many individuals will eventually become "criminals."[14]

To the extent that a society makes crime a reasonable alternative for a large number of its members from all classes, that society is itself not very reasonably or humanely organized and bears some degree of responsibility for the crime it encourages. Since the criminal law is put forth as the minimum requirements that can be expected of any "reasonable man," its enforcement amounts to a denial of the real nature of the social order to which Gordon and the others point. Here again, by blaming the individual criminal, the criminal justice system serves implicitly but dramatically to acquit the society of its criminality.

## The Bonus of Bias

We now consider the additional ideological bonus that is derived from the criminal justice system's bias against the poor. This bonus is a product of the association of crime and poverty in the popular mind. This association, the merging of the "criminal classes" and the "lower classes" into the "dangerous classes," was not invented in America. The word "villain" is derived from the Latin *villanus*, which means a farm servant. And the term "villein" was used in feudal England to refer to a serf who farmed the land of a great lord and who was literally owned by that lord.[15] In this respect, our present criminal justice system is heir to a long tradition.

The value of this association was already seen when we explored the "average citizen's" concept of the Typical Criminal and the Typical Crime. It is quite obvious that throughout the great mass of middle America, far more fear and hostility are directed toward the predatory acts of the poor than the rich. Compare the fate of politicians in recent history who call for tax reform, income redistribution, prosecution of corporate crime, and any sort of regulation of business that would make it better serve American social goals with that of politicians who erect their platform on a call for "law and order," more police, less limits on police power, and stiffer prison sentences for criminals—and consider this in light of what we have already seen about the real dangers posed by corporate crime and "business-as-usual."

It seems clear that Americans have been systematically deceived as to what are the greatest dangers to their lives, limbs and possessions. The very persistence with which the system functions to apprehend and punish poor crooks and ignore or slap on the wrist equally or more dangerous individuals is testimony to the sticking power of this deception. That Americans continue to tolerate the gentle treatment meted out to white-collar criminals, corporate price

fixers, industrial polluters, and political-influence peddlers while
voting in droves to lock up more poor people faster and longer indicates the degree to which they harbor illusions as to who most threatens them. It is perhaps also part of the explanation for the continued
dismal failure of class-based politics in America. American workers
rarely seem able to forget their differences and unite to defend their
shared interests against the rich whose wealth they produce. Ethnic
divisions serve this divisive function well, but undoubtedly the vivid
portrayal of the poor—and, of course, the blacks—as hovering birds
of prey waiting for the opportunity to snatch away the workers' mea-
ger gains serves also to deflect opposition away from the upper
classes. A politician who promises to keep working class communities free of blacks and their prisons full of them can get their votes
even if the major portion of his or her policies amount to continuation of favored treatment of the rich at their expense.

The most important "bonus" derived from the identification of
crime and poverty is that it paints the picture that the threat to decent
middle Americans comes from those below them on the economic
ladder, not those above. For this to happen the system must not only
identify crime and poverty, but *it must also fail to reduce crime so that
it remains a real threat.* By doing this, it deflects the fear and discontent of middle Americans, and their possible opposition, away from
the wealthy. The two politicians who most clearly gave voice to the
discontent of middle Americans in the post-World War II period
were George Wallace and Spiro Agnew. Is it any accident that their
politics was extremely conservative and their anger reserved for the
poor (the welfare chiselers) and the criminal (the targets of law and
order)?

There are other bonuses as well. For instance, if the criminal justice system functions to send out a message that bestows legitimacy
on present property relations, the dramatic impact is greatly en-
hanced if the violator of the present arrangements is without property. In other words, the crimes of the well-to-do "redistribute" property among the haves. In that sense, they do not pose a symbolic
challenge to the larger system in which some have much and many
have little or nothing. If the criminal threat can be portrayed as coming from the poor, then the punishment of the poor criminal becomes
a morality play in which the sanctity and legitimacy of the system in
which some have plenty and others have little or nothing is dramatically affirmed. It matters little who the poor criminals really victim-
ize. What counts is that middle Americans come to fear that those
poor criminals are out to steal what they own.

There is yet another bonus for the powerful in America, produced by the identification of crime and poverty. It might be thought that the identification of crime and poverty would produce sympathy for the criminals. My suspicion is that it produces or at least reinforces the reverse: *hostility toward the poor.*

Indeed, there is little evidence that Americans are very sympathetic to poor criminals. Very few Americans believe poverty to be a cause of crime (6 percent of those questioned in a 1981 survey, although 21 percent thought unemployment was a cause).[16] Other surveys find that most Americans believe that the police should be tougher than they are now in dealing with crime (83 percent of those questioned in a 1972 survey); that courts do not deal harshly enough with criminals (83 percent of those questioned in a 1980 survey)[17]; that a majority of Americans would like to see the death penalty for convicted murderers (67 percent of those questioned in 1980)[18]; and that most would be more likely to vote for a candidate who advocated tougher sentences for lawbreakers (83 percent of those questioned in a 1972 survey).[19] Indeed, the experience of Watergate seems to suggest that sympathy for criminals begins to flower only when we approach the higher reaches of the ladder of wealth and power. For some poor ghetto youth who robs a liquor store, five years in the slammer is our idea of tempering justice with mercy. When a handful of public officials try to walk off with the U.S. Constitution, a few months in a minimum security prison will suffice. If the public official is high enough, resignation from office and public disgrace tempered with a $60,000-a-year pension is punishment enough.

My view is that since the criminal justice system, in fact and fiction, deals with *individual legal* and *moral guilt*, the association of crime with poverty does not mitigate the image of individual moral responsibility for crime, the image that crime is the result of an individual's poor character. My suspicion is that it does the reverse: It generates the association of poverty and individual moral failing and thus *the belief that poverty itself is a sign of poor or weak character.* The clearest evidence that Americans hold this belief is to be found in the fact that attempts to aid the poor are regarded as acts of charity rather than as acts of justice. Our welfare system has all the demeaning attributes of an institution designed to give handouts to the undeserving and none of the dignity of an institution designed to make good on our responsibilities to our fellow human beings. If we acknowledged the degree to which our economic and social institutions themselves breed poverty, we would have to recognize our own responsibilities toward the poor. If we can convince ourselves that the poor are poor because of their own shortcomings, particularly moral shortcomings like incontinence and indolence, then we need acknowledge no such responsibility to the poor. Indeed, we can go further and pat ourselves on the back for our generosity in handing out the little that we do, and of course, we can make our recipients go through all the indignities that mark them as the undeserving objects of our benevolence. By and large, this has been the way in which Americans have dealt with their poor.[20] It is a way that enables us to avoid asking the question of why the richest nation in the world continues to produce massive poverty. It is my view that this conception of the poor is subtly conveyed by the way our criminal justice system functions.

Obviously, no ideological message could be more supportive of the present social and economic order than this. It suggests that poverty is a sign of individual failing, not a symptom of social or economic injustice. It tells us loud and clear that massive poverty in the midst of abundance is not a sign pointing toward the need for fundamental changes in our social and economic institutions. It suggests that the poor are poor because they deserve to be poor, or at least because they lack the strength of character to overcome poverty. When the poor are seen to be poor in character, then economic poverty coincides with moral poverty and the economic order coincides with the moral order. As if a divine hand guided its workings, capitalism leads to everyone getting what they morally deserve!

If this association takes root, then when the poor individual is found guilty of a crime, the criminal justice system acquits the society of its responsibility not only for crime *but for poverty as well.*

With this, the ideological message of criminal justice is complete. The poor rather than the rich are seen as the enemies of the majority of decent middle Americans. Our social and economic institutions are held to be responsible for neither crime nor poverty and thus are in need of no fundamental questioning or reform. The poor are poor because they are poor of character. The economic order and the moral order are one. And to the extent that this message sinks in, the wealthy can rest easily—even if they cannot sleep the sleep of the just.

Thus, we can understand why the criminal justice system creates the image of crime as the work of the poor and fails to reduce it so that the threat of crime remains real and credible. The result is ideological alchemy of the highest order. The poor are seen as the real threat to decent society. The ultimate sanctions of criminal justice dramatically sanctify the present social and economic order, and *the poverty of criminals makes poverty itself an individual moral crime!*

Such are the ideological fruits of a losing war against crime whose distorted image is reflected in the criminal justice carnival mirror and widely broadcast to reach the minds and imaginations of America.

## IDEOLOGY, OR HOW TO FOOL ENOUGH OF THE PEOPLE ENOUGH OF THE TIME

### What Is Ideology?

The view that the laws of a state or nation are made to serve the interests of those with power, rather than to promote the well-being of the whole society, is not a new discovery made in the wake of Watergate. It is a doctrine with a pedigree older even than Christianity itself. Writing during the fourth century B.C., virtually at the dawn of Western thought, Plato expressed this view through the lips of Thrasymachus.[21] A more contemporary and more systematic formulation of the idea is found in the works of Karl Marx. Written during the nineteenth century, not long after the dawn of western industrialism, Marx wrote in *The Communist Manifesto* that the bourgeoisie—the class of owners of businesses and factories, the class of capitalists—has

> conquered for itself, in the modern representative State, exclusive political sway. The executive of the modern State is but a committee for managing the common affairs of the whole bourgeoisie.[22]

Anyone who thinks this is a ridiculous idea ought to look at the backgrounds of our political leaders. The vast majority of the President's cabinet, the administrators of the federal regulatory agencies, and the members of the two houses of Congress come from the ranks of business or are lawyers who serve business. Many still maintain their business ties or law practices, with no sense of a conflict of interest with their political role.[23] If either Thrasymachus or Marx is right, there *is* no conflict with their political role, since that role is to protect and promote the interests of business.

It is clear that the most powerful criminal justice policymakers come from the have-plenties, not from the have-littles. It is no surprise that legislators and judges—those who make the laws that define criminality and those who interpret those laws—are predominantly members of the upper classes, if not at birth, then surely by the time they take office. One study of justices appointed to the U.S. Supreme Court between 1933 and 1957 found that 81 percent were sons of fathers with high social status occupations and that 61 percent had been educated in schools of high standing. Richard Quinney has compiled background data on key members of criminal justice policymaking and policy-advising committees and agencies, such as the President's Commission on Law Enforcement and Administration of Justice, the National Advisory Commission on Civil Disorders, the National Commission on the Causes and Prevention of Violence, the Senate Judiciary Committee's Subcommittee on Criminal Laws and Procedures (the subcommittee had a strong hand in shaping the Omnibus Crime Control and Safe Streets Act of 1968), the Law Enforcement Assistance Administration, the Federal Bureau of Investigation and, last but not least, the U.S. Department of Justice. With few exceptions, Quinney's report reads like a *Who's Who* of the business, legal, and political elite. For instance, 63 percent of the members of the President's Crime Commission had business and corporate connections.[24]

It should be noted that there is considerable evidence that the American criminal justice system has been used throughout its history in rather unsubtle ways to protect the interests of the powerful against the lower classes and political dissenters. The use of the FBI and local police forces to repress dissent by discrediting, harassing, and undermining dissident individuals and groups has been recently revealed. The FBI, often with active cooperation or tacit consent of local police, has engaged in literally hundreds of illegal burglaries of the offices of law-abiding left-wing political parties,[25] and in political sabotage against the Black Panthers (e.g., "a Catholic priest, the Rev. Frank Curran, became the target of FBI operations because he permitted the Black Panthers to use his church for serving breakfasts to ghetto children").[26] It conducted a campaign to discredit the late Martin Luther King, Jr. ("the FBI secretly categorized . . . King as a 'Communist' months before it ever started investigating him").[27] Although directors of the FBI have said that the bureau is "truly sorry" for these past abuses and that they are over, later reports indicate that they still continue.[28]

These acts of repression are only the latest in a long tradition. The first organized uniformed police force in the English-speaking world was established in London in 1829. They came to be called "bobbies" because of the role played by Sir Robert Peel in securing passage of the London Metropolitan Police Act that established the force. The first full-time uniformed police force in the United States was set up in New York City in 1845.[29] It was also in the period from the 1820s to the 1840s that the movement to build penitentiaries to house and reform criminals began in New York and Pennsylvania and spread rapidly through the states of the young nation.[30] That these are also the years that saw the beginnings of a large industrial working class in the cities of England and America is a coincidence too striking to ignore.

The police were repeatedly used to break strikes and harass strikers.[31] The penitentiaries were mainly used to house the laborers and foreigners (often one and the same) whom the middle and upper classes perceived as a threat.[32] Throughout the formative years of the American labor movement, public police forces, private police such as the Pinkertons, the National Guard, and regular army troops were repeatedly used to protect the interests of capital against the attempts of labor to organize in defense of its interests. The result was that "the United States has had the bloodiest and most violent labor history of any industrial nation in the world"—with most of the casualties on the side of labor.[33]

Marx, of course, went further. Not only are the laws of a society made to protect the interests of the most powerful economic class, but also, Marx argued, the prevailing ways of thinking about the world—from economic theory to religion to conventional moral ideas about good and evil, guilt and responsibility—are shaped in ways that promote the belief that the existing society is the best of allpossible worlds. Marx wrote that

> the ideas of the ruling class are in every epoch the ruling ideas: i.e. the class which is the ruling material force of society, is at the same time its ruling intellectual force. The class which has the means of material production at its disposal, has control at the same time over the means of mental production.[34]

In simple terms, because those who have economic power own the newspapers, endow the universities, finance the publication of books and journals, and (in our own time) control the television and radio industries, they have a prevailing say in what is said, heard, and thought by the millions who get their ideas—their picture of reality—from these sources. And this does not mean that the controllers of the "means of mental production" consciously deceive or manipulate those who receive their message. What it means is that the picture of reality held by these controllers—held, no doubt sincerely, to be an accurate representation of reality—will be largely the picture of reality that fills the heads of the readers and viewers of the mass media. And recognizing this involves no disrespect of the so-called "common person." It is simply a matter of facing reality. The average man or woman is almost wholly occupied with the personal tasks of earning a living, piloting a family, and the like. He or she lacks the time (and usually the training) necessary to seek out and evaluate alternative sources of information. They are lucky when they have the time to catch a bit of news on television or in the papers. Moreover, except when there is division of opinion among those who control the media, the average person is so surrounded by unbroken "consensus" that he or she takes it simply as the way things are, with no particular reason even to consider the possibility that there are other sides of the issue to be considered, much less to seek these out. And then, even if people do come up with alternative sources of information, there are no general forums available for the sharing of views among members of the public. What we call mass communication is communication *to* the masses, not among them.

Consequently, the vast majority of people will accept, as a true picture of reality, the picture held by those who control the media. And this is likely to be a distorted picture, even if those who create it act with the best of intentions and sincerity. The point is that, for a wide variety of reasons, people will tend to view the world in ways that make their own role in it (particularly the advantages and privileges they have in it) seem morally just, indeed, part of the best of all possible worlds. Thus without any intention to deceive at all, those who control the content of the mass media are virtually certain to convey a picture of reality that supports the existing social order.

As a result, even in a society such as ours, where freedom of expression has reached a level probably unparalleled in history, there is almost never any *fundamental* questioning of our political-economic-legal institutions in the mass media, that is, television and radio, the major newspapers, or the news weeklies such as *Time* or *Newsweek*. There is much criticism of individuals and of individual policies. But how often does one find the mass media questioning whether the free enterprise system is really the best choice for America or whether our political and legal arrangements systematically promote the domination of society by the owners of big business? These issues are rarely, if ever, raised. Instead, it is taken for granted that, although they need some reform tinkering from time to time, our economic institutions are the most productive, our political institutions the most free, and our legal institutions the most just *there can be.*

In other words, even in a society as free as ours, the ideas that fill the heads of most Americans and shape their picture of reality either explicitly or implicitly convey the message that our leaders are pursuing the common good (with only occasional lapses into personal venality—note how we congratulate ourselves on how "the system is working" when we expose these "aberrations" and then return to business as usual). Thus, we are told that the interests of the powerful coincide with the common interests of us all[35]—that "what's good for General Motors is good for the country." Where this picture of reality shows up some blemishes, they will always be portrayed as localized problems that can be remedied without fundamental overhaul of the entire social order, aberrations in an otherwise well-functioning social system. Indeed, the very willingness to publicize these blemishes "proves" that there is nothing fundamentally wrong with the social system since if the media are free, willing and able to portray the blemishes, they would surely portray fundamental problems with the social system if there were any—and since they do not, there must not be any! When ideas, however unintentionally, distort reality in a way that justifies the prevailing distribution of power and wealth, hides society's injustices, and thus secures uncritical allegiance to the existing social order, we have what Marx called *ideology.*[36]

Ideology is not conscious deception. People may spout ideology simply because it is all they know or all they have been taught or because they do not see beyond the "conventional wisdom" that surrounds them. This can be just as true of scholars who fail to see beyond the conventional assumptions of their disciplines as it is of laymen who fail to see beyond the oversimplifications of what is commonly called "common sense." Such individuals do not mouth an ideology out of a willful desire to deceive and manipulate their fellows, but rather because their own view of reality is distorted by untruths and half-truths—and criminal justice is one source of such distortion.

It should be noted in passing that not everyone uses the term "ideology" as I have, to point to what is necessarily deceptive. Some writers speak of ideology as if it meant any individual or group's "belief system" or "value system" or *Weltanschauung*, that is, "world view."[37] I do not intend to quibble about semantics. However, such a moral neutralization of the concept of "ideology" strikes me as unnecessarily dulling an instrument that thinkers like Marx and others have sharpened into an effective tool for cutting through the illusions that dog our political life. Such tools are few and hard to find. Once found, they should be carefully preserved, especially when concepts such as "belief system" or "world view" are available to perform the more neutral function.

### The Need for Ideology

A simple and persuasive argument can be made for the claim that the rich and powerful in America have an interest in conveying an ideological message to the rest of the nation. The have-nots and have-littles far outnumber the have-plenties. This means, to put it rather crudely, the have-nots and the have-littles could have more if they decided to take it from the have-plenties. This, in turn, means that the have-plenties need the cooperation of the have-nots and the have-littles. And since the have-plenties are such a small minority that they could never *force* this cooperation on the have-nots and have-littles, this cooperation must be voluntary. And for the cooperation to be voluntary, the have-nots and the have-littles must believe that it would not be right or reasonable to take away what the have-plenties have. In other words, they must believe that for all its problems the present social, political, and economic order, with its disparities of wealth and power and privilege, is about the best that human beings can do. More specifically, the have-nots and have-littles must believe that they are not being exploited by the have-plenties. Now this seems to me to add up to an extremely plausible argument that ours is a social system that requires for its continued operation a set of beliefs necessary to secure the allegiance of the less well-off majority. And these beliefs must be in some considerable degree false, since the distribution of wealth and power in the United States is so evidently arbitrary and unjust. Ergo, the need for ideology.

A disquisition on the inequitable distribution of wealth and income in the United States is beyond the scope and purpose of this book. This subject, as well as the existence of a "dominant" or "ruling" class in America, has been documented extensively by others.[38] I will only make two points here. First, there are indeed wide disparities in the distribution of wealth and income in the United States. Second, these disparities are so obviously unjust that it is reasonable to assume that the vast majority of people who must struggle to make ends meet only put up with them because they have been sold a bill of goods, that is, an ideology.

In 1979, the richest 20 percent of American families received 41.6 percent of the income received by all families, while the poorest 60 percent of American families received 34.4 percent of the total income. In crude terms, this means that while the wealthiest 44 million Americans had two-fifths of the money pie to themselves, the least wealthy 132 million Americans had to share a third of that pie among them. At the extremes, the figures are even more outrageous. The richest 5 percent received 15.7 percent of the total income, which was three times the amount received by the poorest 20 percent of families, who received 5.3 percent of total income, and nearly as much as the lowest 40 percent of families, who received 16.9 percent. This means that the richest 5 percent of families—maybe 9 million people—had nearly as much money to divide among themselves as the roughly 88 million persons who make up the bottom 40 percent.[39]

The distribution of *wealth* (property such as stocks and land that generate income and tend to give one a say in major economic decisions) is even worse than the distribution of income.[40] An article in the November 1974 issue of *Survey of Current Business* reports that, in 1971,

> the 1 percent of U.S. families (including single individuals) with the largest personal income accounted for 47 percent of dividend income received and 51 percent of the market value of stock owned by all families, while the 10 percent of families with the largest income accounted for 71 percent of dividend income and 74 percent of market value.[41]

I offer no complicated philosophical argument to prove that these disparities are unjust, although such arguments abound for those who are interested.[42] It is a scandal that in a nation as rich as ours, some 25 million people should live below what the government conservatively defines as the poverty level and that many millions more must scramble to make ends meet.[43] It is tragic that in our wealthy nation so many millions cannot afford a proper diet, a college education, a decent place to live, and good health care. We know too much about the causes of wealth and poverty to believe that the rich become rich because of their talent or contribution to society or that the poor are poor because they are lazy or incapable. Since we are nowhere near offering all Americans a good education and an equal opportunity to get ahead, we have no right even to suggest that the distribution of income reflects what people have truly earned. The distribution of income in America is so fundamentally shaped by factors such as race, educational opportunity, and the economic class of one's parents,[44] that few people who are well off can honestly claim that they deserve *all* that they have. Those who think they do should ask themselves where they would be today if they had been born to migrant laborers in California or to a poor black family in the Harlem ghetto.

Enough said. I take it, then, as established that the disparities of wealth and income in America are wide and unjustified. For the vast majority, the many millions struggling hard to satisfy basic needs, to acquiesce to the vast wealth of a small minority, it is necessary that the majority come to believe that these disparities are justified, that the present order is the best that human beings can accomplish, and that they are not being exploited by the have-plenties. In other words, the system requires an effective ideology to fool enough of the people enough of the time.

This account of the nature and need for ideology, coupled with the historical inertia explanation of the persistence of criminal justice in its current form and the analysis of the ideological benefits produced by the criminal justice system, adds up to an explanation of the continued failure of criminal justice in America. In the remainder of this chapter, I will supplement this explanation with what I call a "structural" explanation.

## A STRUCTURAL EXPLANATION OF CRIMINAL JUSTICE IN AMERICA

There is another way of explaining the persistence of the one-on-one model of crime and the unwillingness to label criminal such things as occupational hazards or air pollution. This explanation relies heavily on Marx's theory of the capitalist mode of production and argues that the structure of a capitalist society is such that the current division between criminal and noncriminal is built into that structure—that is, it is a division built into the way capitalism works and the way capitalism naturally appears to its participants. This explanation does not supplant the explanation from historical inertia; rather it lends it additional support because it explains how in a capitalist society one would be prone to see acts of one-on-one harm as the standard form of crime and not to see indirect harms, such as occupational hazards, as crimes at all. Moreover, the explanation is the very opposite of a conspiracy theory. Insofar as the criminal justice system broadcasts a picture of reality supportive of the social system, this explanation shows that that picture is just the natural picture one would have as a participant in a capitalist society—it is, so to speak, "read off" the face of capitalism, and thus requires no assumption that those in control are intentionally deceptive or manipulative. In this view, capitalist ideology, far from being conscious lies or distortions, is just the way capitalism looks. It is—from the standpoint of Marxian theory—a distortion nonetheless. And this distortion does confer benefits on those in power, but it does not come into existence because those in power intentionally bring it into existence in order to reap those benefits.

One note before beginning. The world of Marxian scholarship is crisscrossed by polemics that touch on virtually every feature of Marx's theory. What I plan to do here is to present in simplified form a sketch of a Marxian explanation of the shape of criminal justice. My purpose is not to settle all the outstanding theoretical disputes but to introduce the reader into a realm of theorizing that is usually either ignored or caricatured or presented so dogmatically that only those already convinced will attend to it. Consequently, while I will present an interpretation of Marxism that others may dispute, I will not try to defend this interpretation against others.[45]

Marx maintained that in every society, at least since the beginnings of settled agricultural communities, the labor that produces the means of existence for all is performed only by some members of the society. They produce a surplus over what they need for themselves and their families, and this surplus goes to support their masters, the nonproducers. There is, consequently, in every such society, a profound conflict of interest between two groups: the producers and the nonproducers, since the former could work less if they only had to fulfill their own needs. Moreover, the extra work they do to produce surplus for the nonproducers is done essentially without compensation, since the producers have already gotten what they are going to get from the work they did for their own needs. This is why Marx says near the beginning of *The Communist Manifesto* that, "the history of all hitherto existing society is the history of class struggles. Freeman and slave, patrician and plebeian, lord and serf . . . carried on an uninterrupted, now hidden, now open fight."[46] This is also why Marx maintains that the real difference between forms of society lies in the means by which the nonproducers extract the surplus product of the producers.[47] This difference in turn is determined by the relation between the producers and the *means of production*, those things such as land and tools and raw materials that enable one to engage in production at all.

In capitalism, workers do not own means of production. Their only possibility of producing a living lies in hiring themselves out to someone who does own means of production, that is, a capitalist. Consequently, they enter into a contractual agreement with the capitalist, in which a worker offers to work some number of hours and the capitalist offers to pay in return some number of dollars as a wage. Workers, of course, cannot eat their wage; what they can do with it is buy the products of those workers who produce consumer goods, food, clothing, and so on. Now if you think of this from the standpoint of the whole society, all workers receive wages with which they purchase the wage-goods produced by those workers who produce consumer goods. But only a part of the labor force is producing consumer goods; others are producing machines and the like. Thus *all* the workers are paid with the product of the labor of *some* of the workers. Or to put it in other terms, *part* of the labor that *all* the workers do comes back to them in the form of wage-goods, the consumer goods that make up their standard of living. In short, *with this part of their labor, the workers pay themselves!* The remainder of the labor in society does not return to the laborers; it (its products, that is) belongs to the capitalists. And of course, for *this* labor, the workers receive no compensation, since they have already received all the compensation they are going to get in the form of their wages.

Think of the total social workday, that is, all the labor done by all the laborers in society in a given eight-hour day. Now, if we suppose that half of the labor force is engaged in producing wage-goods, this means that *half* of the social workday—four hours—is spent producing the goods that *all* the workers receive for working the *whole* social workday. The remaining four hours of work is surplus labor (surplus over that labor necessary to meet the workers' needs), and this surplus goes to the capitalists for free.

Marx illustrates this by asking us to think of an individual worker's day. Suppose a worker is hired to work an eight-hour day at $5 an hour, or $40 for the day. He or she produces in that day, let us say, a chair that the capitalist sells for $100. Assume that the raw materials that went into the chair, the wear and tear on the machinery, and so on, cost the capitalist $20. After paying the worker's wage of $40, the capitalist is left with $40 of profit. Where does this profit come from? Marx assumes that the chair is really worth $100 when the capitalist sells it. Marx's explanation of the source of the profit is that the worker adds $80 worth of value to the raw materials in transforming them into a chair worth $100. Now notice that this means that the worker is producing value at the rate of $10 an hour. And that means that a laborer produces the equivalent of his or her wage *during the first four hours of the workday.* During the remainder of the day, he or she works, produces value, but receives no compensation for it. Capitalists' profit, then, arises because workers work some number of hours for them gratis![48] If you think that the capitalist earns the $40 profit because of designing the chair or thinking of producing it, remember that a capitalist can always hire someone to do these things and still make a profit. Thus, even if capitalists did at one time do such work, once the system is going for a while, they need no longer do anything to reap a profit. They can sit back and have workers work for them and pay themselves!

Now Marx does not merely believe that this process shortchanges workers. He believes that they are *coerced* to work for free. This is why Marx speaks of workers in capitalism as "wage-slaves."[49] But the coercion here is of a special sort, since unlike the slaveowner of old (or even the feudal lord), capitalists cannot use or threaten force to get the worker to work for them. The capitalist must offer the workers a wage which they are free to reject, at least free in the sense that no one will shoot or whip them if they refuse. The coercion, then, is not of the ordinary overt sort in which one person threatens to injure another directly. What coerces workers into working for free is the fact that the capitalists own all the means of production and thus workers *must* work for some capitalist if they are to work, and thus to live, at all. The coercion of capitalism is built into the structure of capitalism that allows relatively few people to have exclusive control over the means of work for everyone. That is to say, in capitalism, it is the *class structure* itself, the fact that there is a class of owners of means of production and a class of nonowners, that is coercive. This quite literally gives the capitalists a stranglehold on the rest of the population.

This is hard for us to see since we grow up in a world in which some people own the means of production and thus this situation seems quite normal—at least as normal as the fact that some people are strong or healthy and others are weak or sickly. Consequently, since the owners of means of production are not allowed to use or threaten overt force against the workers to get them to work, it appears that the relations between the capitalists and workers are free—the very opposite of slavery. This is particularly so since there are several capitalists, so the worker who does not like the terms offered by one can go to another, and the first has no power to stop him. In sum, as long as ownership of means of production seems normal and natural, and the workers and the capitalists trade labor for wages in the absence of visible coercion, their relations seem free.

Imagine, however, a society where there were only a few sources of oxygen owned by a small number of people and that others in the society had to work for the oxygen-owners in order to get a chance to breathe. Even if no overt force were used in arranging the "labor-for-breath" exchanges, it would be quite clear that the workers were slaves to the oxygen-owners. However, this is only so clear because we would regard it as quite bizarre for some to control all the oxygen; thus we would see quite easily that they had a literal stranglehold on the rest. But, imagine that we grew up in a society in which it were regarded as normal that a few owned all the oxygen-sources. Then, we would see it as we currently see private ownership of means of production, that is, as a piece of good fortune that some people happened to have. If, in such a world, workers entered into agreements with the oxygen-owners, trading labor for breath, agreements from which all overt force was prohibited such that if a worker did not like one oxygen-owner's terms, he could freely refuse them and go to a different oxygen-owner and try to strike up a deal, it would appear that the relations between workers and oxygen-owners were free, the very opposite of slavery. This, for Marxism, is just the way it is with capitalism: Capitalism is a coercive system, a form of slavery, but it appears to be a free system because on one hand ownership of means of production appears normal and on the other hand overt force is prohibited in the transactions between capitalists and workers. Or to put it more simply, in capitalism all relations between capitalists and workers are exchanges free of the use or threat of force and thus all such relations naturally *look* free.

Consider, in this respect, the difference between feudalism and capitalism. The feudal serf owns means of production after a fashion. That is, he owns his own tools and has traditional rights to some plot of land. He has no need to sell his labor to the feudal lord, since he can produce the means of his subsistence himself. Thus the only way that the feudal lord can extract surplus from the serf is by the threat and use of overt force. Under threat of such force, the serf is required to farm an additional plot of land whose output goes to the lord. In such a system, there is no doubt that the serf is in part the slave of the lord, forced to work for him for free. Capitalism, on the other hand, by freeing the workers of means of production, frees the capitalists of the need to threaten or use overt force to get the workers to work for them for free. All the capitalists need do is wait for the fact that the workers own no means of production to have its effect: The workers will have no choice but to work for the capitalists; and if they work for the capitalists, they will have to give the capitalists more labor than that which produces their wages, or else the capitalists will have no reason to hire them in the first place. In short, capitalism is a system of coerced labor as is feudalism; the difference is that in feudalism the coercion is by means of overt force and thus visible, while in capitalism overt force has been eliminated and coercion operates invisibly through the class structure of society itself.[50]

Having made this theoretical detour, let us now return to the question posed in this book: Why, for instance, are the ordinary direct forms of assault and killing counted as criminal while occupational hazards are not, even though they are at least as dangerous? To answer this, recall that the Defender of the Present Legal Order objected to labeling unprevented occupational hazards as crimes because workers are not subjected to these hazards by force, in the way that victims of crimes are. That is, in criminal assault or homicide one person uses force directly to impose a dangerous and harmful situation on another against his or her will. The victims of occupational disease, on the other hand, were not forced to work in dangerous conditions. They chose to in accepting their jobs, and no one held a gun to their heads to make them do this. Since the worker has consented to work in dangerous conditions, the maintenance of these conditions by the employer is not directly coercive in the way that criminal assault or homicide are, and thus not seen as criminal assault or homicide.

If this is the correct rendering of the conventional view, then, according to the Marxian account sketched above, occupational hazards are not seen as criminal in capitalism precisely because the class relation between employer and employee is not seen as coercive. On the other hand, ordinary assault and killing correspond to just the kinds of exercises of overt force that are prohibited from economic relations. In short, the division between criminal and noncriminal dangers corresponds precisely to the division between what is naturally seen as coercive in capitalism and what is naturally not seen as coercive. And this applies not only to occupational hazards, but to such conditions as air pollution, chemical contamination, inadequate emergency care, and poverty, as well, since all of these appear as voluntarily accepted risks of modern life as long as the social structure itself is not seen as coercive. Once it is seen that the relation between the owners of means of production and their employees is a coercive one, then the conditions of the employees' (and their families') existence would not look like something they had voluntarily accepted—they would look much more like conditions imposed by force.

In sum, capitalist social relations are characterized by the absence of acts of overt force between economic agents. Capitalists do not use direct force to coerce workers into accepting terms of employment. Indeed, if capitalists did do this, they would be blocked by another segment of the population organized outside the immediate realm of production, namely, the state. Capitalism establishes a kind of "demilitarized zone" between workers and their employers (a zone of the sort that did not exist under feudalism), and this demilitarized zone is policed by the state. The laws on the books are to this demilitarized zone as maps are to actual terrain. If we can see the nature of this social reality that the law represents, we can see the source of the prevailing notion of what is and what is not criminal. What I have referred to as the demilitarized zone between economic agents functions as a kind of lighted backdrop against which acts of overt force are thrown into relief as normative violations and worthy objects of state repression, while the indirect coercion built into the capitalists' exclusive control of the means of production falls behind the lighted backdrop and is not seen. If this is the real structure of social relations under capitalism, then it follows that people socialized into such relations who consequently regard them as just the natural shape of things, will naturally come to see acts of overt visible force as crimes, that is, as acts rightfully prohibited. These people equally naturally will *not* come to see the relationship between owners of means of production and everyone else as coercive. Among such people, it will be merely commonsense that fatal stabbing or shooting is murder while fatal disease resulting from conditions in the workplace is not.

This account explains how the current shape of the criminal justice system, what is criminal and what is not, is "read off" the structure of the capitalist social relations. Naturally, it explains the phenomenon in its broad contours; the actual details of the law and the policies surrounding the law are the outcome of myriad struggles within these contours. Thus, for example, while occupational hazards are largely seen as shared social risks, they are not ignored by the law. Rather they are treated as regulatory matters, which is how we deal with problems for which the question of how to solve them most efficiently is more important than the question of culpability. On the other hand, since there is at least some partial recognition that the employee's choice to accept a job is less than ideally free, there is some movement toward treating some occupational hazards as crimes, though not as grave ones. Leaving such details aside, I contend that the Marxian account just offered explains why we continue to have and regard as natural and obvious a criminal justice system that takes the model of "one-on-one" harms as its standard and fails to treat as criminal a wide variety of indirect harms that threaten society as much or more than these. And it explains it without any assumption that this is the conscious aim of the powers-that-be.

# 5

# Criminal Justice or Criminal Justice: A Matter of Moral Conviction

What are states without justice but robber-bands enlarged?

**St. Augustine,** Confessions

. . . unjust social arrangements are themselves a kind of extortion, even violence. . . .

**John Rawls,** A Theory of Justice

. . . the policeman . . . moves through Harlem, therefore, like an occupying soldier in a bitterly hostile country; which is precisely what, and where he is, and is the reason he walks in twos and threes.

**James Baldwin,** Nobody Knows My Name

## THE CRIME OF JUSTICE

Robbers, extortionists, occupying soldiers are terms used to characterize those who enforce an unjust law and an unjust order. It would be a mistake to think that this is merely a matter of rhetoric. There is a very real and very important sense in which those who use force unjustly or who use force to protect an unjust social order are no different from a band of criminals or an occupying army. In this chapter, I want to prove that this is true.

Without this proof, you are likely to think that what has been described in the first three chapters and accounted for in the fourth amounts to no more than another call for reform of the criminal justice system to make it more effective and more fair, when in fact it is much more. A criminal justice system that functions like ours—that imposes its penalties on the poor and not equally on all who threaten society, that does not protect us against threats to our lives and possessions equal to or graver than those presently defined as "crimes," and that fails even to do those things that could better protect us against the crimes of the poor—*is morally no better than the criminality it claims to fight.*

At the end of this chapter, I propose some reforms of the system. However, these should not be taken as proposals aimed merely at improving the effectiveness or fairness of American criminal justice. If the argument of this chapter is correct, then these proposals represent the necessary conditions for establishing the moral superiority of criminal justice to criminality. They are the conditions that must be fulfilled if the criminal justice system is to be acquitted of the indictment implicit in the above statements of Baldwin, Rawls, and St. Augustine.

The argument that follows will be set forth in dialogue form, since this is the form closest to the way we argue among (and within) ourselves and thus is most accessible and most easily understood. Further, I assume that there are readers who may be willing to believe the criticisms thus far presented but are reluctant to accept the more profound indictment implied by these criticisms. By using the dialogue form, I hope to anticipate and respond to their objections.

Before beginning, I will sketch out the terrain in which the dialogue will take place and give you an idea of the route that will be followed in traversing that terrain.

What is common to the charge implicit in the statements of Baldwin, Rawls and St. Augustine is the idea that *injustice transforms a legal system into its opposite.* What is common to the robber, the extortionist, and the occupying soldier is that each uses force (or the threat of force) to coerce other people to do things against their own interests. The robber and the extortionist use force to make other people hand over things of value. The occupying soldier uses force to subject one people to domination by another.

A legal system, of course, also uses force. But its defenders maintain that it uses force to protect people's control over the things they value and over their own destinies. That is, they claim that the legal system protects what people possess against robbers and extortionists and protects their autonomy against anyone who would try to impose their will on them by force. In short, although both a legal system and its opposite, either criminality or military domination, use force, the moral superiority of the legal system lies in the fact that it uses force to secure the interests of the people subject to its force, while criminals and occupation troops use force to subject some people to the interests of others.

The moral legitimacy of a legal system and the lack of legitimacy of crime and military domination hinge, then, on the question of whether or not coercion is being used to enhance people's own interests. Ordinarily, when anyone is forced to serve as an instrument for the purposes of others, we call this tyranny or exploitation—or, in a word, *injustice*. In the absence of some compelling moral reason, force used to coerce people into serving the interests of others at the expense of their own is *morally no better than criminal force*. Since a legal system purports to do the reverse—to use force to protect every-one's interest in freedom and security by preventing and rectifying violations of those interests—legal systems call themselves *systems of justice*.[1] With this, they assert that the force used under color of law is morally opposite from, and morally superior to, the force used by criminals or conquerors.

This adds up to something that should be obvious but is not. *A criminal justice system is criminal to the extent that it is not a system of justice*. And the requirements of justice are the familiar ones. A criminal justice system serves justice to the extent that it protects equally the interests and rights of all and to the extent that it punishes equally all who endanger these interests or violate these rights. To the extent that it veers from these goals, the criminal justice system is guilty of the same sacrificing of the interests of some for the benefit of others that it exists to combat. It is therefore, morally speaking, guilty of crime.

The experience of the twentieth century has taught us that we should not take for granted that every legal system is a system of justice. Hitler's Germany and Stalin's Russia, as well as contemporary South Africa, are testimony to the fact that what is put forth as law may well be outrageously unjust. We have come to recognize that truth implicit in the statements of Baldwin, Rawls, and St. Augustine: that what is put forth under color of law may be morally no better than crime or tyranny. Therefore, we can no longer uncritically take for granted that our own legal order is just merely because it is legal. We must subject it to the moral test of whether it serves and protects the interests of all to make sure that it is not injustice disguised as justice, criminality wearing the mask of law.

It is, of course, not my aim to place the American legal system on par with that of Hitler's Germany or Stalin's Russia. As I have acknowledged more than once already, there is much in the system that is legitimate and many are caught by the system who should be. Rather my claim is this:

- *To the extent that* the American criminal justice system *fails* to implement policies that could significantly reduce crime and the suffering it produces (as argued in Chapter 1).
- *To the extent that* the American criminal justice system *fails* to protect Americans against the gravest dangers to their lives and property (as argued in Chapter 2).
- *To the extent that* the American criminal justice system apprehends and punishes individuals, not because they are dangerous, but because they are *dangerous and poor* (as argued in Chapter 3).
- *Then, to that same extent,* the American criminal justice system fails to give all Americans either protection or justice, aids and abets those who pose the greatest dangers to Americans, and uses force in ways that do not serve equally the interests of all who are subject to that force, and *thus its use of force is morally no better than crime itself.*

Let us now join the dialogue between the Critic and the Defender of the Present Legal Order. By now neither of them needs any introduction.

**Defender:**  See here, Critic, I've been listening quite patiently to you and I'm willing to agree to much of what you've said so far, but now I think you are letting your emotions get the best of you. I admit that our criminal justice system is far from perfect. I admit it may even be in need of a major overhaul. But to call it *criminal* is either just rhetoric or—if you mean it literally—confusion. A crime is a violation of the law. A legal system may be unjust, but to call it "criminal" is to ask for confusion, since a legal system can't violate the law—it is the law!

**Critic:**  How foolish do you think I am? Surely you don't take me to be saying that the legal system is criminal in the sense of breaking the law.

**Defender:**   Then say what you mean. If I'm confused, it's because your argument leads to confusion.

**Critic:**   Maybe so. Then let me try again. My point is that if what I've said about the system is true. . . . You grant that what I have said in the first three chapters is true, don't you?

**Defender:**   Yes, yes. I already said I did. Get on with it.

**Critic:**   Well, then, if that's true, it means that the criminal justice system is *morally indistinguishable from criminality*. That is, its use of force is morally wrong for the same reasons that make the criminal's use of force morally wrong. And what is morally indistinguishable from criminality is essentially criminal in every respect other than the technical one of being a violation of the criminal law.

**Defender:**   A mere technicality, is it? I suppose I'm splitting hairs to point out that a crime is a violation of the law.

**Critic:**   You're not splitting hairs, but you are missing an important point. Crime is morally wrong because it uses force in ways that hurt people without moral justification and because it uses the threat of force to make people do what they might not otherwise freely choose to do. Now the criminal justice system also uses force in ways that hurt people. . . .

**Defender:**   You mean the use of force to arrest suspects or to confine convicts?

**Critic:**   Yes. But also it uses the threat of force to limit the freedom of just about everyone else.

**Defender:**   Here I take it that you are referring to the fact that the system threatens punishment as a way of forcing people to comply with the criminal law.

**Critic:**   Right again. And this means not only complying with law but putting up with the social and economic arrangements that the law protects. Just as the criminal law limits the ways in which homosexuals express their sexual desires, so it limits the ways in which the poor can alleviate the miseries of poverty or the powerless can gain more control over their lives. For instance, we've seen that the system allows harmful business practices such as pollution and inadequate occupational safety to exist. Now if the victims of these practices took action in their own self-defense against these practices, they would come up against the very property rights that the criminal justice system protects. But this means that by enforcing laws against theft and assault and the rest, *the criminal justice system is using force in ways that protect those harmful practices.* All of which means that the criminal justice system uses force in ways that directly produce considerable suffering, for example, the suffering of those who languish in prison cells or of those who must seriously limit their freedom in fear of imprisonment—and it uses force in ways that indirectly produce considerable suffering—for example, the suffering of these who receive the short end of the stick in the economic system, which the criminal justice system protects with force and the threat of force.

**Defender:**   What you're saying is obvious. Get to the point.

**Critic:**   Yes, of course. The point is obvious also. Both crime and criminal justice use force and the threat of force in ways that directly and indirectly lead to human suffering. If there is a difference, it must be a *moral* difference.

**Defender:**   Not a *legal* difference? Isn't it enough that the criminal's use of force is against the law and the criminal justice system's use of force is legal?

**Critic:**   That's not enough, because the question we are asking is: What makes the use of force under color of law morally superior to the use of force outside the law? And enough evil has been perpetrated in the name of law to prove that a legal difference is not enough. Do you think that Hitler's actions were not criminal just because they were allowed by Nazi law?

**Defender:**   No.

**Critic:**   Then we must ask what the moral justification is that makes the criminal justice system's use of force superior to the criminal's.

**Defender:**   But the answer is obvious. What the enforcers of law do is morally right because it is necessary to protect society. You do believe there is a right of self-defense, don't you.

**Critic:**   Yes, of course.

**Defender:**   You do believe that the right to self-defense is a moral justification for the use of force, even deadly force, in one's defense, don't you?

**Critic:**   Yes, again.

**Defender:**   Well, that's enough. A criminal justice system is a society's form of self-defense. Since those who attack it use force, sometimes deadly force, the society has the right to use that much force in its defense—and it does this through the criminal justice system domestically, just as it does it through the military internationally.

**Critic:**   Don't leave justice out of the picture.

**Defender:**   Certainly, self-defense is neither the sole goal nor the sole justification for the system. The system is also justified in using force to do justice—to punish the evildoer and so forth. And this is compatible with the goal of self-defense, since if other potential criminals see that actual criminals receive their just deserts, then hopefully they'll think twice about crime.

**Critic:**   But sometimes the goal of justice seems to go against that of society's self-defense, doesn't it? For example, when a person is acquitted by reason of insanity we are hardly made safer. Nor are we made safer when an otherwise guilty person is released because the evidence that would convict him was the result of an illegal search.

**Defender:**   I think these are some of the best aspects of our system. They prove that we are willing to accept some risks rather than punish those who are not responsible for their acts or convict someone unfairly—even if he or she did commit a crime. I admit there is some tension between the goals of justice and self-defense, just as there is tension in an individual between the goals of freedom and security or between the ideals of integrity and satisfaction. But you and I don't have to resolve this tension. All I want to maintain is that what the criminal justice system does is morally superior to what criminals do, because it is done in the name of the ideals of justice and self-defense.

**Critic:**   Thanks.

**Defender:**   Thanks for what?

**Critic:**   For proving my point.

**Defender:**   Proving your . . . ?

**Critic:**   I agree that the moral credentials of criminal justice are to be found in the moral goals of justice and protection of society. Indeed, I would argue that a criminal justice system really aimed at achieving justice and protecting society would be using force to promote *everyone's* interests—and that would make it clearly superior to crime or conquest, which use force to promote particular interests. But my whole argument so far is that one can barely comprehend criminal justice policy if one looks at it as aimed at justice and the protection of society. After all, it refuses to make changes that might reduce what are now labeled serious crimes—those on the FBI Index. It refuses to treat as crimes acts that are at least as dangerous to society as these. And others that it does label crimes, such as the illegal machinations of corporate executives, it treats delicately, if at all. So much for protecting society. As for justice, the system punishes some people for acts that are not at all harmful, such as homosexuality or prostitution, and allows others who gravely endanger society to go unpunished. And then, of course, that criminals are mainly punished, not because they are criminals, but because they are *poor* criminals is itself a howling injustice. The system does not use force in everyone's interest: It imposes force disproportionately upon the poor while leaving society vulnerable to the harmful acts of the well-off. So if the moral difference between the criminal's use of force and the criminal justice system's use of force lies in justice and self-defense—as you have so eloquently argued—my point is made.

**Defender:**   While you were just holding forth, it occurred to me what's been bothering me about your argument. Your mistake finally dawned on me.

**Critic:**   Well please tell me what it is. If I am mistaken, I'll gladly revise my views. I get no pleasure from thinking that the criminal *justice* system is a *criminal* justice system.

**Defender:**   You admitted earlier that you accept that most if not all the people who end up in prison are probably guilty of the crime or crimes that got them there.

**Critic:**   It's hard to know these things with certainty, but I start from the assumption that those people did commit the acts that they were sentenced for and that they are *legally* guilty of those crimes. So?

**Defender:**   So? So that's the difference. The victims of criminal force are innocent, but the victims of the force used by the criminal justice system are not at all innocent. So even if the system functions unjustly or ineffectively, as long as it uses force against people who have done wrong, it is morally different from crime. Suppose you're right that the system punishes some killers and not others. We may think it is unjust that the poor guy who shoots his neighbor goes to prison, while the executive responsible for deadly occupational hazards goes free. But that poor murderer can't complain about his imprisonment. He can't cry injustice, since, after all, he did kill someone and deserves punishment regardless of what happens to anyone else. I think this is why the criminal justice system may be accused of exercising force unjustly *but not criminally*—this is why I think your argument rests on a confusion. The system may be unjust and it may be ineffective in protecting us, but the objects of its force are not innocent victims. This is the moral difference between the criminal justice system and criminality.

**Critic:**    I admit that some of the "victims" of the criminal justice system get what they deserve. But I think it is a mistake to think that the only victims of criminal justice policy are the people who get locked up. The criminal justice system is responsible for the victims of the acts that it doesn't use force to prevent. Since it is the institution that uses force to prohibit harmful acts, what it doesn't prohibit, *it permits*. Indeed, since it is the *only* institution allowed to use force, what it permits, *it protects*. The criminal justice system has many victims, and most of them are clearly innocent.

**Defender:**    Who are the innocent victims of criminal justice?

**Critic:**    Well, first, and least controversially, there are the *millions* of citizens who fork over more than $25 billion a year (on pain of imprisonment) in taxes to pay for the false illusion of protection and justice. *This is robbery in the name of criminal justice.* Then there are the hundreds of thousands of citizens who are killed or injured by safety hazards and all the other acts that the system either winks at or closes it eyes to entirely. These people are victimized not merely because the system neglects to use force to protect them but even more so because the system uses force to protect the wealth and power of those who harm them. Add to them the thousands who are victimized by the crimes of heroin addicts and of ex-convicts who can't get a decent job and by the crimes that are facilitated and intensified by the availability of guns. *An entire FBI Index of property "crimes" and violent "crimes" result from criminal justice policy.* And the victims are innocent.

**Defender:**    And the criminals in prison—are they also innocent victims?

**Critic:**   All those who are either punished or live in fear of punishment for *victimless crimes*, that is, for acts that harm no one against his or her will, those who are punished for using marijuana or heroin, for prostitution or homosexual behavior and the like are innocent victims of the criminal justice system.

**Defender:**   What of those who are punished for crimes with victims?

**Critic:**   I would say that for many of them, their moral guilt is questionable, and to that extent they are victimized by the system.

**Defender:**   Before, you said that you believe that most of those now serving jail or prison sentences are guilty of the crimes for which they were convicted.

**Critic:**   I believe that most are *legally* guilty. I think the extent of their *moral* guilt is questionable. So many of those in our prisons are poor that it seems reasonable to doubt that they would have committed the crimes that got them in prison if they had not suffered the disabilities and disadvantages of poverty. If this is so, who is morally responsible for the crimes of the poor? The poor who didn't choose their poverty or the affluent who choose to do little or nothing to rectify it? We've seen that there is reason to believe that a society like ours provokes crime in all economic classes, although most intensely in the lowest classes. If this is so, can you be so sure that the criminals punished by the system are not in a more profound sense really innocent victims of the system, at least in the sense that they are not morally responsible for the social conditions that have made crime such a reasonable and tempting option for them?[2]

**Defender:**   I think you are being a bit maudlin about criminals. Many of them are pretty nasty, not at all as innocent as you picture them.

**Critic:**   I knew you would say that. But I have no illusions about those criminals. I don't doubt that many are dangerous and nasty and that we need to be protected against them. This, however, shouldn't be used as an excuse for ignoring the social sources of their nastiness. And if those sources are to be found in the poverty our society allows, in the selfishness our society encourages, and in the institutions our criminal justice system protects, then there is a profound sense in which our criminals are our victims. The punishment we heap upon them is just a continuation of the pains we have allowed them to suffer since birth, for no fault of their own.

**Defender:**   Poverty is no excuse for hurting other people—certainly not other poor people.

**Critic:**   Look, I agree with you. My point is not that all criminals are innocent but rather that the moral guilt of many criminals is less because of the social conditions that are part of their existence. Some may well be morally guilty of their crimes but for others, there is reason to believe that their guilt is at least shared by the society that allows crime-producing conditions to flourish. My point is that if you add to these all the victims of the system's action and inaction who are clearly innocent, the inescapable conclusion is that of all the hundreds of thousands of victims of our criminal justice policies and practices, many are clearly innocent, many are of questionable guilt, and a small fraction of the total are really getting what they deserve. *This is enough, I think, to make the case that the criminal justice system is morally no better than crime.* That the system is more *criminal* than *just.*

At this point the dialogue breaks off.

## REHABILITATING CRIMINAL JUSTICE IN AMERICA

The criminal justice system in America is morally indistinguishable from criminality because it exercises force and imposes suffering on human beings *while violating its own morally justifying ideals: protection and justice.* Once this is understood, the requirements for rehabilitating the system follow rather directly. The system must institute policies that make good on its claim to protect society and to do justice. In the remainder of this chapter I will briefly suggest the outlines of a "treatment strategy" for *helping the system go straight.* It cannot be reiterated too frequently that these proposals are not offered as a means of *improving* the system. Nor am I under any illusion that these proposals will be easily adopted or implemented. They are presented as the necessary requirements for establishing the criminal justice system's moral difference from, and moral superiority to, *crime*; and, even if not implemented or not likely to be implemented, they stand as a measure against which this moral difference and superiority can be judged. The proposals fall under the headings of the two ideals that justify the existence of a criminal justice system. These ideals are that the criminal justice system protect us against the real dangers that threaten us and that it not be an accomplice to injustice in the larger society. In order to realize these ideals, it is necessary that the harms and injustices done by the criminal justice system itself be eliminated.

### Protecting Society

First, it must be acknowledged that every day that we refuse to implement those strategies that have a good chance of cutting down on the crimes people fear—the crimes on the FBI Index—the system is an accomplice to these crimes and bears responsibility for the suffering they impose.

**We must enact and vigorously enforce stringent gun controls.**

Americans are armed to the teeth. The handgun is the most easily concealed, the most effective, and the deadliest weapon there is. Its ubiquity is a constant temptation to would-be crooks who lack the courage or skill to commit crimes without weapons or to chance hand-to-hand combat. Its ubiquity also means that any dispute may be transformed into a fatal conflict beyond the desires or expectations of the disputants. Trying to fight crime while allowing America to remain an armed camp is like trying to teach a child to walk and tripping him each time he stands up. In its most charitable light, it is hypocrisy. Less charitably, it is complicity in murder.[3]

**We must legalize the production and sale of heroin and treat addiction as a medical problem.**

Although most observers seem to agree that the British system of dispensing heroin to registered addicts is superior to our own punitive system, a number of experts have gone even further. Norval Morris and Gordon Hawkins urge that narcotics use be decriminalized and that drugs be sold in pharmacies by prescription. Arnold Trebach urges that doctors be permitted to prescribe heroin for the treatment of addicts and as a powerful painkiller. Philip Baridon recommends that pure heroin—clearly labeled as to contents, recommended dosage, and addictive potential—be sold at a low fixed price in pharmacies, without prescription, to anyone aged 18 or over.[4] I will not enter into debate about the various ways in which heroin can be decriminalized. I make the simple point that when heroin addicts cannot obtain heroin legally, they will obtain it illegally. And since those who sell it illegally have a captive market, they will charge high prices to make their own risks worthwhile. To pay the high prices, addicts must, will, and do resort to crime. Thus, every day in which we keep the acquisition of heroin a crime, we are using the law to protect the high profits of heroin black marketeers, *and* we are creating a situation in which large numbers of individuals are virtually physically compelled to commit theft. Since there is little evidence that heroin is dangerous beyond the fact of addiction itself, there can be little doubt that our present "cure" for narcotics use is more criminal (and criminogenic) than the narcotics themselves.

**We must develop correctional programs that promote rather than undermine personal responsibility, and we must offer ex-offenders real preparation and a real opportunity to make it as law-abiding citizens.**

The scandal of our prisons has been amply documented. Like our attitudes toward guns and heroin, they seem more calculated to produce than reduce crime. The enforced childhood of imprisonment may be the painful penalty offenders deserve, but if it undermines their capacity to go straight after release, we are cutting off our noses to spite our faces. People cannot learn to control themselves responsibly if they have spent years having every aspect of their lives—the hour they wake, the number of minutes they wash, the time and content of eating and working and exercising, the hour at which lights go out—regulated by someone else. Add to this the fact that convicts usually emerge with no marketable skill and little chance of getting a decent job with the stigma of a prison sentence hanging over them. The result is a system in which we never let criminals finish paying their debt to society and give them every incentive to return to crime.

If we are going to continue to punish people by depriving them of their liberty, we must do it in a way that prepares them for the life they will lead when their liberty is returned. Anything less than this is a violation of the Constitution's Eighth Amendment guarantee against "cruel and unusual punishment." Depriving a person of his or her liberty may be an acceptable punishment, but *depriving people of their dignity and a chance to live a law-abiding life when their punishment is supposed to be over is cruel and* (should be, but sadly is not) *unusual!*

Pursuant to the guarantee of the Eighth Amendment, every imprisoned person should have a right to training at a marketable skill as well as a right to compete equally with non-ex-convicts for a job once the punishment is over. This would require that it be illegal to discriminate against ex-convicts in hiring and illegal to require job applicants to state whether or not they had ever been arrested, convicted, and/or imprisoned for a crime. This requirement might have to be modified for particularly sensitive occupations, although on the whole I think it would be fairer and more effective in rehabilitating ex-cons to enact it across the board and to have the government finance or subsidize a fund to ensure against losses incurred as a result of ex-convicts. My hunch is that this would be much less costly than paying to support ex-cons in prison and their families on welfare when they return to crime for lack of a job. Beyond this, prison industries should pay inmates at prevailing wages; this money then could be used for restitution to victims and to purchase privileges and possibly increased privacy or freedom for the prisoners—all of which might tend to give them greater practice at controlling their own lives so that they will be prepared to do so after release.

But none of this will give us a criminal justice system worthy of the name, until we:

### Let the crime fit the harm and the punishment fit the crime.

For the criminal justice system to justify its methods, it must make good on its claim to protect society. This requires that the criminal law be redrawn so that the list of crimes reflects the real dangers that individuals pose to society. Avoidable acts where the actor had reason to know that his or her acts were likely to lead to someone's death should be counted as forms of murder. Avoidable acts where the actor had reason to believe that his or her acts were likely to lead to someone's injury should be counted as forms of assault and battery. Acts that illegitimately deprive people of their money or possessions should be treated as forms of theft regardless of the color of the thief's collar. Crime in the suites should be prosecuted and punished as vigorously as crime in the streets.

The law must be drawn carefully so that individuals are not punished for harm they could not foresee or could not have avoided, or that others have freely consented to risk. The pursuit of security must not swamp the legitimate claims of liberty. However, within these guidelines, we must rid the law of the distinction between *one-on-one* harm and *indirect* harm  *and treat all harm-producing acts in proportion to the actual harm they produce.*[5] *We must enact and implement punishments that fit the harmfulness of the crime without respect to the class of the criminal.* There is, for instance, general agreement that incarceration functions as an effective deterrent to corporate crime where the threat of imprisonment is believed.[6] And to be believed, it must be used.

The other side of this coin is the decriminalization of "victimless crimes," acts such as prostitution, homosexuality, gambling, vagrancy, drunkenness, and of course, drug use. As long as these acts only involve persons who have freely chosen to participate, they represent no threat to the liberty of any citizen. But this also means that there is generally no complainant for these crimes, no person who feels harmed by these acts and who is ready and able to press charges and testify against the wrongdoers. Therefore, police have to use a variety of shady tactics involving deception and bordering on entrapment, which undermine the public's respect for the police and the police officers' respect for themselves. In any event, the use of such low-visibility tactics increases the likelihood of corruption and arbitrariness in the enforcement of the law. Beyond this, since these acts produce no palpable, undeniable, tangible harm to others, laws against them appear to be no more than the imposition of some people's ideas of virtue on others, rather than laws that really protect society. To make good on its claim to protect society, the criminal justice system must not only treat the dangerous acts of business executives as crimes, but it must also decriminalize those acts that are not clearly dangerous.[7]

Over 100 years ago, John Stuart Mill formulated a guiding principle, still relevant in our time, for the design of legislation in a society committed to personal liberty:

> *That principle is, that the sole end for which mankind are warranted, individually or collectively, in interfering with the liberty of action of any of their number, is self-protection. That the only purpose for which power can be rightfully exercised over any member of a civilized community, against his will, is to prevent harm to others.*[8]

Although the principle has had to be modified in recognition of the ways in which individuals can cause future harm to themselves because of present injudicious choices, particularly in a complex modern society where people must deal with machines and chemicals beyond their understanding,[9] the heart of the principle is still widely accepted. This is the notion that a necessary condition of any justifiable legal prohibition is that it prohibit an act that does harm to someone, possibly the actor himself. Since priority should be given to freedom of action, this harm should be *demonstrable* (i.e., detectable by some widely agreed upon means, say, those used by medical science), and it should be of sufficient gravity to outweigh the value of the freedom that is to be legally prohibited.[10]

This principle should not only guide legislators and those engaged in revising and codifying criminal law, but it should be raised to the level of an implicit constitutional principle. The U.S. Supreme Court recognizes certain traditional principles of legality as constitutional requirements even though they are not explicitly written into the Constitution. For instance, some laws have been held unconstitutional because of their vagueness[11] and others because they penalized a condition (like being a drunk or an addict) rather than an action (like drinking or using drugs).[12] It strikes me that the entire tenor of the Bill of Rights is to enshrine and protect individual liberty from the encroachment of the state. But legal philosophers from Mill to the present have argued that to give priority to individual liberty, one must accept some version of the demonstrable harm requirement as a condition for acceptable laws. An act that threatens no harm is no threat to liberty, so a law that prohibits such an act is a limitation on liberty with no counterbalancing gain in liberty to justify it. In this light, it seems reasonable that the Supreme Court should strike down as *unconstitutional* any criminal law that prohibits an act that does not cause demonstrable harm, with the burden of proof lying with the state to demonstrate the palpable harm the law seeks to prevent.

Whether as a legislative or a judicial criterion, however, this principle would undoubtedly rid our law of the excrescences of our puritan moralism. It would bring our law more in line with a realistic view of what is harmful, and it would eliminate the forced induction into criminality of the individuals, mainly those of the lower class, who get arrested for "victimless crimes."

*These changes, taken together, would be likely to reduce dangerous crime and to bring us a legal order that actually punished (and, it is hoped, deterred) all and only those acts that really threaten our lives and possessions and punished them in proportion to the harm they really produce. Such a legal system could be truly said to protect society.*

### Promoting Justice

The changes recommended above would, in part, make the criminal justice system more just, since people would be punished in proportion to the seriousness of their antisocial acts, and the number of innocent persons victimized by those acts would be reduced. Much would still remain to be done to eliminate the disabilities of the poor caught up in the system.

A criminal justice system should arrest, charge, convict, and sentence individuals with an eye only to their crime, not to their class. Any evidence of more frequent arrest or harsher penalties for poor persons than for others accused of the same crime is a grave injustice that tends to undermine the legitimacy of the criminal justice system. Since many of the decisions that work to the disadvantage of the poor—police decisions to arrest, prosecutors' decisions to charge, and judges' decisions on how long to sentence—are exercises of discretion often out of public view, they are particularly resistant to control. Since, unlike prosecutors' or judges' decisions, the police officer's decision *not* to arrest is *not* a matter of record, it is the least visible exercise of discretion and the most difficult to control. Our best hope to make arrests by police more just lies in increased citizen awareness and education of police officers so that they at least become aware of the operation and impact of their own biases and are held more directly accountable to, and by, the public they serve and sometimes arrest.

As for prosecutorial and judicial discretion, two approaches seem potentially fruitful. First, our lawmakers ought to spell out the acceptable criteria that prosecutors may use in deciding whether or what to charge and the criteria that judges may use in deciding whether or what to sentence. The practice of multiple charging (e.g., charging an accused burglar with "the lesser included crimes" of breaking and entering, possession of burglar's tools, etc.) should be eliminated. It is used by prosecutors to "coax" accused persons into pleading guilty to one charge by threatening to press *all* charges. Of all the dubious features of our system of bargain justice, this seems most clearly without justification, since it works to coerce a plea of guilty that should be uncoerced if it is to be legally valid.[13] The law should also set out more specific sentencing ranges, since the present system leads to individuals receiving wildly different sentences for the same crimes—a practice that can only be viewed as arbitrary and capricious, that violates the principle that citizens should know in advance what is in store for them if they break a law, and that produces in convicts disrespect for the law rather than remorse for their violations. In addition to, and in conjunction with, these legislative changes, we ought to require prosecutors and judges to put in writing the reasons they have charged or sentenced in one way rather than another. And they should be required to give an account of their policies and practices to some truly representative body to show that they are fair and reasonable. However we achieve it, it is clear that to make the criminal justice system function justly:

**We must narrow the range in which police officers, prosecutors and judges exercise discretion, and we must develop procedures to hold them accountable to the public for the fairness and reasonableness of their decisions.**

But all these changes still leave standing what is probably the largest source of injustice to the poor in the system: *unequal access to quality legal counsel.* We know that, by and large, privately retained counsel will have more incentive to put in the time and effort to get their clients off the hook, and we know that this results in a situation in which *for equal crimes* those who can retain their own counsel are more likely to be acquitted than those who cannot. Note that as many as 70 percent of the inmates of our state correctional facilities could not afford to retain their own private counsel. The present system of allocating assigned counsel or public defenders to the poor, and privately retained lawyers to the affluent, is little more than a parody of the constitutional guarantee of a *right to counsel* and a clear violation of the constitutional guarantee of *equal protection under the law.*

There are simply no two ways about this. In our system, even though lawyers are assigned to the poor, justice has a price. Those who pay get the choicest cut—those who cannot, get the scraps. About a hundred years ago, before there were public police forces in every town and city, people got "police protection" by hiring private police officers or bodyguards if they could afford it. Protection was available for a price, and so those who had more money were better protected under the law. Today, we regard it as every citizen's right to have police protection, and we would find it outrageous if police protection were allocated to citizens on a fee-for-service basis. *But this is precisely where we stand with respect to the legal protection provided by lawyers!*

Legal protection is not only provided by the police. Attorneys are necessary to protect individuals from losing their freedom at the hands of the law before they have exhausted the legal defenses that are theirs by right. Both police officers and lawyers are essential to the individual's legal protection. It is sheer hypocrisy to acknowledge everyone's right to equal protection under the law by the police and then to allocate protection under the law by lawyers on the basis of what individuals can pay. As long as this continues, we cannot claim that there is anything like equal treatment before the law in the criminal justice system.

**We must transform the equal right to counsel into the right to equal counsel, as far as it is possible.**

Although this would appear to be a clear requirement of the "equal protection" and "due process" clauses of the Constitution, the Supreme Court has avoided it, perhaps because it poses massive practical problems. And surely it does. However, the creation of public police forces to protect everyone probably seemed to pose many practical problems in its time as well.

Certainly it would not be appropriate to use the police as a model for resolving the problem of equal counsel. To establish a governmental legal service for all—in effect to nationalize the legal profession—might make equal legal representation available to all. It would, however, undermine the adversary system by undercutting the independence of the defense attorney from the state. Some form of national legal insurance to enable all individuals to hire private attorneys of their own choice, however, could bring us closer to equal legal protection without compromising the adversarial relationship.

Such insurance would undoubtedly have to be subsidized by the government, as are the police, the courts, and prisons; but it would not necessarily have to be totally paid for out of taxes. People might rightly be expected to pay their legal bills up to some fraction of their income, if they have one. The rest would be paid for by a government subsidy that would pay the difference between what the accused could afford and the going rate for high-quality legal counsel. Nothing in the system need interfere with the freedom of the accused to select the lawyer of his or her choice (an option closer to the hearts of free enterprisers than the present public defender system allows) or interfere with the independence of the lawyer.

Undoubtedly, such a system would be costly. But our commitment to equal justice remains a sham until we are willing to pay this price. Americans have paid dearly to protect the value of liberty enshrined in the Constitution. Is it too much to ask that they pay to realize the ideal of justice enshrined there too?

One final recommendation remains to be made. I have already argued that the criminal justice system, by its very nature, embodies the prevailing economic relations in its laws. This means that it is an error to think of the criminal justice system as an entity that can be reformed in isolation from the larger social order. A criminal justice system is a means to protect that social order, and it can be no more just than the order it protects. A law against theft may be enforced with an even and just hand. But if it protects an unjust distribution of wealth and property, the result is *injustice evenly enforced.* A criminal justice system cannot hold individuals guilty of the injustice of breaking the law if the law itself supports and defends an unjust social order.

**We must establish a more just distribution of wealth and income and make equal opportunity a reality for all Americans.**

Without economic and social justice, the police officer in the ghetto is indeed an occupying soldier with no more legitimacy than his or her gun provides. Without economic and social justice the criminal justice system is the defender of injustice and is thus morally indistinguishable from the criminal. *A criminal justice system can be no more just than the society its laws protect.* Along with the other recommendations I have made in this chapter, the achievement of economic and social justice is a necessary condition for establishing the criminal justice system's moral superiority to *crime.*

\*     \*     \*

Every step toward domestic disarmament, toward decriminalization of heroin and "victimless crimes," toward criminalization of the dangerous acts of the affluent and vigorous prosecution of "white-collar" crimes; every step toward creating a correctional system that promotes human dignity, toward giving ex-offenders a real opportunity to go straight, toward making the exercise of power by police officers, prosecutors, and judges more reasonable and more just, toward giving all individuals accused of crime equal access to high-quality legal expertise in their defense; every step toward establishing economic and social justice is a step that moves us from a system of *criminal* justice to a system of criminal *justice.* The refusal to take those steps is a move in the opposite direction.

# Notes

## ABBREVIATIONS USED IN THE NOTES

Challenge
The Challenge of Crime in a Free Society: A Report by the President's Commission on Law Enforcement and Administration of Justice (Washington, D.C.: U.S. Government Printing Office, February 1967).

Sourcebook-1974
U.S. Law Enforcement Assistance Administration, National Criminal Justice Information and Statistics Service, Sourcebook of Criminal Justice Statistics-1974, edited by Michael J. Hindelang, Christopher S. Dunn, Alison J, Aumick, and L. Paul Sutton (Washington, D.C.: U.S. Government Printing Office, 1975).

Sourcebook-1981
U.S. Department of Justice, Bureau of Justice Statistics, Sourcebook of Criminal Justice Statistics-1981, edited by Timothy J. Flanagan, David J. van Alstyne, and Michael R. Gottfredson (Washington, D.C.: U.S. Government Printing Office, 1982).

Stat Abst-1981
U.S. Bureau of the Census, Statistical Abstract of the United States: 1981, 102nd edition (Washington, D.C.: U.S. Government Printing Office, 1981).

UCR-1980
Federal Bureau of Investigation, Uniform Crime Reports for the United States: 1980 (Washington, D.C.: U.S. Government Printing Office, 1981). References to other editions of this annual report will be indicated by UCR followed by the year for which the statistics are reported. In general, these reports are published in the fall of the year following the year they cover.

## NOTES TO THE INTRODUCTION

1. See especially, Louis Althusser, "Ideology and Ideological State Apparatuses," in Lenin and Philosophy and Other Essays (London: New Left

Books, 1971), pp. 121–173; and Nicos Poulantzas, *Fascism and Dictatorship* (London: New Left Books, 1974), pp. 299–309. These writers refer back to the pioneering insights of Antonio Gramsci into the ideological functions of state institutions. See Quintin Hoare and Geoffrey Nowell-Smith, eds., *Selections from the Prison Notebooks of Antonio Gramsci* (London: Lawrence and Wishart, 1971); and Carl Boggs, *Gramsci's Marxism* (London: Pluto Press, 1976). For other contemporary analyses of the relationship between the state and ideology, see Ralph Miliband, *The State in Capitalist Society* (New York: Basic Books, 1969), pp. 179–264; and Jürgen Habermas, *Legitimation Crisis* (Boston: Beacon Press, 1975). The Frankfurt School of social theory, of which Jürgen Habermas and Herbert Marcuse are probably the best known representatives, is distinguished by the application of Marxian as well as Freudian theory to the analysis of ideology. See Martin Jay, *The Dialectical Imagination: The Frankfurt School of Critical Theory, 1930–1950* (Boston: Little, Brown, 1973).

## NOTES TO CHAPTER 1

1. Speech of the President to the International Association of Chiefs of Police, New Orleans, Louisiana, September 28, 1981, reported in *Weekly Compilation of Presidential Documents* (July-September, 1981), pp. 1039ff.
2. *UCR-1980*, p. 38; *Sourcebook-1981*, p. 4; *Bureau of Justice Statistics Technical Report: Criminal Victimization in the U.S.* (July 1982), p. 2.
3. *Challenge*, p. 35.
4. *UCR-1980*, p. 38.
5. *Sourcebook-1981*, pp. 4 and 19.
6. Louise I. Shelley, *Crime and Modernization* (Carbondale, Ill.: Southern Illinois University Press, 1981), p. 76.
7. *Stat Abst-1981*, p. 178, Table no. 303.
8. *UCR-1980*, pp. 42–47.
9. Quoted in *Violence: An Element of American Life*, eds. K. Taylor and F. Soady (Boston: Holbrook Press, 1972), p. 49.
10. *UCR-1980*, pp. 42–47, 87–136.
11. *UCR-1980*, pp. 60–86.
12. Table 1 further illustrates the *lack* of correlation between city size and crime rates. Five large metropolitan areas (population over 3 million) and five middle-sized metropolitan areas (population between 1,000,000 and 2,000,000) are listed in order of population, from largest to smallest. Each of these is then numerically ranked (in comparison to the others) by overall crime rate, violent crime rate, and property crime rate. Keep in mind that the ranking is by crime *rate* (i.e., incidence of crime per 100,000 inhabitants), not total volume of crime. If crime were a simple function of population size, we would expect the same

crime *rate* for all urban areas, and thus no ranking would be possible. If soaring crime is a product of modernization, social complexity, industrialization, urbanization, and the like we should expect the largest metropolitan areas—the areas where these symptoms of the modern era have furthest progressed—to have the highest crime rates with the rates decreasing as the population decreases. Table 1, compiled from the FBI's *Uniform Crime Reports* for 1980 (Table 5: "Index of Crime, Standard Metropolitan Statistical Areas, 1980," *UCR-1980*, pp. 60–86), shows that no such relationship is to be found.

Nor does any relationship emerge when cities are compared by population density (number of persons per unit of space) instead of just by population. The President's Crime Commission, reporting on robbery rates in 1965 in the 14 largest cities, shows wildly different rates and virtually no correlation between the size of a city's population or its density and the incidence of robbery. Chicago and Philadelphia are roughly equal in population density, 15,836 and 15,743 persons per square mile respectively, while both are over five times as dense as Houston with 2860 persons per square mile. Nevertheless, Chicago has roughly three times as many robberies per 100,000 people as Philadelphia and Houston have. The 1965 rate for the City of Brotherly Love was 140 per 100,000 persons and for the old Murder Capital it was 135, while Chicago came in at an astounding 421, the highest in the nation. Meanwhile the rate for New York (population density 24,697 persons per square mile) was lower than all three, and Washington, D.C., with roughly one tenth the population (763,956) and half the density (12,442 persons per square mile) of New York City, had over three times as many robberies per capita. Fun City's rate in 1965 was a mere 114 per 100,000, while our nation's capital came in second only to Chicago at 359. The commission goes on to report that "Los Angeles is 1st for rape and 4th for aggravated assault but 20th for murder, with a murder rate less than half that of St. Louis. Chicago has the highest rate for robbery but a relatively low rate for burglary. New York is 5th in larcenies $50 and over, but 54th for larcenies under $50. The risk of auto theft is about 50 percent greater in Boston than anywhere else in the country, but in Boston the likelihood of other kinds of theft is about average for cities over 250,000." *Challenge*, p. 29.
13. *Challenge*, p. 56.
14. *Time*, June 30, 1975, p. 11.
15. The number of Americans aged 15 to 24 arrested in 1974 was 2,959,289. In 1960, it was 1,112,827. In the decade of the 1950s the crime rate increased 60 percent, from a rate of 1162.4 per 100,000 in 1950 to a rate of 1875.8 in 1960. Yet during that same period the number of Americans aged 15 to 24 increased only 9 percent and, as a percentage of the total population, actually decreased from 14.7 percent in 1950 to 13.6 percent in 1960. It was in the decade of the 1960s that the real impact of the postwar baby boom was felt. By 1970 the number of

Americans between the ages of 15 and 24 increased dramatically. In 1970, there were 42 percent more persons aged 15 to 24 than there were in 1960, an increase of over 10 million people. But in the decade between 1960 and 1970, the crime rate increased by 111 percent! And in the same period the number of 15- to 24-year-olds arrested increased by 250 percent, from 1,112,827 to 2,838,230. Figures are from the United States Census Bureau, *Current Population Report*: Series P25, Number 519 and 614; and from the *UCR* for relevant years.

16. *Stat Abst-1981*, p. 26, Table no. 29; *Bureau of Justice Statistics Technical Report: Criminal Victimization in the U.S.*, July 1982, p. 2.

17. Preliminary figures released by the FBI show that crime rates decreased by 4 percent in 1982 compared to 1981. *The Washington Post*, April 20, 1983, p. A3. Serious crime decreased in the Washington, D.C. area in the first three months of 1983 compared to the same period in 1982. "Dr. Charles Wellford, director of the University of Maryland Institute of Criminal Justice and Criminology . . . attributed the decline to demographic changes. 'We are shifting from a very young to an older population,' he said. 'In particular, 15- to 29-year-olds have very high rates of crime. As fewer people are in those categories, there will be lower rates of crime.'" *The Washington Post*, April 29, 1983, p. C1.

18. *The Washington Post*, August 4, 1975, p. A2.

19. Ibid., August 17, 1975, pp. A1, A4.

20. Jeffrie G. Murphy, "Marxism and Retribution," *Philosophy & Public Affairs*, 2, No. 3 (Spring 1973), p. 237.

21. *Stat Abst-1981*, p. 438, Table no. 730.

22. *The Washington Post*, September 6, 1982, p. 2; the report was issued by the Full Employment Action Council (a coalition of religious, civil rights, and union groups) and the National Policy Exchange (an economic research and educational organization).

23. *The Washington Post*, September 14, 1982, pp. 1 and 4.

24. *Economic Report of the President*, February 1982 (Washington, D.C.: U.S. Government Printing Office, 1982), p. 271, Table B-33.

25. *The New York Times*, September 5, 1981, p. 7:1.

26. Robert Johnson and Hans Toch, "Introduction," in Johnson and Toch, eds., *The Pains of Imprisonment* (Beverly Hills, Calif.: Sage Publications, 1982), pp. 19–20.

27. Franklin Zimring, *Firearms and Violence in American Life* (Washington, D.C.: U.S. Government Printing Office, 1968), pp. 6–7. (Emphasis added.)

28. Address by the Honorable Edward H. Levi, attorney general of the United States, before the Law Enforcement Executives Conference, April 6, 1975.

29. *Challenge*, pp. 239 and 4 (emphasis added).

30. *UCR-1980*, pp. 7, 11, 13.

31. Presidential News Conference, June 16, 1981; see also "Reagan Denounces Gun Control Laws," *The Washington Post*, May 7, 1983, p. A8.

**32.** Zimring, *Firearms and Violence in American Life*, Chapter 11.

**33.** Arnold S. Trebach, *The Heroin Solution* (New Haven: Yale University Press, 1982), pp. 3–4 and 246.

**34.** United States Department of Health, Education and Welfare, Public Health Service, National Institute on Alcohol Abuse and Alcoholism, Special Action Office for Drug Abuse Prevention, *Social Cost of Drug Abuse* (Washington, D.C., 1974), pp. 20–21.

**35.** "The largest study ever made of drug abuse in this country shows that two widely available legal drugs—alcohol and the tranquilizer Valium—are responsible for the greatest amount of drug-related illness, the government reported yesterday." Stuart Auerbach, "2 Drugs Widely Abused," *The Washington Post*, July 9, 1976, p. A1. See also Jeffrey H. Reiman, "Prostitution, Addiction, and the Ideology of Liberalism," in *Contemporary Crises* 3 (1979), pp. 53–68.

**36.** *Social Cost of Drug Abuse*, p. 25.

**37.** Robert L. DuPont, "Operation Trip-Wire: A New Proposal Focused on Criminal Heroin Addicts," speech, Federal Bar Association Convention, Washington, D.C., October 1, 1977, p. 11; quoted in Trebach, p. 247.

**38.** Trebach, p. 248.

**39.** *Sourcebook-1981*, pp. 464 and 485.

**40.** Trebach, p. 246.

**41.** Troy Duster, *The Legislation of Morality: Law, Drugs, and Moral Judgment* (New York: The Free Press, 1970), pp. 3, 7, inter alia.

**42.** Cf. Philip C. Baridon, *Addiction, Crime, and Social Policy* (Lexington, Mass.: Lexington Books, 1976), pp. 4–5.

**43.** *Time*, June 30, 1975, p. 17. (Emphasis added.)

**44.** Kai T. Erikson, *Wayward Puritans* (New York: John Wiley, copyright © 1966), p. 4. Reprinted by permission of John Wiley & Sons, Inc.

**45.** Ibid. p. 11.

**46.** Ibid. pp. 13–15. (Emphasis added.)

## NOTES TO CHAPTER 2

**1.** *The Washington Star*, March 14, 1976, pp. A1, A9.

**2.** Ibid., p. A9.

**3.** Gerald R. Ford, President of the United States, "To Insure Domestic Tranquility: Mandatory Sentence for Convicted Felons," speech delivered at the Yale Law School Sesquicentennial Convocation, New Haven, Connecticut, April 25, 1975, in *Vital Speeches of the Day*, XXXXI, No. 15 (May 15, 1975), p. 451.

**4.** *The Washington Post*, September 16, 1975, p. C1.

**5.** Ibid.; see also The Maryland-National Capital Parks and Planning Commission, *Crime Analysis 1975: Prince George's County* (August 1975), p. 86.

6. *UCR-1974*, p. 186.
7. *UCR-1980*, p. 200.
8. *The Washington Post*, September 16, 1975, p. C1; and *Crime Analysis 1975: Prince George's County* (August 1975), p. 86.
9. *UCR-1974*, p. 191.
10. *Stat Abst-1981*, p. 26, Table no. 29; and *UCR-1980*, p. 204.
11. Speech to International Association of Chiefs of Police, September 28, 1981.
12. Out of 1,289,524 persons arrested for FBI Index Crimes in 1974, 1,043,155, or over 80 percent were males. See *UCR-1974*, p. 190. In Prince George's County, males "represented three of every four serious crime defendants." *Crime Analysis 1975: Prince George's County*, p. 3.
13. Out of 1,474,427 persons arrested for FBI Index Crimes in 1974, 1,267,955 were "city arrests" and 420,682 were "suburban" (suburban arrest figures include arrests in suburban cities, and thus overlap with statistics for city arrests). *UCR-1974*, p. 180.
14. Jeffrie G. Murphy, "Marxism and Retribution," *Philosophy & Public Affairs*, 2, No. 3 (Spring 1973), p. 237. Cf. Samuel Jordan, "Prison Reform: In Whose Interest?" *Criminal Law Bulletin*, 7, No. 9 (November 1971), pp. 779–787: "Of the 1.2 million criminal offenders handled each day by some part of the United States correctional system, 80 percent are members of the lowest 12 percent income group—or black and poor," quoted in Jessica Mitford, *Kind and Usual Punishment* (New York: Alfred A. Knopf, 1973), p. 289.
15. *Challenge*, p. 44; see also p. 160.
16. John N. Mitchell, "Crime Prevention: Citizen Participation," speech delivered before the Conference on Crime and the Urban Crisis of the National Emergency Committee of the National Council on Crime and Delinquency, San Francisco, California, February 3, 1969, in *Vital Speeches of the Day*, XXXV, No. 10 (March 1, 1969), p. 290.
17. See note 11, above.
18. See note 15, above.
19. This transformation has been noted by Erving Goffman in his sensitive description of total institutions, *Asylums* (Garden City, New York: Doubleday, 1961):

    > The interpretative scheme of the total institution automatically begins to operate as soon as the inmate enters, the staff having the notion that entrance is *prima facie* evidence that one must be the kind of person the institution was set up to handle. A man in a political prison must be traitorous; a man in a prison must be a law-breaker; a man in a mental hospital must be sick. If not traitorous, criminal, or sick, why else would he be here? (p. 84)

    So too, a person who calls forth the society's most drastic weapons of defense must pose the gravest danger to its well-being. Why else the reaction? The point is put well and tersely by D. Chapman: "There is a circular pattern in thinking: we are hostile to wicked people, wicked people are punished, punished people are wicked, we are hostile to punished people because they are wicked." "The Stereotype of the Criminal and the Social Consequences," *International Journal of Criminology and Penology,* 1 (1973), p. 16.

20. Richard Quinney, *The Social Reality of Crime* (Boston: Little, Brown, 1970). In his later work, for example, *Critique of Legal Order: Crime Control in Capitalist Society* (Boston: Little, Brown, 1973), and *Class, State & Crime* (New York: McKay, 1977), Quinney moves clearly into a Marxist problematic and his conclusions dovetail with many in this book. In my own view, however, Quinney has not yet accomplished a satisfactory synthesis between the "social reality" theory and his later Marxism. Elsewhere, I have examined Quinney's theory from the standpoint of moral philosophy. See Jeffrey H. Reiman, "Doing Justice to Criminology: Reflections on the Implications for Criminology of Recent Developments in the Philosophy of Justice," in *Issues in Criminal Justice: Planning and Evaluation,* eds., Marc Riedel and Duncan Chappell (New York: Praeger, 1976), pp. 134–142.

21. Quinney, *Social Reality of Crime,* p. 15.

22. *The Washington Post,* January 11, 1983, p. C10.

23. Sir James Fitzjames Stephen, from his *History of the Criminal Law of England,* II (1883), excerpted in *Crime, Law and Society,* eds., Abraham S. Goldstein and Joseph Goldstein (New York: The Free Press, 1971), p. 21.

24. Troy Duster, *The Legislation of Morality: Law, Drugs and Moral Judgment* (New York: The Free Press, 1970), pp. 3–76.

25. Norval Morris and Gordon Hawkins, *The Honest Politician's Guide to Crime Control* (Chicago: The University of Chicago Press, 1970), p. 2.

26. *Challenge,* p.7.

27. *UCR-1980,* pp. 7, 20, and 38.

28. *UCR-1980,* p. 179.

29. See David Wise, *The Politics of Lying: Government Deception, Secrecy and Power* (New York: Vintage Books, 1973), pp. 61–67.

30. *The President's Report on Occupational Safety and Health* (Washington, D.C.: U.S. Government Printing Office, 1972).

31. See, for instance, Joseph A. Page and Mary-Win O'Brien, *Bitter Wages: Ralph Nader's Study Group Report on Disease and Injury on the Job* (New York: Grossman, 1973); Rachel Scott, *Muscle and Blood* (New York: E. P. Dutton, 1974); and Jeanne M. Stellman and Susan M. Daum, *Work Is Dangerous to Your Health* (New York: Vintage Books, 1973). See also Fran Lynn "The Dust in Willie's Lungs," *The Nation,* 222, No. 7 (February 21, 1976), pp. 209–212; and Joel Swartz, "Silent Killers at Work," *Crime and Social Justice,* 3 (Summer 1975), pp. 15–20.

32. *President's Report on Occupational Safety and Health,* p. 111.

33. *Report of the President to the Congress on Occupational Safety and*

*Health, 1980* (August 4, 1981), p. 86; reporting on deaths and illnesses for 1979.

**34.** Ibid., p. 91. Robert Johnson, who has conducted extensive interviews with present and former textile workers suffering from brown lung, indicates that another reason for the underreporting of occupational diseases is that workers are often hesitant to admit symptoms for fear of being seen as "defective" or "worn out" and therefore losing their jobs (personal communication).

**35.** U.S. Department of Labor, Assistant Secretary for Policy, Evaluation and Research, *An Interim Report to Congress on Occupational Diseases*, 1980, p. 1. For further discussion of the shortcomings of official statistics on occupational disease and death, see Daniel Berman, *Death on the Job* (New York: Monthly Review Press, 1978), pp. 38ff.

**36.** Richard Doll and Richard Peto, "The Causes of Cancer: Quantitative Estimates of Avoidable Risks of Cancer in the United States Today," *Journal of the National Cancer Institute* 66, No. 6 (June 1981), p. 1245.

**37.** Letter from Schweiker to B. J. Pigg, Executive Director of the Asbestos Information Association, dated April 29, 1982.

**38.** Thomas C. Brown, *Occupational Respiratory Disease—A Statistical Overview for the American Lung Association Occupational Health Task Force*, April 1980, p. 1.

**39.** "An unknown, but quite possibly substantial, proportion of the 75% of heart disease risk which is presently unaccounted for could be related to work and its attendant hazards, particularly stress" (Nicholas Ashford, *Crisis in the Workplace: Occupational Disease and Injury* [Cambridge, Mass.: MIT Press, 1976], p. 93). Note that heart disease is responsible for 750,000 deaths a year, almost twice the toll from cancer.

**40.** P. Derr, R. Goble, R. E. Kasperson, and R. W. Kates, "Worker/Public Protection: The Double Standard," *Environment* 23, no. 7 (September 1981), p. 9.

**41.** U.S. Department of Justice, *Bureau of Justice Statistics Technical Report: Criminal Victimization in the U.S.* (July 1982), p. 3.

**42.** Susan Q. Stranahan, "Why 115,000 Workers Will Die This Year," *Boston Sunday Globe*, March 21, 1976, p. A4.

**43.** National Safety Council, *Accident Facts*, 1981 edition, pp. 23–24.

**44.** Page and O'Brien, *Bitter Wages*, p. 16.

**45.** Testimony of Peter Henle, Deputy Assistant Secretary for Policy Evaluation and Research, given before the Labor Standards Subcommittee of the House Committee on Education and Labor, 96th Congress, First Session, May 26, 1979. Chronic brown lung is a severely disabling occupational respiratory disease. For a description of its impact on its victims, see Robert Johnson, "Labored Breathing: Living with Brown Lung," paper presented at the Annual Meeting of the American Society of Criminology, Fall 1982, Toronto, Canada. See also, Page and O'Brien, *Bitter Wages*, p. 18.

**46.** Page and O'Brien, p. 23; and Scott, *Muscle and Blood*, p. 196

47. Scott, pp. 45–46; cf. Page and O'Brien, p. 25.
48. Page and O'Brien, p. 37.
49. Ibid., p. 45.
50. The quotations in this paragraph are from Stranahan, p. A4. See also *Report of the President to the Congress on Occupational Safety and Health, 1980*, p. 42.
51. U.S. Department of Labor, Assistant Secretary for Policy, Evaluation and Research, *An Interim Report To Congress on Occupational Diseases*, submitted to Congress June 1980, pp. 112–114.
52. Page and O'Brien, *Bitter Wages*, p. 71.
53. Ibid., p. 74. (Emphasis added).
54. Scott, *Muscle and Blood*, pp. 35–36.
55. Ibid., pp. 109, 111
56. Ibid., p. 112.
57. Page and O'Brien, *Bitter Wages*, p. 73.
58. Ibid., p. 73.
59. *Report of the President to the Congress on Occupational Safety and Health, 1980*, p. 43.
60. Joann Lublin, "Workplace Perils: Occupational Diseases Receive More Scrutiny Since the Manville Case," *Wall Street Journal*, December 20, 1982, p. 1.
61. George Miller (Democratic representative from California), "OSHA Sure is Backsliding," *The Washington Post*, January 30, 1902, p. A21
62. Douglas Feaver, "Accidents Up, Citations Down in Coal Fields," *The Washington Post*, February 3, 1982, p. A21.
63. "OSHA Shift Means Cutback in its Inspections," *The Washington Post*, February 3, 1982, p. A21.
64. "OSHA Plans Sharp Reduction in Medical Records," *The Washington Post*, July 19, 1982, p. A 11.
65. Christine Russell, "Nader Group Calls OSHA Too Lax," *The Washington Post*, November 9, 1982, p. A19; see also, Saundra Saperstein, "Critics Say Worker Safety is Undermined," *The Washington Post*, February 23, 1982, p. A20.
66. Anthony Robbins, "Can Reagan Be Indicted for Betraying Public Health?," *American Journal of Public Health* 73, No. 1 (January 1983), p. 13.
67. *Challenge*, p. 52. (Emphasis added.) See also p. 3 for then prevailing homicide rates.
68. *The Washington Post*, July 16, 1975, p. A3.
69. George A. Silver, M.D., "The Medical Insurance Disease," *The Nation*, 222, No. 12 (March 27, 1976), p. 369.
70. Ibid., p. 371.
71. *Newsweek*, March 29, 1976, p. 67. Lest anyone think this is a new problem, compare this passage written in a popular magazine about 30 years ago:
    In an editorial on medical abuses, the *Journal of the Medical Association of Georgia* referred to "surgeons who paradoxically are often

cast in the role of the supreme hero by the patient and family and at the same time may be doing the greatest amount of harm to the individual."

Unnecessary operations on women, stemming from the combination of a trusting patient and a split fee, have been so deplored by honest doctors that the phrase "rape of the pelvis" has been used to describe them. The American College of Surgeons, impassioned foe of fee-splitting, has denounced unnecessary hysterectomies, uterine suspensions, Caesarian sections. [Howard Whitman, "Why Some Doctors Should Be in Jail," *Colliers*, October 30, 1953, p. 24.]

72. *Stat Abst-1981*, Table no. 180.
73. *UCR-1980*, p. 12.
74. Silver, p. 369. Silver's estimates are extremely conservative. Some studies suggest that between 30,000 and 160,000 individuals die as a result of drugs prescribed by their doctors. See Boyce Rensberger, "Thousands a Year Killed by Faulty Prescriptions," *The New York Times*, January 28, 1976, pp. 1, 17. If we assume, with Silver, that at least 20 percent are unnecessary, then this puts the annual death toll from unnecessary prescriptions at between 6000 and 32,000 persons. For an in-depth look at the recklessness with which prescription drugs are put on the market and the laxness with which the Food and Drug Administration exercises its mandate to protect the public, see the series of eight articles by Morton Mintz, "The Medicine Business," in *The Washington Post*, June 27, 28, 29, 30, July 1, 2, 3, 4, 1976.
75. *Economic Report of the President*, February 1982, Table B-53: "Consumer Price Indexes, Selected Expenditure Classes," pp. 292–293.
76. Lewis Regenstein, *America the Poisoned* (Washington, D.C.: Acropolis Books, 1982), pp. 246–247.
77. National Institutes of Health, *1980 NCI Fact Book*, pp. 12 and 24.
78. Morton Mintz, "Cancer Scientist Quits in Policy Split," *The Washington Post*, April 30, 1976, p. A2.
79. "The New War on Cancer, Part I," *The Washington Star*, May 23, 1976, p. A10.
80. Morton Mintz, "3 Lawyers Leave EPA in Protest," *The Washington Post*, February 6, 1976, p. A1. The three lawyers are Jeffrey H. Howard, Frank J. Sizemore III, and William E. Reukauf. All were assigned to regulation of pesticides and toxic substances.
81. "The Environmental Protection Agency and the Regulation of Pesticides," Staff Report to the Senate Subcommittee of Administrative Practice and Procedure, Washington, D.C., December 1976; cited in Regenstein, *America the Poisoned*, pp. 119–120.
82. Ibid.
83. Quoted in Beatrice Hunter, *The Mirage of Safety* (New York: Charles Scribner's Sons, 1975), p. 147.

84. Quoted in Stuart Auerbach, "N.J.'s Chemical Belt Takes Its Toll: $4 Billion Industry Tied to Nation's Highest Cancer Death Rate," *The Washington Post*, February 8, 1976, p. A1.
85. Bill Richards, "Arsenic: A Dark Cloud Over 'Big Sky Country,' " *The Washington Post*, February 3, 1976, pp. A1, A5.
86. Quotations in this paragraph are from "N.J.'s Chemical Belt Takes Its Toll," *The Washington Post*, February 8, 1976, p. A1.
87. Lester B. Lave and Eugene P. Seskin, "Air Pollution and Human Health," *Science*, 169, No. 3947 (August 21, 1970), pp. 723–733, especially p. 730. The source for the 1974 mortality rates for lung cancer, respiratory disease (excluding cancer), and cardiovascular disease is the Department of Health, Education and Welfare.
88. Lave and Seskin, p. 728.
89. Robert Mendelsohn and Guy Orcutt, "An Empirical Analysis of Air Pollution Dose-Responsive Curves," *Journal of Environmental Economics and Management* (June 1979), pp. 85–106; cited in Regenstein, *America the Poisoned*, p. 194.
90. Regenstein, *America the Poisoned*, p. 195.
91. *Toxic Chemicals and Public Protection*, A Report to the President by the Toxic Substances Strategy Committee, Council on Environmental Quality, Washington, D.C. (May 1980), p. 6; quoted by Regenstein, *America the Poisoned*, p. 184. See also p. 170 in Regenstein.
92. Regenstein, pp. 136–137.
93. Regenstein, pp. 215–216 and 239. For an account of Reagan's successful attempt to fill the leadership positions of the EPA with former anti-regulation lawyers and lobbyists for industry, see ibid., pp. 377–379. See also Jacqueline Warren and Ross Sandler, "EPA's Failure to Regulate Toxic Chemicals," *Environment* 23, No. 10 (December 1981), pp. 2–4.
94. Anthony Robbins, "Can Reagan Be Indicted . . . ?," p.13.
95. C. Everett Koop and Joanne Luoto, " 'The Health Consequences of Smoking: Cancer,' Overview of a Report of the Surgeon General," *Public Health Reports* 97, No. 4 (July-August 1982), pp. 318–324.
96. Samuel Epstein, *The Politics of Cancer* (San Francisco: Sierra Club Books, 1978), p. 165.
97. Anthony Robbins, "Can Reagan be Indicted . . ?," p. 12.
98. Koop and Luoto, see note 95, above.
99. Saul R. Kelson, James L. Pullella, and Anders Otterland, "The Growing Epidemic: A Survey of Smoking Habits and Attitudes Toward Smoking Among Students in Grades 7 Through 12 in Toledo and Lucas County (Ohio) Public Schools, 1964–1971," *The American Journal of Public Health*, 65, No. 9 (September, 1975), pp. 923–938; cited in James Fallows "Cigarettes: A Menace We Love to Ignore; Bankrupt Policies, Public and Private," *The Washington Star*, February 29, 1976, p. E4.
100. Fallows, p. E4.
101. Ibid., p. E4

102. *Business Week* (December 20, 1982), p. 55.
103. Hunter, *The Mirage of Safety*, p. 4.
104. Quoted in Hunter, p. 2.
105. Hunter, pp. 40–41, 64–65, 85, 148–151, *inter alia*.
106. Ibid., p. 119.
107. Ibid., pp. 123–124.
108. Ibid., pp. 127–140.
109. Ibid., pp. 102–103.
110. Ibid., pp. 162–176.
111. Regenstein, p. 246.
112. Ibid., p. 251.
113. Ibid., p. 128. The National Institute of Allergy and Infectious Diseases reports that 17 out of every 100 persons suffers from a major allergy.
114. Hunter, p. 162.
115. Regenstein, p. 253.
116. At the very least, "we" includes all those who earn considerably above the median income for the nation (around $21,000 for a family in 1980) and who resist, or vote for candidates who resist, moves to redistribute income significantly.
117. William Ryan, *Blaming the Victim* (New York: Random House, 1971), p. 162.
118. Monroe Lerner, "Social Differences in Physical Health," in *Poverty and Health: A Sociological Analysis*, eds., John Kosa et al. (Cambridge: Harvard University Press, 1969); cited in Edward S. Greenberg, *Serving the Few: Corporate Capitalism and the Bias of Government Policy* (New York: John Wiley & Sons, 1974), p. 156.
119. Greenberg, *Serving the Few*, p. 156.
120. Aaron Antonovsky, "Class and the Chance for Life," in *Inequality and Justice*, ed., Lee Rainwater (Chicago: Aldine Publishing Co., 1974),p. 177.
121. S. Leonard Syme and Lisa F. Berkman, "Social Class, Susceptibility and Sickness," *American Journal of Epidemiology*, 104, No. 1 (July, 1976), pp. 1, 4.
122. K. Mahaffey, J. Annest, J. Roberts, R. Murphy, "National Estimates of Blood Lead Levels: United States, 1976–1980," *The New England Journal of Medicine* 307, No. 10 (September 2, 1982), pp. 573–579. The editorial is on p. 615.
123. Mary Grace Kovar, "Health Status of U.S. Children and Use of Medical Care," *Public Health Reports* 97, No. 1 (January-February 1982) pp. 3–15, esp. p. 8.
124. *Stat Abst-1981*, p. 118, Table #189.
125. E. Stockwell, J. Wicks, D. Adamchak, "Research Needed on Socioeconomic Differentials in U.S. Mortality," *Public Health Reports* 93, No. 6 (November-December 1978), pp. 666–672, esp. p. 668.
126. J. Berg, R. Ross, H. Latourette, "Economic Status and Survival of Cancer Patients," *Cancer* 39, No. 2 (February 1977), pp. 467–477, esp.

p. 468. See also the similar findings in L. Lipworth, T. Abelin, R. Connelly, "Socioeconomic Factors in the Prognosis of Cancer Patients," *Journal of Chronic Diseases* 23 (1970), pp. 105–116.

127. Study by Howard University sociologist John Reid, published by the Population Reference Bureau on December 13, 1982; reported in Spencer Rich, "Study Finds Black Economic Growth Not Enough," *The Washington Post*, December 14, 1982, p. A3; also *Stat Abst-1981*, p. 432, Table #720.

128. *Stat Abst-1981*, p. 73, Table #111.

129. Rich, "Study Finds . . . " (see note 127, above).

130. Anthony Robbins, "Can Reagan Be Indicted . . . ?," pp. 12-13.

131. National Institutes of Health, *Cancer Patient Survival Experience* (June 1980), pp. 4–5.

132. Ross, et al., op. cit., note 126, above, p. 474.

133. Rich, "Study Finds . . ." (see note 127, above).

134. Richard Allen Williams, M.D., reports that "there is no reason why the life span of the White should differ from that of the Black," in his *Textbook of Black-Related Diseases* (New York: McGraw-Hill, 1975), p. 2.

135. See note 133, above.

136. This is indeed a minimum, since the level of health for whites in America comes nowhere near our technological potential. "We rank only 15th in the world in infant mortality, and only 16th in average life expectancy. Twenty countries have less heart disease, and 12 have fewer cases of ulcers, diabetes, cirrhosis of the liver, and hypertension. Deaths among women in childbirth exceed that of 106 other countries." Greenberg, *Serving the Few*, pp. 154–155. What this means is that the case that I have been making that poverty kills blacks an average of six years before their time is a conservative one arrived at by comparing black life expectancy with white. However, if we compared American life expectancy with that of, say, Sweden, it could be argued that Americans of all races die before they would if we provided them the health care that we are capable of providing.

## NOTES TO CHAPTER 3

1. *Challenge*, p. 44.

2. Ronald Goldfarb, "Prisons: The National Poorhouse," *The New Republic*, November 1, 1969, pp. 15–17.

3. Philip A. Hart, "Swindling and Knavery, Inc.," *Playboy*, August 1972, p. 158.

4. Compare the statement of Professor Edwin H. Sutherland, one of the major luminaries of twentieth-century criminology: "First, the administrative processes are more favorable to persons in economic comfort than to those in poverty, so that if two persons on different economic levels are equally guilty of the same offense, the one on the lower level is more likely to be arrested, convicted, and committed to an institu-

tion. Second, the laws are written, administered and implemented primarily with reference to the types of crimes committed by people of lower economic levels." E. H. Sutherland, *Principles of Criminology* (Philadelphia: Lippincott, 1939), p. 179.

5. For example, in 1972 when blacks made up 11.3 percent of the national population, they accounted for 42.5 percent of the population of the nation's jails. U.S. Bureau of the Census, Current Population Reports, Special Studies, Series P-23, No. 54, *The Social and Economic Status of the Black Population in the United States, 1974* (Washington, D.C.: U.S. Government Printing Office, 1975), pp. 11 and 173.

6. Edwin H. Sutherland and Donald R. Cressey, *Criminology*, 9th edition (Philadelphia: Lippincott, 1974), p. 133. The following studies are cited (p. 133, note 4) in support of this point: Edwin M. Lemert and Judy Rosberg, "The Administration of Justice to Minority Groups in Los Angeles County," *University of California Publications in Culture and Society*, 2, No. 1 (1948), pp. 1–28; Thorsten Sellin, "Race Prejudice in the Administration of Justice," *American Journal of Sociology*, 41 (September, 1935), pp. 212–217; Sidney Alexrad, "Negro and White Male Institutionalized Delinquents," *American Journal of Sociology* 57 (May, 1952) pp. 569–574; Marvin E. Wolfgang, Arlene Kelly, and Hans C. Nolde, "Comparison of the Executed and the Commuted Among Admissions to Death Row," *Journal of Criminal Law, Criminology, and Police Science*, 53 (September, 1962), pp. 301–311; Nathan Goldman, *The Differential Selection of Juvenile Offenders for Court Appearance* (New York: National Council on Crime and Delinquency, 1963); Irving Piliavin and Scott Briar, "Police Encounters with Juveniles," *American Journal of Sociology*, 70 (September, 1964) pp. 206–214; Robert M. Terry, "The Screening of Juvenile Offenders," *Journal of Criminal Law, Criminology, and Police Science*, 58 (June 1967), pp. 173–181. See also Ramsey Clark, *Crime in America* (New York: Simon and Schuster, 1970), p. 51: "Negroes are arrested more frequently and on less evidence than whites and are more often victims of mass or sweep arrests"; and Donald Taft, *Criminology*, 3rd edition (New York: Macmillan, 1956), p. 134: "Negroes are more likely to be suspected of crime than are whites. They are also more likely to be arrested. If the perpetrator of a crime is known to be a Negro the police may arrest all Negroes who were near the scene—a procedure they would rarely dare to follow with whites. After arrest Negroes are less likely to secure bail, and so are more liable to be counted in jail statistics. They are more liable than whites to be indicted and less likely to have their cases nol prossed or otherwise dismissed. If tried, Negroes are more likely to be convicted. If convicted they are less likely to be given probation. For this reason they are more likely to be included in the count of prisoners. Negroes are also more liable than whites to be kept in prison for the full terms of their commitments and correspondingly less likely to be paroled."

7. For an overview of this double distortion, see Thomas J. Dolan, "The Case for Double Jeopardy: Black and Poor," *International Journal of Criminology and Penology*, 1 (1973), pp. 129–150.
8. *Black Population in the U.S.*, (see note 5, above), pp. 41, 172. Furthermore, 12 percent of black jail inmates and 11 percent of the whites had prearrest incomes of $2000 to $2999 per year, and 33 percent of the blacks and 32 percent of the whites had prearrest incomes of $3000 to $7499 per year. Stuart Nagel writes that "generally, the poor suffer even more discrimination than Negroes in criminal justice; and Negroes may suffer more from lack of money than from race." "The Tipped Scales of American Justice," in *Law and Order: The Scales of Justice*, ed., Abraham S. Blumberg (Aldine-Transaction, 1970), p. 40.
9. *Sourcebook-1981*, p. 463.
10. Isidore Silver, "Introduction" to the Avon edition of *The Challenge of Crime in a Free Society* (New York: Avon Books, 1968), p. 31.
11. *Challenge*, p. 43. (Emphasis added.) The study referred to is James S. Wallerstein and C. J. Wyle, "Our Law-abiding Lawbreakers," *Probation*, XXV (April, 1947), pp. 107–112.
12. This is the conclusion of Austin L. Porterfield, *Youth in Trouble* (Fort Worth: Leo Potishman Foundation, 1946); Fred J. Murphy, M. Shirley, and H. L. Witmer, "The Incidence of Hidden Delinquency," *American Journal of Orthopsychiatry*, XVI (October, 1946), pp. 686–96; James F. Short, Jr., "A Report on the Incidence of Criminal Behavior, Arrests, and Convictions in Selected Groups," *Proceedings of the Pacific Sociological Society*, 1954, pp. 110–18 [published as Vol. XXII, No. 2, of *Research Studies of the State College of Washington* (Pullman, Washington, 1954)]; F. Ivan Nye, James F. Short, Jr. and Virgil J. Olson, "Socioeconomic Status and Delinquent Behavior," *American Journal of Sociology*, 63 (January, 1958), pp. 381–389; Maynard L. Erikson and Lamar T. Empey, "Class Position, Peers and Delinquency," *Sociology and Social Research*, 49 (April, 1965), pp. 268–282; William J. Chambliss and Richard H. Nagasawa, "On the Validity of Official Statistics—a Comparative Study of White, Black, and Japanese High-School Boys," *Journal of Research in Crime and Delinquency*, 6 (January, 1969), pp. 71–77; Eugene Doleschal, "Hidden Crime," *Crime and Delinquency Literature*, 2, No. 5 (October, 1970), pp. 546–572; Nanci Koser Wilson, *Risk Ratios in Juvenile Delinquency* (Ann Arbor, Michigan: University Microfilms, 1972); and Maynard L. Erikson, "Group Violations, Socioeconomic Status and Official Delinquency," *Social Forces*, 52, No. 1 (September, 1973), pp. 41–52.
13. This is the conclusion of Martin Gold, "Undetected Delinquent Behavior," *Journal of Research in Crime and Delinquency*, 3, No. 1 (1966), pp. 27–46; and of Sutherland and Cressey, *Criminology*, 9th edition (Philadelphia: Lippincott, 1974), pp. 137 and 220.
14. Cf. Larry Karacki and Jackson Toby, "The Uncommitted Adolescent: Candidate for Gang Socialization," *Sociological Inquiry*, 32 (1962), pp.

203–215; William R. Arnold, "Continuities in Research—Scaling Delinquent Behavior," *Social Problems*, 13, No. 1 (1965), pp. 59–66; Harwin L. Voss, "Socio-economic Status and Reported Delinquent Behavior," *Social Problems*, 13, No. 3 (1966), pp. 314–324; LaMar Empey and Maynard L. Erikson, "Hidden Delinquency and Social Status," *Social Forces*, 44, No. 4 (1966), pp. 546–554; Fred J. Shanley, "Middle-class Delinquency as a Social Problem," *Sociology and Social Research*, 51 (1967), pp. 185–198; Jay R. Williams and Martin Gold, "From Delinquent Behavior to Official Delinquency," *Social Problems*, 20, No. 2 (1972), pp. 209–229.

15. Empey and Erikson, "Hidden Delinquency and Social Status," pp. 549, 551. Nye, Short, and Olson also found destruction of property to be committed most frequently by upper-class boys and girls. "Socioeconomic Status and Delinquent Behavior," p. 385.

16. Op. cit., footnote 14, above.

17. Eugene Doleschal and Nora Klapmuts, "Toward a New Criminology," *Crime and Delinquency Literature*, 5 (December, 1973), p. 611.

18. Gold, "Undetected Delinquent Behavior," p. 37.

19. Ibid., p. 44. Doleschal, reviewing a later work of Martin Gold [*Delinquent Behavior in an American City* (Belmont, Calif.: Brooks-Cole, 1970)], reports that "while the official figures on delinquency in Flint [Michigan] set the ratio of lower-class to middle-class delinquents at 8 to 1, Gold found that among the 20 percent most delinquent, there were about three lower-class boys for every two middle-class boys." Doleschal, "Hidden Crime," p. 556.

20. Comparing socioeconomic status categories "scant evidence is found that would support the contention that group delinquency is more characteristic of the lower-status levels than other socioeconomic status levels. . . . In fact, *only arrests seem to be more characteristic of the low-status category* than the other categories." Erikson, "Group Violations, Socioeconomic Status and Official Delinquency," p. 15. (Emphasis added.)

21. Gold, "Undetected Delinquent Behavior," p. 28. (Emphasis added.)

22. Ibid., p. 38.

23. Terence P. Thornberry, "Race, Socioeconomic Status and Sentencing in the Juvenile Justice System," *The Journal of Criminal Law and Criminology*, 64, No. 1 (1973), pp. 90–98.

24. Goldfarb, "Prisons: The National Poorhouse," p. 17.

25. *UCR-1980*, p. 202.

26. Doleschal and Klapmuts, "Toward a New Criminology," p. 614, reporting the conclusions of Ross L. Purdy, *Factors in the Conviction of Law Violators: The Drinking Driver* (Ann Arbor, Michigan: University Microfilms, 1971).

27. Gerald Robin, "The Corporate and Judicial Disposition of Employee Thieves," *Wisconsin Law Review*, No. 3 (Summer, 1967), p. 693.

28. See for example D. Chapman, "The Stereotype of the Criminal and the Social Consequences," *International Journal of Criminology and Penology*, 1, (1973), p. 24.

29. This view is widely held, although the degree to which it functions as a self-fulfilling prophecy is less widely recognized. Versions of this view can be seen in *Challenge*, p. 79; Jerome Skolnick, *Justice Without Trial* (New York: John Wiley, 1966), pp. 45–48, 217–218; and Jessica Mitford, *Kind and Usual Punishment*, p. 53. Piliavin and Briar write in "Police Encounters with Juveniles":

> Compared to other youths, Negroes and boys whose appearance matched the delinquent stereotype were more frequently stopped and interrogated by patrolmen—often even in the absence of evidence that an offense had been committed—usually were given more severe dispositions for the same violations. Our data suggest, however, that these selective apprehension and disposition practices resulted not only from the intrusion of long-held prejudices of individual police officers but also from certain job-related experiences of law-enforcement personnel. First, the tendency of police to give more severe dispositions to Negroes and to youths whose appearance correspond to that which police associated with delinquents partly reflected the fact, observed in this study, that these youths also were much more likely than were other types of boys to exhibit the sort of recalcitrant demeanor which police construed as a sign of the confirmed delinquent. Further, officers assumed, partly on the basis of departmental statistics, that Negroes and juveniles who "look tough" (e.g. who wear chinos, leather jackets, boots, etc.) commit crimes more frequently than do other types of youths. [p. 212]

Cf. Albert Reiss, *The Police and the Public* (New Haven: Yale University Press, 1971). Reiss attributes the differences to the differences in the actions of complainants.

30. Richard J. Lundman, for example, found higher arrest rates to be associated with "offender powerlessness." "Routine Police Arrest Practices: A Commonweal Perspective," *Social Problems*, 22, No. 1 (October, 1974), pp. 127–141.

31. *Vital Speeches of the Day* (July 1, 1981), pp. 485–487.

32. Marshall Clinard and Peter Yeager, *Corporate Crime* (New York: Free Press, 1980), p. 8.

33. "Crime in the Suites: On the Rise," *Newsweek* (December 3, 1979), pp. 117–121, esp. p. 117.

34. "Corporate Crime: The Untold Story," *U.S. News and World Report* (September 6, 1982), pp. 25–29, esp. p. 25.

35. Chamber of Commerce of the United States, *A Handbook on White Collar Crime* (Washington, D.C., 1974), p. 6. Copyright © 1974 by the

Chamber of Commerce of the United States. Table reprinted by permission of the Chamber of Commerce of the United States.

**36.** *UCR-1980*, p. 179.

**37.** The President's Commission on Law Enforcement and Administration of Justice, *Task Force Report: Crime and Its Impact—an Assessment* (Washington, D.C.: U.S. Government Printing Office, 1967), pp. 103–104.

**38.** Gilbert Geis, "Upperworld Crime," in *Current Perspectives on Criminal Behavior*, ed., Abraham S. Blumberg (New York: Knopf, 1974), p. 126.

**39.** Sutherland and Cressey, *Criminology*, p. 41. (Emphasis added.)

**40.** Clinard and Yeager, *Corporate Crime*, p. 113.

**41.** Ibid., pp. 124–125.

**42.** *Task Force Report: Crime and Its Impact*, p. 107.

**43.** Hart, "Swindling and Knavery, Inc.," p. 158.

**44.** *UCR-1980*, p. 191.

**45.** See, for example, Theodore G. Chiricos, Phillip D. Jackson, and Gordon P. Waldo, "Inequality in the Imposition of a Criminal Label," *Social Problems*, 19, No. 4 (Spring, 1972), pp. 553–572.

**46.** Abraham S. Blumberg, *Criminal Justice* (Chicago: Quadrangle, 1967), p. 33. Even for the middle-class defendant, the state with its greater financial, investigatory, and legal personnel resources, holds the advantage over the accused—so the poor person is doubly disadvantaged. Cf. Abraham S. Goldstein, "The State and the Accused: Balance of Advantage in Criminal Procedure," in *Crime, Law and Society*, eds., Goldstein and Goldstein, pp. 173–206.

**47.** *Sourcebook-1981*, p. 462.

**48.** See, for example, C. E. Ares, A. Rankin, and J. H. Sturz, "The Manhattan Bail Project: An Interim Report on the Use of Pre-Trial Parole," *NYU Law Review*, 38 (1963), p. 67; C. Foote, "Compelling Appearances in Court-Administration of Bail in Philadelphia," *University of Pennsylvania Law Review*, 102 (1954), pp. 1031–79; and C. Foote, "A Study of the Administration of Bail in New York City," *University of Pennsylvania Law Review*, 106 (1958), p. 693. For statistics on persons held in jail awaiting trial, see *Black Population in the U.S.*, (see note 5, above) p. 171; and U.S.L.E.A.A., *Survey of Inmates of Local Jails 1972—Advance Report* (Washington, D.C.: U.S. Government Printing Office, 1974), pp. 5 and 8.

**49.** Blumberg, *Criminal Justice*, pp. 28–29; *Challenge*, p. 134; and Donald J. Newman, *Conviction: The Determination of Guilt or Innocence Without Trial* (Boston: Little, Brown, 1966), p. 3.

**50.** A good summary of these developments can be found in Joel Jay Finer, "Ineffective Assistance of Counsel," *Cornell Law Review*, 58, No. 6 (July, 1973), pp. 1077–1120.

**51.** See, for example, Dallin H. Oaks and Warren Lehman, "Lawyers for the Poor," in *Law and Order: The Scales of Justice*, ed., A. Blumberg, pp. 92–93; also Jerome H. Skolnick, "Social Control in the Adversary System," in *Criminal Justice: Law and Politics*, ed., Cole (Belmont, Calif.: Duxbury, 1972), p. 266. "The National Legal Aid and Defender Association has suggested that experienced attorneys handle no more than 150 felony cases per year, rather than . . . the case load of over 500 felony cases per attorney with which some public defender offices in major cities are burdened." Finer, "Ineffective Assistance of Counsel," p. 1120.

52. In several essays, Abraham S. Blumberg has described the role of the public defender as an officer of the court bureaucracy rather than as a defender of the accused. See his "Lawyers with Convictions," in *Law and Order: The Scales of Justice*, pp. 51–67; "The Practice of Law as Confidence Game: Organizational Cooptation of a Profession," in *Criminal Law in Action*, ed., William J. Chambliss (Santa Barbara, Calif.: Hamilton Publishing Co., 1975), pp. 262–275; and his book *Criminal Justice* (Chicago: Quadrange, 1967), esp. pp. 13–115.

53. Jonathan D. Casper, "Did You Have a Lawyer When You Went to Court? No, I Had a Public Defender," in *Criminal Justice: Law and Politics*, ed., Cole, pp. 239–240.

54. Blumberg, "Lawyers with Convictions," pp. 62–65; and his *Criminal Justice*, pp. 92–93.

55. Ibid.; percentages are rounded to nearest whole number.

56. Oaks and Lehman, "Lawyers for the Poor," p. 95.

57. Of those defendants who were *convicted* in U.S. District Courts in 1971, 46 percent had assigned lawyers (including public defenders); of those *acquitted*, 37.5 percent had assigned counsel; and of those *dismissed*, only 33.3 percent had assigned counsel. *Sourcebook-1974*, p. 388.

58. Robert Johnson, *Condemned to Die: Life Under Sentence of Death* (New York: Elsevier, 1981), p. 138; Stephen Gettinger, *Sentenced to Die: The People, the Crimes, and the Controversy* (New York: Macmillan, 1979), p. 261.

59. Blake Fleetwood and Arthur Lubow, "America's Most Coddled Criminals," *New Times* (September 19, 1975), pp. 26–29. *New Times Magazine*, copyright © 1975. Reprinted by permission of *New Times Magazine*.

60. Lesley Oelsner, "Wide Disparities Mark Sentences Here," *The New York Times*, September 27, 1972, p. 1. Stuart Nagel writes, "The reasons for the economic class sentencing disparities, holding crime and prior record constant, are due possibly to the quality of legal representation that the indigent receive and probably to the appearance that an indigent defendant presents before a middle-class judge or probation officer." "Disparities in Sentencing Procedure," *UCLA Law Review*, 14 (August, 1967), p. 1283.

61. Oelsner, p. 1.

62. Nagel, "The Tipped Scales of American Justice," p. 39.
63. Doleschal and Klapmuts, "Toward a New Criminology," p. 613; reporting the findings of Terence Patrick Thornberry, *Punishment and Crime: The Effect of Legal Dispositions on Subsequent Criminal Behavior* (Ann Arbor, Mich.: University Microfilms, 1972); see footnote 23, above.
64. Terence P. Thornberry, "Sentencing Disparities in the Juvenile Justice System," *Journal of Criminal Law and Criminology* 70, No. 2 (Summer 1979), pp. 164–171, esp. p. 170.
65. Steven H. Clarke and Gary G. Koch, "The Influence of Income and Other Factors on Whether Criminal Defendants Go to Prison," *Law and Society Review* (Fall 1976), pp. 57–92, esp. pp. 81, 83–84.
66. Alan J. Lizotte, "Testing the Conflict Model of Criminal Justice," *Social Problems* 25, No. 5 (1978), pp. 564–580, esp. p. 564.
67. *Sourcebook-1981*, pp. 463, 477, 490.
68. Henry Allen Bullock, "Significance of the Racial Factor in the Length of Prison Sentences," in *Crime and Justice in Society*, ed., R. Quinney (Boston: Little, Brown, 1969), p. 425; also, Marvin E. Wolfgang and Marc Riedel, "Race, Judicial Discretion and the Death Penalty," in *Criminal Law in Action*, ed., Chambliss, p. 375.
69. William J. Bowers and Glenn L. Pierce, "Racial Discrimination and Criminal Homicide Under Post-Furman Capital Statutes," in H. A. Bedau, ed., *The Death Penalty in America* (New York: Oxford University Press, 1982), pp. 206–224.
70. William J. Chambliss and Robert B. Seidman, "Sentencing and Sentences," in *Criminal Law in Action*, ed., Chambliss, p. 339; reporting the findings of Mary Owen Cameron, *The Booster and the Snitch: Department Store Shoplifting* (New York: Free Press, 1964).
71. "Blacks Receive Stiffer Sentences," *The Boston Globe*, April 4, 1979, pp. 1 and 50f.
72. Randall Thomson and Matthew Zingraff, "Detecting Sentencing Disparity: Some Problems and Evidence," *American Journal of Sociology* 86, No. 4 (1981), pp. 869–880, esp. p. 875.
73. J. Unnever, C. Frazier, J. Henretta, "Race Differences in Criminal Sentencing," *The Sociological Quarterly* 21 (Spring 1980), pp. 197–205, esp. p. 204.
74. Marvin E. Wolfgang, Arlene Kelly, and Hans C. Nolde, "Comparison of the Executed and the Commuted Among Admissions to Death Row," in *Crime and Justice in Society*, ed., Quinney, pp. 508, 513.
75. "Antitrust: Kauper's Last Stand," *Newsweek*, June 21, 1976, p. 70. On December 21, 1974, the "Antitrust Procedures and Penalty Act" was passed, striking out the language of the Sherman Antitrust Act, which made price-fixing a misdemeanor punishable by a maximum sentence of one year in prison. According to the new law, price-fixing is a felony punishable by up to three years in prison. Since prison sentences were a rarity under the old law and usually involved only 30 days in jail

when actually imposed, there is little reason to believe that the new law will strike fear in the hearts of corporate crooks.

76. Clinard and Yeager, *Corporate Crime*, pp. 291–292.
77. Ibid., p. 153.
78. Ibid., p. 287.
79. Ibid., p. 291.
80. Marvin E. Frankel, *Criminal Sentences: Law Without Order* (New York: Hill and Wang, 1972), p. 24, footnote.
81. *Justice in Sentencing: Papers and Proceedings of the Sentencing Institute for the First and Second U.S. Judicial Circuits*, eds., Leonard Orland and Harold R. Tyler, Jr. (Mineola, N.Y.: Foundation Press, 1974), pp. 159–160. (Emphasis added.)
82. Michael C. Jensen, "Watergate Donors Still Riding High," *The New York Times*, August 24, 1975, sec. 3, pp. 1, 7. Copyright © 1975 by The New York Times Company. Reprinted by permission.
83. Tom Wicker, *A Time to Die* (New York: Quadrangle, 1975), pp. 311, 314.
84. Ibid., p. 310.
85. *Sourcebook-1974*, p. 470.
86. U.S. Department of Justice, U.S. Law Enforcement Assistance Administration, National Criminal Justice Information and Statistics Service, *Survey of Inmates of Local Jails: Advance Report* (Washington, D.C.: U.S. Government Printing Office, 1974), pp. 3, 4, 16.
87. U.S. Department of Justice, U.S. Law Enforcement Assistance Administration, National Criminal Justice Information and Statistics Service, *Survey of Inmates of State Correctional Facilities, 1974*, No. SD-NPS-SR-2 (Washington, D.C.: U.S. Government Printing Office, March, 1976), pp. 1, 2, 4, 5, 6, 9, and 25.
88. U.S. Department of Justice, *Bureau of Justice Bulletin: Prisoners 1925–81* (December 1982), pp. 2–3; see also, Kevin Krajick, "Annual Prison Population Survey: The Boom Resumes," *Corrections Magazine* (April 1981), pp. 16–20.
89. *Sourcebook-1981*, p. 463.
90. U.S. Department of Justice, *Bureau of Justice Bulletin: Prisons and Prisoners* (January 1982), p. 2.

## NOTES TO CHAPTER 4

1. *Challenge*, p. 44.
2. U.S. Department of Justice, *Criminal Victimization in the United States, 1979* (A National Crime Survey Report), September 1981, p. 4.
3. Ibid., p. 5.
4. Ibid., p. 31, Table no. 14.
5. Ibid., p. 39, Table no. 25.

6. A report to the Federal Communications Commission estimates that by the time the average American child reaches age 14, he or she has seen 13,000 human beings killed by violence on television. Although a few of these are probably killed by science fiction monsters, the figure still suggests that the extent of the impact of the televised portrayal of crime and the struggle against it, on the imaginations of Americans, is nothing short of astounding. See Eve Merriam, "We're Teaching Our Children that Violence is Fun," in *Violence: An Element of American LIfe*, eds., K. Taylor and F. Soady, Jr. (Boston: Holbrook Press, 1972), p. 155. For a list of the 20 police programs (which does not include detective programs and other shows in which the fight against crime is the theme) aired on ABC, CBS, and NBC, the three major networks, see Center for Research on Criminal Justice, *The Iron Fist and the Velvet Glove: An Analysis of the U.S. Police*, pp. 194–195.

7. Richard A. Cloward and Lloyd E. Ohlin, *Delinquency and Opportunity: A Theory of Delinquent Gangs* (New York: The Free Press, 1960), esp. pp. 77–107.

8. Ibid., p. 81.

9. Ibid., p. 105.

10. Ibid., p. 107.

11. Ibid., p. 105.

12. Willem Bonger, *Criminality and Economic Conditions*, abridged and with an introduction by Austin T. Turk (Bloomington, Ind.: Indiana University Press, 1969), pp. 7–12, 40–47. Willem Adriaan Bonger was born in Holland in 1876 and died by his own hand in 1940 rather than submit to the Nazis. His *Criminalité et conditions économiques* first appeared in 1905. It was translated into English and published in the United States in 1916. Ibid., pp. 3–4.

13. David M. Gordon, "Capitalism, Class and Crime in America," *Crime and Delinquency* (April 1973), p. 174.

14. Ibid., p. 174.

15. William and Mary Morris, *Dictionary of Word and Phrase Origins*, II (New York: Harper and Row, 1967), p. 282.

16. *Sourcebook-1981*, p. 192.

17. Ibid., p. 205.

18. Ibid., pp. 210–211.

19. *Sourcebook-1974*, pp. 203, 204, 223, 207; see also p. 177.

20. Historical documentation of this can be found in David J. Rothman, *The Discovery of the Asylum: Social Order and Disorder in the New Republic* (Boston: Little, Brown, 1971); and in Frances Fox Piven and Richard A. Cloward, *Regulating the Poor: The Functions of Public Welfare* (New York: Pantheon, 1971), which carries the analysis up to the present.

21. *The Republic of Plato*, trans. F. M. Cornford (New York: Oxford University Press, 1945), p. 18 [I. 338]. Plato was born in Athens in the year 428 B.C. (or 427, depending on the reckoning) and died there in 348 B.C.

(or 347). Scholars generally agree that at least Book One of *The Repub-lic* (the section in which Thrasymachus speaks) was written between the death of Socrates in 399 B.C. and Plato's first journey to Sicily, from which he returned in 388 B.C. (or 387). See Frederick Copleston, S. J., *A History of Philosophy, Volume I: Greece and Rome* (Westminster, Maryland: The Newman Press, 1946), pp. 127–141.

22. Karl Marx and Fredrich Engels, *Manifesto of the Communist Party,* in *The Marx-Engels Reader,* ed., Robert C. Tucker (New York: W. W. Norton, 1972), p. 337. Marx was born in Trier, Prussia (now in West Germany) on May 5, 1818, and died on March 14, 1883. The *Manifesto* was first published in London in February, 1848—when Marx was nearly 30 years old. Ibid., pp. xi-xiv.

23. An article on congressional ethics in *Newsweek* (June 14, 1976) makes the point so graphically that it is worth quoting at length:

> . . . Some of the Hill's most powerful veterans have long earned part of their income from outside business interests—and may be tempted to vote with their own bank accounts in mind when legislation affecting those interests has come before Congress. House whip Thomas P. (Tip) O'Neill is active in real estate and insurance in Massachusetts, Minority Leader John Rhodes of Arizona is a director and vice-president of a life insurance company and scores of other senior members are involved with the banking industry, oil and gas companies and farming operations. Do these connections destroy their judgment? Not necessarily, argues Russell Long of Louisiana, chairman of the powerful Senate Finance Committee and a reliable defender of oil interests—who nevertheless refuses to disclose the size of his personal oil and gas holdings, most of them inherited from his father, former Gov. Huey Long. "A long time ago I became convinced that if you have financial interests completely parallel to your state, then you have no problem," says Long. "If I didn't represent the oil and gas industry, I wouldn't represent the state of Louisiana."
>
> Even more difficult to trace is the influence of representatives who keep their law practices—and their clients, many of whom do business with the Federal government—when they become members of Congress. [p. 25]

See Richard Quinney, *Critique of Legal Order: Crime Control in Capitalist Society* (Boston: Little, Brown, 1973), pp. 82–84, for an account of the financial interests and corporate connections of the members of the influential Committee for Economic Development—the domestic policy counterpart of the Council on Foreign Relations. For similar information on the members of various committees and councils that shape American foreign policy, see G. William Domhoff, "Who Made American Foreign Policy, 1945–1963?" in *Corporations and the Cold War,* ed., David Horowitz (New York: Monthly Review Press, 1969), pp. 25–69.

24. J. A. Schmidhauser, "The Justices of the Supreme Court: A Collective Portrait," *Midwest Journal of Political Science* 3 (1959), pp. 2–37, 40–49, cited in William J. Chambliss and Robert B. Seidman, *Law, Order, and Power* (Reading, Mass.: Addison-Wesley, 1971), p. 96; and Richard Quinney, *Critique of Legal Order: Crime Control in Capitalist Society* (Boston: Little, Brown, 1973), pp. 60–82, 86–92.

25. "F.B.I. Burglarized Leftist Offices Here 92 Times in 1960–66, Official Files Show," *The New York Times*, March 29, 1976, p. 1; "Burglaries by FBI Listed in Hundreds," *The Washington Post*, July 16, 1975, p. 1. See also *Cointelpro: The FBI's Secret War on Political Freedom*, ed., Cathy Perkus, introduction by Noam Chomsky (New York: Monad Press, 1975).

26. "Hill Panel Raps FBI's Anti-Panthers Tactics," *The Washington Post*, May 7, 1976, pp. A1, A22.

27. "FBI Labeled King 'Communist' in '62," *The Washington Post*, May 6, 1976, pp. A1, A26.

28. "Kelley Says FBI Is 'Truly Sorry' for Past Abuses," *The Washington Post*, May 9, 1976, pp. A1, A14; "FBI Break-ins Still Go On, Panel Reports," *The Washington Post*, May 11, 1976, pp. A1, A16; and "The FBI: Bag Jobs," *Newsweek*, July 4, 1976, pp. 84–85.

29. James F. Richardson, *Urban Police in the Untied States* (Port Washington, N.Y.: Kennikat Press, 1974), pp. 8–13, 22. See also Richardon's *The New York Police: Colonial Times to 1901* (New York: Oxford University Press, 1970).

30. Rothman, *The Discovery of the Asylum*, pp. 57–108, esp. 79–81. Cf. Michel Foucault, *Discipline and Punish: The Birth of the Prison* (London: Allen Lane, 1977).

31. Richardson, *Urban Police*, pp. 158–161. See also R. Boyer and H. Morais, *Labor's Untold Story* (New York: United Electrical, Radio & Machine Workers of America, 1976).

32. Rothman, pp. 253–254.

33. Philip Taft and Philip Ross, "American Labor Violence: Its Causes, Character, and Outcome," in *The History of Violence in America*, eds., H. D. Graham and T. R. Gurr (New York: Bantam, 1969), pp. 281–395, esp. pp. 281, 380; and Richard E. Rubenstein, *Rebels in Eden: Mass Political Violence in the United States* (Boston: Little, Brown, 1970), p. 81, inter alia. See also Center for Research in Criminal Justice, *The Iron Fist and the Velvet Glove* (Berkeley, Calif. 1975), pp. 16–19.

34. Marx, *The German Ideology*, in *The Marx-Engels Reader*, ed., Tucker, p. 136.

35. Each new ruling class "is compelled, merely in order to carry through its aim, to represent its interest as the common interest of all the members of society," Marx, *The German Ideology*, in *The Marx-Engels Reader*, ed., Tucker, p. 138.

36. Marx was not the first to use the term "ideology." The term was coined by Antoine Destutt de Tracy, who was among the intellectuals named

in 1795 to direct the researches of the newly founded Institut de France. The *idéologues* of the Institut generally believed that existing ideas were prejudices rooted in individual psychology or in political conditions and that the path to liberation from these prejudices and thus toward a rational society lay in a science of ideas (literally, an "ideaology") which made human beings aware of the sources of their ideas. Thomas Jefferson introduced the theory of ideology in America. He tried (albeit unsuccessfully) to have Destutt de Tracy's theory made part of the original curriculum of the University of Virginia. See George Lichtheim, "The Concept of Ideology," *History and Theory*, 4, No. 2 (1965), pp. 164–195; and *Ideology, Politics, and Political Theory*, ed., Richard H. Cox (Belmont, Calif.: Wadsworth, 1969), pp. 7–8. Needless to say, Marx used the term "ideology" in ways that neither Destutt de Tracy nor Jefferson anticipated.

37. Lichtheim's essay provides a good discussion of the philosophical antecedents of the gradual separation of the notion of *ideology* from that of *false consciousness*. Undoubtedly, this separation is of a piece with the current wisdom that insists that all views of the world are conditioned and rendered partial by the limits of the viewer's historical and social vantage point, and thus shrinks from trying to say anything *true* about the human condition. An illuminating contemporary example of this "current wisdom" applied to the criminal justice system is Walter B. Miller, "Ideology and Criminal Justice Policy: Some Current Issues," *Journal of Criminal Law and Criminology*, 64, No. 2 (1973), pp. 141–162. I shall use the concept of ideology in the Marxian sense, that is, to include that of false consciousness.

38. What follows is just a smattering of the literature documenting either the wide and abiding disparities of wealth in America or the existence of a very small, not necessarily organized, group of individuals who, in addition to being extremely wealthy, make most of the economic and political decisions that shape America's destiny: G. William Domhoff, *Who Rules America?* (Englewood Cliffs, N.J.: Prentice-Hall, 1967); Richard C. Edwards, Michael Reich, and Thomas E. Weisskopf, *The Capitalist System: A Radicial Analysis of American Society* (Englewood Cliffs, N.J.: Prentice-Hall, 1972); John Kenneth Galbraith, *The New Industrial State* (New York: Signet Books, 1968); Edward S. Greenberg, *Serving the Few: Corporate Capitalism and the Bias of Government Policy* (New York: John Wiley, 1974); Gabriel Kolko, *Wealth and Power in America: An Analysis of Social Class and Income Distribution* (New York: Praeger, 1962); C. Wright Mills, *The Power Elite* (New York: Oxford University Press, 1956); Joseph A. Pechman and Benjamin A. Okner, *Who Bears the Tax Burden?* (Washington, D.C.: The Brookings Institution, 1974); Philip M. Stern, *The Rape of the Taxpayer* (New York: Vintage Books, 1974).

39. *Stat Abst-1981*, p. 438, Table no. 730.

40. Alan S. Blinder, "The Level and Distribution of Economic Well-Be-

ing," in Martin Feldstein, ed., *The American Economy in Transition* (Chicago: University of Chicago Press, 1980), p. 466.

41. Marshall E. Blume, Jean Crockett, and Irwin Friend, "Stock-ownership in the United States: Characteristics and Trends," *Survey of Current Business*, 54, No. 11 (November, 1974), p. 17. (Emphasis added.)

42. Undoubtedly, the most interesting recent work on this topic is John Rawls's *A Theory of Justice* (Cambridge, Mass.: Harvard University Press, 1971). The noted British philosopher Stuart Hampshire has called it the most important work in moral philosophy since the Second World War. It is sure to exert considerable influence on theoretical discussions of political, legal, and economic justice. Rawls's approach is essentially "naturalistic." That is, he takes the "good" to be that which people rationally desire, and the "moral good" to be that which would best serve *all* people's rational desires. Based on this, he takes justice to be those social (legal, political, economic, etc.) arrangements that best serve the interests of all. To reach specific principles of justice, he asks for those principles that it would be rational for all people to agree to if each could not use force or influence to tailor the principles to his or her own interest. On the question of the distribution of income or wealth, this way of questioning leads to the principle that economic inequalities are only just if they work to everyone's advantage, for instance, as incentives that work to raise the level of productivity and thus the level of well-being for all. It would be the task of government to rectify inequalities that exceed this point, by means of taxes and transfers. I cannot, of course, do justice here to what Rawls takes 600 pages to explain and defend. However, I offer this short summary to suggest that the disparities of income in America are far from just in the light of contemporary moral philosophy. Clearly, those disparities are far greater than anything that could be claimed to be *necessary* to increase the well-being of all. Indeed, one would have to be blind not to see that they are not increasing the well-being of all. For a discussion of Rawls' principle of economic justice, see Jeffrey H. Reiman, "The Labor Theory of the Difference Principle," *Philosophy & Public Affairs* 12, No. 2 (Spring 1983), pp. 133–159. Robert Nozick has replied to Rawls in a book entitled *Anarchy, State and Utopia* (New York: Basic Books, 1974), which no doubt represents the free enterprise system's theory of justice. Nozick holds that no theory (such as Rawls's) that calls for government intervention to rectify income distribution can be just. His argument is that if people acquire their property (including money) legitimately, then they have the right to spend or sell it as they wish. If this leads to disparities in wealth, one cannot alter this outcome without denying that those spenders or sellers had the right to dispose of their property or money as they saw fit. I shall not try to answer Nozick here. It should be noted, however, that his view starts from the assumption that the property or money that is sold or spent was acquired legitimately. In light of the fact that so much American

property was stolen at gunpoint from Indians or Mexicans and so much wealth taken from the hides of black slaves, it is questionable whether Nozick's theory can be applied in the American context. It might require a redistribution of wealth just so that we could reach the starting point at which we could say that individuals own what they own legitimately. For a discussion of Nozick's theory, see Jeffrey H. Reiman, "The Fallacy of Libertarian Capitalism" *Ethics* 92 (October 1981), pp. 85–95.

**43.** *Stat Abst-1981*, p. 445, Table no. 745.

**44.** One study reports that "among high school graduates with *equal* academic ability, the proportion going on to college averages nearly 25 percentage points lower for males (and nearly 35 for females) in the bottom socioeconomic quarter of the population than in the top quarter." And another indicates that "the sons of families in the top fifth of the socioeconomic pyramid have average incomes 75 percent higher than those coming from the bottom fifth." Arthur M. Okun, *Equality and Efficiency* (Washington, D.C.: The Brookings Institution, 1975), p. 81 and p. 75.

**45.** For a more detailed statement of Marxian theory, its relationship to criminology, and its capacity to account for current developments in criminal justice policy, see Jeffrey H. Reiman and Sue Headlee, "Marxism and Criminal Justice Policy," *Crime & Delinquency* (January 1981), pp. 24–47; see also David F. Greenberg and Drew Humphries, "Economic Crisis and the Justice Model: A Skeptical View," *Crime & Delinquency* (October 1982), pp. 601–609; and Jeffrey H. Reiman, "Marxist Explanations and Radical Misinterpretations: A Reply to Greenberg and Humphries," *Crime & Delinquency* (October 1982), pp. 610–617.

**46.** Karl Marx and Friedrich Engels, *The Communist Manifesto* (Baltimore: Pengiun Books, 1967), p. 79.

**47.** Karl Marx, *Capital* (New York: International Publishers, 1967), vol. 1, p. 217.

**48.** Marx, *Capital*, vol. 1, p. 534.

**49.** Marx, *Capital*, vol. 3, p. 595.

**50.** Marx, *Capital*, vol. 1, p. 715.

## NOTES TO CHAPTER 5

**1.** Although I think this way of looking at the legal system, at justice, and at the moral legitimacy of the law, is common to most moral and legal philosophers, it should be acknowledged that my own formulation bears a heavy debt to the conceptions of justice and morality developed by John Rawls, Kurt Baier, and Herbert Morris. See John Rawls, *A Theory of Justice* (Cambridge, Mass.: Harvard University Press, 1971); Kurt Baier, *The Moral Point of View: A Rational Basis of Ethics* (New York: Random House, 1965); and Herbert Morris, "Persons and Punishment," in A. I. Melden, ed., *Human Rights* (Belmont, Calif.: Wadsworth, 1970), pp. 111–134. On the issue of the legitimacy of states (i.e., political-legal systems), see Robert Paul Wolff, *In Defense of Anarchism* (New York: Harper & Row, 1970 and 1976), Jeffrey H. Reiman, *In Defense of Political Philosophy* (New York: Harper & Row, 1972), Reiman, "Autonomy, Authority, and Universalizability," in *The Personalist* (January, 1978), pp. 85–92; and Reiman "Anarchism and Nominalism: Wolff's Latest Obituary for Political Philosophy," in *Ethics* (October, 1978). On the issue of the legitimacy and moral justification of police authority in particular, see Jeffrey H. Reiman, "Police Autonomy vs. Police Authority: A Philosophical Perspective," in *The Police Community*, eds., Jack Goldsmith and Sharon S. Goldsmith (Pacific Palisades, Calif.: Palisades Publishers, 1974), pp. 225–233; and Roger Wertheimer, "Are the Police Necessary?", in *The Police in Society*, eds., Emilio C. Viano and Jeffrey H. Reiman, (Lexington, Mass.: Lexington Books, 1975), pp. 49–60.

2. This is an important point both practically and theoretically. Moral guilt for breaking a law does not arise in a vacuum. One's moral guilt for breaking a law is only as great as one's moral obligation to comply with it. Contemporary moral philosophers generally maintain that one's moral obligation to comply with laws is a function of the benefits one receives from the social order that the legal system protects and makes possible. The social contract metaphor certainly suggests this, since a contract has at least two sides. One is bound to fulfill his or her part of a contract to the extent that the other parties to the contract fulfill theirs. If we conceive of the obligation to obey the laws as each individual's obligation to do his or her part in the social contract, then quite clearly one's obligation is only strong to the extent that one's own contribution to the contract is matched with contributions by the others which are commensurate in value. In short, this means that one is obligated if the terms of the contract are fair and if everyone, on the whole, is also keeping their part of the bargain. Arguing from such a framework, John Rawls concludes that "the duty to comply is problematic for permanent minorities that have suffered from injustice for many years." *A Theory of Justice*, p. 355. Applying Rawls's theory to the question of the obligation of deprived minorities to obey laws which result in economic injustice towards them, Phillip H. Scribner maintains that "just as we are not obligated to acquiesce in the denial of our basic liberties, we are not required to cooperate in our own exploitation." "On the Duty to Obey an Unjust Law," in *The Police in Society*, eds., Viano and Reiman, p. 43. Michael Walzer, treating the subject from a somewhat different perspective, concludes that "the oppressed do not receive all the . . . benefits [of the political community] because they are not counted equally. They are in a special and very difficult position that may best be defined by suggesting that they possess within the state the liberty to refuse, to say no to the laws they

have not been able to join in making. They possess the liberty to refuse because they have themselves been refused full participation in the democratic community." "The Obligations of Oppressed Minorities," in *Obligations: Essays on Disobedience, War and Citizenship* (New York: Simon and Schuster, 1970), p. 69. All this adds up to one conclusion: *The obligation to obey the law is decreased when one is on the receiving end of injustice, and therefore the moral guilt for disobeying the law must decrease as well.*

3. See the thoughtful recommendations for gun control and their rationale in Norval Morris and Gordon Hawkins, *The Honest Politician's Guide to Crime Control* (Chicago: University of Chicago Press, 1970), pp. 63–71.

4. Morris and Hawkins, pp. 3, and 8–10; Arnold S. Trebach, *The Heroin Solution* (New Haven: Yale University Press, 1982), pp. 267–270; and Philip C. Baridon, *Addiction, Crime, and Social Policy* (Lexington, Mass.: Lexington Books, 1976), p. 88.

5. For a convincing argument that there is no moral difference between directly caused and indirectly caused harm, see John Harris, "The Marxist Conception of Violence," *Philosophy & Public Affairs*, 3, No. 2 (Winter, 1974), pp. 192–220; and Jonathan Glover, *Causing Death and Saving Lives* (Hammondsworth, England: Penguin, 1977), pp. 92–112.

6. These are the words of a former director of the fraud division of the Department of Justice: "No one in direct contact with the living reality of business conduct in the United States is unaware of the effect the imprisonment of seven high officials in the Electrical Machinery Industry in 1960 had on the conspiratorial price fixing in many areas of our economy; similar sentences in a few cases each decade would almost completely cleanse our economy of the cancer of collusive price fixing and the mere prospect of such sentences is itself the strongest available deterrent to such activities." Gordon B. Spivak, "Antitrust Enforcement in the United States: A Primer," *Connecticut Bar Journal*, 37 (September, 1963), p. 382.

7. See Chapter One, "The Overreach of the Criminal Law," in Morris and Hawkins, pp. 1–28; Herbert Packer, *The Limits of the Criminal Sanction* (Stanford, Calif.:Stanford University Press, 1968); and Jeffrey H. Reiman, "Can We Avoid the Legislation of Morality?," in *Legality, Morality and Ethics in Criminal Justice*, eds., Nicholas N. Kittrie and Jackwell Susman (New York: Praeger, 1979), pp. 130–141.

8. John Stuart Mill, *On Liberty* (1859), (New York: Appleton-Century Crofts, 1973), p. 9.

9. See, for example, Gerald Dworkin, "Paternalism," in *Morality and the Law*, ed., Richard Wasserstrom (Belmont, Calif.: Wadsworth, 1971), pp. 107–126; and Joel Feinberg, "Legal Paternalism," in *Today's Moral Problems*, ed., Richard Wasserstrom (New York: Macmillan, 1975), pp. 33–50.

10. See, for instance, the excellent discussion of the principle in Peter T.

Manicas, *The Death of the State* (New York: Putnam, 1974), Chapter V: "The Liberal Moral Ideal," pp. 194–241; and H. L. A. Hart, *Law, Liberty and Morality* (New York: Vintage Books, 1963).

11. The standard laid down in *Conally v. General Constr. Co.*, 269 U.S. 385, 391, 70 L. Ed. 322, 46 S. Ct. 126 (1926) is "whether or not the vagueness is of such a character 'that men of common intelligence must necessarily guess at its meaning.' " See also *Lanzetta et al. v. State of New Jersey, 306*, U.S. 451, 83 L. Ed. 888, 59 S. Ct. 618 (1939), where the Supreme Court struck down a New Jersey statute that made it a felony for anyone not engaged in any lawful occupation to be a member of a gang, etc., because the terms of the statute were "vague, indefinite and uncertain" and thus "repugnant to the due process clause of the Fourteenth Amendment." Both cases are cited and discussed in Jerome Hall, *General Principles of Criminal Law*, 2nd edition (New York: Bobbs-Merrill, 1960), pp. 36–48. For a constitutional and philosophical argument for treating Mill's harm principle as an implied constitutional principle, see David A. J. Richards, *Sex, Drugs, Death, and the Law: An Essay on Human Rights and Overcriminalization* (Totowa, N.J.: Rowman and Littlefield, 1982), pp. 1–34, *inter alia*.

12. See *Robinson v. California*, 370 U.S. 66 (1962), where the court held that a state law penalizing a person for a "status" such as addiction constitutes "cruel and unusual punishment" in violation of the Eighth Amendment. Cited and discussed in Nicholas N. Kittrie, *The Right to be Different: Deviance and Enforced Therapy* (Baltimore: The Johns Hopkins Press, 1971), pp. 35–36, inter alia.

13. I have already pointed out that the vast majority of persons convicted of crimes in the Untied States are not convicted by juries. They plead guilty as the result of a "bargain" with the prosecutor (underwritten by the judge), in which the prosecutor agrees to drop other charges in return for the guilty plea. Kenneth Kipnis argues that the entire system of bargain justice is a violation of the ideal of justice, since it amounts to coercing a guilty plea and often to punishing an offender for a crime other than the one he or she has committed. It is an argument worth considering. See Kenneth Kipnis, "Criminal Justice and the Negotiated Plea," *Ethics, 86*, No. 2 (January, 1976), pp. 93–106.

# Index

# About the Author

Jeffrey Reiman was born in Brooklyn, New York in 1942. He received his B.A. in Philosophy from Queens College in 1963, and his Ph.D. in Philosophy from The Pennsylvania State University in 1968. He joined the faculty of The American University's School of Justice in Washington, D.C. in 1970, when it was called the Center for the Administration of Justice. The School of Justice is a multidisciplinary department devoted to teaching and research in all areas of social justice with special emphasis on criminal justice. Dr. Reiman currently holds a joint appointment in the School of Justice and the Department of Philosophy and Religion. In addition to *The Rich Get Richer and the Poor Get Prison*, he is the author of *In Defense of Political Philosophy*, and numerous articles in philosophy and criminal justice journals and anthologies.